Adventure
Motorcycling Manual

First edition published in January 2008
Reprinted in 2010
Second edition published in June 2013

A catalogue record for this book is available from the British Library

ISBN 978 0 85733 352 0

Library of Congress catalog card no 2013932257

Published by Haynes Publishing,
Sparkford, Yeovil, Somerset BA22 7JJ, UK
Tel: +44 1963 442030 Fax: +44 1963 440001
E-mail: sales@haynes.co.uk
Website: www.haynes.co.uk

Haynes North America Inc., 861 Lawrence Drive,
Newbury Park, California 91320, USA

Printed and bound in the USA

📷 Joe Pichler

Dedication

For my mum who sacrificed a great deal to, amongst other things, purchase me my first motorcycle in 1985 – my first step on the road to the passion that is adventure motorcycling.

To my wife Tanya, daughter Hannah and family back in South Africa for all their tremendous support while this book has taken shape.

Acknowledgements

I would like to thank the following people for their support and expertise:

Elspeth Beard, Paul Blezard, Nik Boseley, Herman Botha, Roger Burnett, Steve Cain, Tony Carter, Walter Colebatch, Steve Coombs, Dave Dew, Su Downham, Andy Dukes, Matt Durrans, Johan Engelbrecht, Cora Forssman, Neil Fullerton, Paul Gowen, John Griffiths, Scott Grimsdall, Steve Hatt, Wendy Hearn, Tony Jakeman, Brock Jamison, Allan Johnson, Grant Johnson, Matt Kay, Judy Kennedy, Damien Kimberley, Derick Lategan, Dave Lomax, Kylie Maebus, Sam Manicom, Suzi Mewes, Colin Mileman, Mark Montecillo, Ian Oliver, Helge Pedersen, Liz Peel, Josef Pichler, Clinton Pienaar, Nick Plumb, Lois Pryce, Benka Pulko, Dave Rawlings, Beth Robinson, Richard Samuels, Julia Sanders, Kevin Sanders, Nick Sanders, Shaun Sisterson, Chris Smith, Harley Stevens, Bernd Tesch, Geoff van der Merwe, Waldo van der Waal, Paul Walker, Ross Walker, Marc Webb, Juergen Weisz, Mick Wheeler, Sherri Jo Wilkins, Ian Willoughby

With special thanks to:
Ted Simon
For the inspiration I gained from reading *Jupiter's Travels*, for the time he took out of his busy schedule to meet me and for agreeing to write the foreword to my first book.
Greg Baker
To my close friend for his companionship, technical expertise and passion – long may the adventures continue.
Steve Eilertsen
For his contribution to a number of the topics discussed in the book. His website – www.flamesonmytank.co.za – is a tremendous resource for adventure motorcyclists, covering a wide range of relevant topics.
Adam Lewis and Danny Burroughs
To the two intrepid round-the-world travellers for their insight and photography used in this book. By the time the book is published they will be halfway through their journey. Together they epitomise the spirit of adventure motorcycling today and I wish them the very best on the long ride home.

Mark Hughes – Editorial Director at Haynes Publishing
For his belief in the project from the start and wonderful support throughout the editorial process.
Lee Parsons – Senior Designer at Haynes Publishing
For the outstanding design and interpretation of the subject matter.

Adventure

Haynes®

Motorcycling Manual

Everything you need to plan and complete the journey of a lifetime

Robert Wicks
Foreword by **Ted Simon**

Second Edition

Equipment ■ Legal documentation ■ Riding techniques ■ Maintenance ■ Navigation ■ Emergencies ■ Routes

Contents

Robert Wicks

Foreword by Ted Simon

We are all different, thank goodness, but those of us who ride bikes have one thing in common: we are willing consciously to accept risk. In a society that puts so much emphasis on trying to protect us from ourselves, the motorcycle is an obvious symbol of rebellion. Having said that, we fall naturally into two groups.

Some bikers use the machine quite deliberately to take their lives in their hands and push their luck to the limit. I admire the courage of racers. I'm astonished at their ability to skirt death by such fine margins. I couldn't do it, partly because in body and mind I'm not suited to it, but mostly because I'm not really interested in speed. I belong to the other group. I would rather go far than go fast.

To those who know me through *Jupiter's Travels* it might seem that my existence began with that journey, but in reality it was more of a culmination. I had already led quite a full life, including a fair amount of travel. Growing up in Britain through World War 2, confined to the island and hearing about exotic locations from Casablanca to Guadalcanal, I was desperate to see it all for myself. As soon as the war was over I made my first trip through France on a bicycle, determined to see if the Mediterranean was really blue, and that trip was in its way just as hairy as the Jupiter journey.

Curiosity was always the driving impulse. As the years passed I got many more glimpses of the world, but it was never enough. I really needed to see it all.

Perhaps the closest I've come to genius was on that day in 1973 when I realised that the motorcycle was the perfect vehicle for adventure. Not having ridden a bike before, I greatly exaggerated the dangers, and it's just as well that I did because I had to learn the art of motorcycle travel as I went, but I came to understand fairly soon that it was not a lottery: I could control the risk by being alert, aware, and very clear about my priorities, which were to survive and arrive.

North Africa was my training ground. After three months I came out of Ethiopia confident that I could defend myself. I had assembled a battery of instincts that seemed to work for me, and my life with the bike was transformed. We moved on, effortlessly it seemed despite breakdowns and interruptions, through the Americas, Australia and Asia, and I satisfied much of my curiosity about the world, but the greatest prize was quite unexpected. It was what I learned about myself.

The same qualities you need to survive on a bike are the ones that make travel through foreign countries and cultures so rewarding. It's a perfect fit. The act of taking control of your own destiny raises your consciousness, makes it easier to relate to strangers, and makes you more interesting in their eyes.

This book will tell you much of what I had to learn on the road, and just reading it will sharpen your appetite, but finally it will be you who takes charge. Every journey is unique. You have only to take the plunge.

Ted Simon

January 2008

← **Ted Simon –
he conquered
the world and
has inspired
countless others
to do the same**
📷 Ted Simon

AUTHOR'S NOTE

Over a period of four years in the 1970s Ted Simon rode 63,000 miles (101,000km) through 54 countries in one of the greatest adventure rides of all time. It culminated in the bestseller, *Jupiter's Travels*, a book which would inspire countless adventurers, including myself. In 2001 at the age of 69, Ted decided to retrace his journey and his latest account, entitled *Dreaming of Jupiter*, will surely inspire a new generation of adventure motorcyclists.

Introduction

← **Riding high in the mountains of Oman**
📷 Robert Wicks

Growing up in rural South Africa in the mid-1970s, Ted Simon rode, quite literally, past our front door without me knowing. He was already well into his epic journey around the world and it was only once I had read *Jupiter's Travels* that the possibility of exploring the world by motorcycle really dawned on me.

When I met Ted for the first time and asked him to autograph my original copy of *Jupiter's Travels*, he wrote these simple words: "I'm glad it worked". Ted's wonderful story opened my eyes and kick-started an insatiable desire to explore the world, wherever possible on two wheels.

From a solo trip in the desert for weeks to a few days off the beaten track closer to home, adventure motorcycling means different things to different people. It requires commitment – physical, mental and financial – but the rewards are far greater and somehow we all take something unique from the experience. In a world where there are very few new frontiers and little escape from the mundane, adventure motorcycling for some represents a rebellion of sorts; a refusal to accept the drudgery of modern life and an escape from the hell that is reality TV, social networking and chasing up the corporate ladder.

Writing this book has reminded me about the special camaraderie that we as motorcyclists enjoy. No matter what bike you ride or where you're headed, friends are easily made and problems solved. The overwhelming response from the adventure motorcycling community at large to my research for this book is indicative of that same spirit.

Adventure motorcycling has brought me closer to the world around me, it's made me appreciate different cultures, taught me new skills, forged unexpected new friendships and opened up opportunities such as writing this book. I still pinch myself when I think there are now five books in the Haynes Adventure Motorcycling series that have inspired people to take the plunge and head off.

Make no mistake, adventuring on two wheels will change your life. It will fuel a latent desire to explore and it will change the way you think about yourself and others. Few other pursuits are likely to have such a profound effect.

Ted's book certainly inspired me and, in the same way, I hope the words and images that follow do the same for you.

Life is worth living; I hope you enjoy the read.

Robert Wicks
June 2013

The Origins of Adventure

Motorcycling

← **The epitome of adventure motorcycling – Helge Pedersen crosses the Darien Gap**

📷 Helge Pedersen

It was frowned upon, it was deemed impossible and it was considered highly risky, but in the early 1900s a small number of intrepid adventurers conceived the notion of using a motorcycle to explore the world.

New Yorker Carl Stevens Clancy appears to have been the first motorcyclist to circumnavigate the globe – evidence from his 1913 expedition shows he rode his four-cylinder Henderson 18,000 miles (29,000km) through Scotland, England, Ireland, Belgium, France, Germany, Italy, northern Africa, India, Japan and across the United States, from San Francisco to New York.

Writing for the *Toronto Star* newspaper, journalist Allan Johnson recalls: "By the 1920s, it was not uncommon for European riders to undertake long, adventurous motorcycling trips to the less-travelled points of the Middle East, India and Australia, usually with heavy sidecar outfits and backed by the motorcycle manufacturer. The intent was, of course, to advertise the ruggedness and reliability of a particular brand's product. There was much publicity immediately after a successful journey, but the memory of nearly all these expeditions has faded."

In 1928, one such pioneer was Stanley Glanfield, who embarked on a world tour on his Coventry-built Rudge Whitworth motorcycle combination. The journey would take him just eight months and would cover an astonishing 18,000 miles (29,000km) passing through 16 countries and across four continents. The 'combination' included a 3.5hp single-cylinder motorcycle and a bespoke sidecar, specially fitted out to carry spares and provisions for the trip.

The term 'adventure motorcycling' is relatively new and was coined by Chris Scott, one of the key personalities at the forefront of the modern era whose books *Desert Travels*, *Sahara Overland* and in particular the *Adventure Motorcycling Handbook* (now in its fifth edition) have given immense assistance and inspiration to aspiring adventure motorcycle riders for many years, and confirmed him as an expert in the field. Indeed, in 1997 he originated the term 'adventure motorcycling' to describe overland travel by motorcycle which he defines as "a challenging journey into the wilderness or a significantly strange country". He views the motorcycle as a tool with which "to escape from the mundane and predictable".

Over the last 25 years Scott has undertaken nearly 30 expeditions through the Sahara and regularly provides advice to many individuals' hare-brained projects, as well as adventure tour operators and television production

The Long Way Round expedition took the concept of adventure motorcycling into millions of homes around the globe

📷 Provided courtesy of Long Way Down

companies such as Michael Palin's *Sahara* series.

Not long after Glanfield's successful trip, American Robert Edison Fulton Jr. set out in 1932 on a customised Douglas T6 twin motorcycle for his own 18-month, 40,000 mile (64,000km) odyssey that included Turkey, Syria, Iraq, Afghanistan, India, Sumatra, Malaysia, Siam, Indonesia, China, and Japan. His machine also included a sidecar for carrying equipment, an extra large fuel tank, a secret hiding place for his revolver and enough room in his luggage for a motion-picture camera and 40,000ft (12,200m) of film. Following a crash he discarded the sidecar and relied on a small suitcase fixed to the handlebars for his clothing. His account of the trip, entitled *One Man Caravan*, was published in 1937 and has become one of the most famous accounts of adventure motorcycling to date.

To attempt an expedition such as that of Glanfield or Fulton today would be quite an achievement but to have succeeded in the 1920s and 1930s when motorcycles were considerably less reliable, roads – where they existed – were often badly maintained, spares were almost non-existent and fuel supplies were at best sporadic, is nothing short of an achievement of epic proportions.

The publicity that was to surround Glanfield's triumphant return journey would signal continuing success for Rudge as a manufacturer and, in a similar way, BMW's support of the now famous *Long Way Round* and *Long Way Down* adventures by Ewan McGregor and Charley Boorman, generated an unprecedented amount of publicity for the German manufacturer. These expeditions had a remarkable impact on sales of BMW's GS machines and, more importantly, propelled the notion of adventure motorcycling into more homes than ever before through an engaging television series and a range of commercial spin-offs including mobile phone downloads, a popular website, a hugely successful book, DVD and merchandise range.

The pair started from London in April 2004 and completed a round-the-world journey across some of the most beautiful, and at times dangerous terrain in the world. The route would take them through France, Belgium, Germany, the Czech Republic, Slovakia, Ukraine, Russia, Kazakhstan, Mongolia, Siberia, Alaska and Canada before arriving 115 days later at their final destination, New York City.

McGregor's celebrity was a huge draw card and created a significant following around the world. The pair recently completed the *Long Way Down* from the northern tip of Scotland to the most southerly tip of Africa. As with *Long Way Round*, they stopped off along the way to visit UNICEF projects to raise awareness and funds for children. Few can doubt the profound effect these high profile trips have had on adventure motorcycling.

During their *Long Way Round* expedition, the pair met Ted Simon who was also undertaking his own adventure – this time retracing his steps from his now legendary trip in the 1970s. Ted continues to provide inspiration to many riders and must take at least some of the credit for bringing adventure motorcycling to the fore with his grand adventures.

Another of the more contemporary figures, who would have been rather unaccustomed to the media attention and support crews which followed the *Long Way* expeditions is Norwegian, Helge Pedersen.

He epitomises the sense of wanderlust, and in the elite community of today's global explorers, Helge stands at the pinnacle of achievement, having journeyed throughout the world for ten years on his trusted BMW R 80 GS, visiting over 75 countries and covering 250,000 miles (402,500km) in the process.

He concluded his book, *10 Years on 2 Wheels*, with these words: "Going around the world on two wheels has been, like every sort of endeavour in life, a school, where wisdom is picked up along the way – in my case along the road. I had many experiences born of trial and error. The sheer volume of impressions I experienced was enormous. It took some time to absorb it all and a few years have now passed. I had indeed realised my childhood dream when I returned from Africa. Later I came up with new dreams and strove to realise them as well, one by one. Some I did; others remain dreams. Some of those I hope – I believe – will come true. Others will always be dreams…and who would want to run out of dreams?"

Pedersen now runs GlobeRiders, a diversified and successful motorcycle adventure touring and multimedia company based in Seattle, Washington.

Other key figures include Bernd Tesch who started travelling in 1955 at the age of 14. Since then he has travelled more than 210,000 miles (340,000km) across numerous countries by various modes of transport, at least 125,000 miles (200,000km) of which have been by motorcycle. After he crossed Africa in 1971, he published the first German *Globetrotter Guide* – a comprehensive guide for individual travellers to the African continent. This led him to establish 'Globetrotters Central' in 1977, a veritable one-stop-shop for adventure bikers with a

↑ Clockwise from top left – Stanley Glanfield's 'Combination' 📷 Coventry Transport Museum**, Robert Edison Fulton's Douglas T6 Twin** 📷 White Horse Press**, Simon Millward's 'Overlander'** 📷 Coventry Transport Museum **and Ted Simon's Triumph Tiger** 📷 Coventry Transport Museum

range of services including an online mail order catalogue of adventure motorcycling books and specialist motorcycle panniers, travel equipment, survival training workshops and motorcycle meetings for world travellers.

From a sporting perspective, adventure motorcycling is best epitomised by the Dakar Rally and other similar rally raid endurance events which typically take place in extreme desert locations. Widely regarded as the toughest off-road challenge, the Dakar Rally started back in 1977 when Thierry Sabine got lost on his motorcycle in the Libyan desert during a race from Abidjan to Nice. He returned to France knowing he had been defeated by the dunes but promised himself that he would share this experience with as many people as possible. This led him to conceive the idea of an extraordinary event from Paris across the Sahara to Dakar in Senegal. The plan quickly became reality and Sabine would often say of the rally: "A challenge for those who go; a dream for those who stay behind." Today the Dakar Rally is a major global sporting event attracting more than 13,600 participants since its inception. The 2007 event saw 245 motorcycles, 180 cars and 85 trucks take to the start line, with around 80 per cent of the field made up of amateurs.

The endurance element which forms such an important part of events such as the Dakar Rally has played a role in defining some of the most significant overland rides to date by taking adventure motorcycling to the extreme in terms of the sheer distance covered and time taken to do so.

Take Danny Liska, for instance, a farmer from Nebraska who in 1961 left everything behind in search of adventure and ended up riding his BMW more than 95,000 miles (153,000km) from the Arctic Circle to the tip of South America. Liska is included in the *Guinness Book of Motorcycle Facts and Feats* as a 'champion rider' along the Pan American Highway. Then, much of the road he travelled on simply didn't exist and what often passed as a 'highway' was nothing more than a gravel track. He followed this up with another significant journey from the Cape in Norway to the Cape in South Africa. Over the two journeys he visited 69 countries and BMW produced a series of advertisements to celebrate his achievements.

Someone else very familiar with the rigours of long distance riding is Nick Sanders – one of the most experienced extreme motorcycle adventurers in the world, he has circumnavigated the globe six times. In 1992 he first rode around the world on an Indian Enfield 500cc Bullet and has been riding professionally ever since. His various expeditions culminated in his solo speed circumnavigation on a Yamaha R1 in just 19 days. Over the past seven years he has motorcycled around the world four times, on three occasions riding in excess of 30,000 miles (48,000km). Adventure motorcycling, he says, "will change the way you think about your life". Nick recently led 18 inexperienced riders from Lisbon to Timbuktu riding a Yamaha XT660R.

Of the same surname but no relation to Nick are the husband and wife team of Kevin and Julia Sanders who are best known for their two Guinness World Records for the 'Fastest Circumnavigation of the World by Motorcycle' (2002) and the 'Trans Americas by Motorcycle' (2003). The second record saw the couple start from Deadhorse, Alaska and ride the length of the Americas, some 17,000 miles (27,200km), in less than 35 days.

Soon thereafter Guinness World Records announced that further attempts would no longer be endorsed from a safety perspective – not surprising when you consider that on the first trip Kevin had averaged 1,008 miles (1,600km) a day riding a total of 19,461 miles (31,332km), including a staggering 1,700 miles (2,700km) in less than 28 hours.

After their success the couple founded GlobeBusters as the first overland motorcycle expedition company in the UK specialising in taking riders on amazing journeys to unusual destinations and have notched up hundreds of thousands of miles riding the world over – from Siberia to Colombia, from Iran to Australia, from Finland to Bolivia and back to the UK.

The significant growth in the number of organisations such as GlobeBusters and GlobeRiders is indicative of the development in the adventure motorcycling market.

Long before these record breaking achievements were being recognised, a man by the name of Ed Culberson was defining his own place in the history of adventure motorcycling. His determination to cross the notorious and inhospitable stretch of jungle between Panama and Colombia known as the Darien Gap had become a lifelong obsession. In his personal account of the experience, *Obsessions Die Hard*, he describes how, during one of his earlier journeys of 26,000 miles (42,000km) through 15 Latin American countries, the trip had "revived a restless spirit that made a return to orderly, conventional living seem impossible". Culberson eventually succeeded in crossing the Gap in what can only be described as an amazing tale of human endurance and perseverance. Some years later, Pedersen too would succeed at crossing the Darien, this time from south to north, ranking as his most difficult endeavour to date.

There is also the humanitarian side to adventure motorcycling where the likes of Simon Millward (1965–2005), the well-respected two-wheel activist, decided to realise his dream of riding round the world and raising funds for international medical aid. Simon's 'Millennium Ride' started in 2000 in support of the charities Medecins sans Frontieres and Riders for Health. His hand-built 'Overlander' covered more than 120,000 miles (193,000km) across six continents in five years. He worked on a health project on the remote Indonesian island of Flores and then continued his journey through Latin America and then Africa, all the while continuing with his fundraising. Sadly, Simon lost his life in a road accident in Mali in March 2005. Since his passing, his family and close colleagues have worked to ensure that his legacy and vision for sustainable healthcare delivery in developing countries survives through the Motorcycle Outreach organisation.

In his book entitled *Riding the World*, motorcycle journalist and photographer Gregory Frazier says adventure motorcycling "allows people to escape daily routines, to seek answers to life's questions and to challenge themselves".

It is this quest to get away from it all, to escape the routines and the monotony of work and to accept the challenge of riding into the unknown that makes adventure motorcycling such a fascinating subject. This is by no means a definitive history and there are countless other explorers, journeys and feats which have all contributed in their own special way and are not mentioned here. Hopefully, what this brief introduction does is provide at least an insight into what adventure motorcycling means to some and thereby inspire others toward their own journey of a lifetime.

Another day in the office – Joe Pichler is KTM's leading adventure ambassador and has travelled the world on two wheels

📷 Joe Pichler

Before Leaving Home

Adam Lewis

Practicalities

A section of tarmac brings welcome relief in Bolivia
Chris Smith

reparing well in advance for any overland adventure is where half the battle is won – get it right here and the chances of something going wrong on the trip can be reduced significantly, though not completely eradicated.

It's important to get certain bits nailed down early – paperwork, budgets, routes, kit and bike preparation. Much of this is time consuming, particularly the paperwork, and you will need to keep on top of the project in between your work, family life and other commitments as the departure date looms ever closer.

You may already have an idea of whether you want to ride solo, with a friend or in a small group. If not, it is worth spending time to research the different options, always bearing in mind what it is that you want to get out of the trip.

Funding your adventure and making sure that you have an accurate budget in place is another important element, as is the timing. Finally, it's imperative to do as much research as possible. The more information you have to hand from a cultural, technical and even geographic perspective, the better placed you will be to deal with the unexpected when out on the road. Determine how best to access the most current and reliable information and then use it to plan appropriately.

Everyone will approach the preparation phase differently, but be careful not to plan too much. There is a fine balance to be had between preparing adequately and taking your planning to a point that it becomes a military-style operation. It's impossible to predict what might happen once you set out – a border crossing may be closed, the bike might break down, you may want to detour to see a special sight or you may fall ill and not be able to ride for a couple of days – any number of issues can rapidly impact on the best laid intentions so it's best not to set out a plan and schedule which are too structured – instead allow yourself a window with an adequate amount of time to complete your objective, making sure that all the vital issues have been covered before you leave home.

Character

Adventure motorcycling appeals to people for very different reasons – some head off to fulfil a lifelong dream, others to convey a message to the world, while many use it simply to get away from the rat race. Whatever the motivation, appreciate that you will be confronted with a number of both mental and physical challenges, particularly on trips of longer duration.

Writing about his experiences in the Darien Gap, Ed Culberson confesses that the journey had subjected him "to long periods of heavy introspection, the kind of thought only solitary travel can produce". There is certainly no magic recipe of personal traits to suit an overland adventure but there are a few key factors to consider:

Attitude – Start small by doing an initial trip over a long weekend, then extend this to a week the next time round to assess if you are happy with what it will take to sustain this type of activity over a longer period of time, further from home and over tougher terrain

Mental toughness – No this is not the Dakar Rally, but at times it may feel like it and at times you may be extending yourself further than you thought possible

Being alone for long stretches – Even if not on a solo trip, one gets a lot of time to think

Determination – It is important to have the end goal in sight at all times

Flexibility – It is vital to be able to adapt as detailed planning can often pale into insignificance

Fitness – Riding a fully-laden adventure bike for long stretches is a physically demanding exercise and in addition to mental toughness, you will need a reasonable level of basic fitness to cope with the demands.

Everyone will have different riding abilities – bear this in mind when forming your group
📷 Metal Mule
📷 Waldo van der Waal

Companions

One of the most important choices to make early on is whether to ride alone, with a friend, or as part of a larger group as it has implications on a number of fronts. If you've had some overland experience then a solo trip can be considered, but if you are new to adventure motorcycling, then joining a larger party in the form of a group of friends or even a commercially operated trip may be the best way of achieving your goal.

Going Solo

Going solo certainly offers maximum flexibility – you can follow your own route, stop when you want to and set a riding pace that you feel comfortable with. The downside is that you are more vulnerable when travelling solo and if you get into any difficulty, mechanical or otherwise, you will either have to fix it yourself or rely on the assistance of passers-by. Drop your bike over in soft sand – it may weigh as much as 660lb (300kg) or more – and you'll soon be wishing you had someone with you to help!

You will of course meet other travellers en route, but travelling overland alone is a far more 'real' experience. There is great satisfaction in a solo achievement, though you will not have anyone to share both the good and bad memories of the trip. You will also have to deal with things directly and will be forced to interact with the local population to get things done. Going solo is not recommended for a first timer, particularly not if the itinerary includes tough remote routes.

Two Up

Travelling with a friend who shares the same goals and expectations can be hugely rewarding. That said, some of

the world's best known expeditions and adventure travels have been undone or at least unhinged by differing personalities and characters so it's important to know the person you're travelling with, understand their expectations and concerns (at the same time sharing yours with him or her), and even go so far as to have a plan in your mind as to how to deal with the situation if it all goes horribly wrong and you decide to part company from one another midway through the ride. In these circumstances, always carefully consider the merits of splitting up, the risks involved and the importance of the friendship before making any decision.

Riding pillion is an option but this has some serious implications — storage space will be severely constrained and the load on the bike will be significant, making it difficult to control over rough terrain and nearly impossible in soft sand.

Groups

Even with the best intentions, it is unlikely that you will be able to establish a large group of people all willing to commit to the same objective, budget and time frame. Initial enthusiasm soon disappears as individuals assess the real implications and you are more likely to end up with a much smaller group than initially planned. If you can successfully get a group together, this has a number of advantages:

↑ **Choose your riding partners carefully as you'll share both the good and the bad times together**
📷 Johan Engelbrecht

- It offers a level of security – there is safety in numbers and with that comes an element of responsibility for one another
- It allows for a broad set of skills – some in the group may be more technically minded while others may be good at navigating, first aid or planning
- It's a great way to build your experience and prepare for a solo trip
- One is able to share experiences, skills, duties and decision making.

On the downside, group travel generally means:
- One doesn't get to interact with locals as much
- There will be a lack of flexibility in the route with different interests across the group
- There may be pressure to meet set objectives
- There may be an uncomfortable group dynamic and personality clashes amongst group members.

Sometimes the smallest thing can trigger a reaction in people, particularly if you are thrust into a Third World environment where there may be limited communications, little or inaccurate information from which to make decisions, climate extremes, disinterested civil servants and a language barrier to deal with. It is vital to discuss the potential for this kind of eventuality in the planning stages and to ensure that you can formulate a successful outcome bearing in mind the risks associated with each potential scenario.

Guided group trips run on a commercial basis aren't always favoured by traditionalists, but the growth and success enjoyed by operators in this part of the market cannot be ignored. If anything, a more structured trip offers several key points worth considering for the beginner, including:
- Less unknowns (costs, for example) and more structure
- The opportunity to travel with and meet like-minded individuals, perhaps even make friends for future trips
- The benefit of local knowledge and perhaps exploring less well-known routes.

Routes

Your final destination and the route you take to get there will be influenced by a number of different factors, including the time you have available, budget, the daily range achievable on your chosen bike and the objectives you set. It may be that you want to ride to a specific point – Timbuktu in Mali for example, or perhaps to Machu Picchu in Peru. Or it may be that you simply want to spend time exploring a particular country or region. Some people will want to traverse entire continents while others will commit to at least a full year for a round-the-world expedition.

Invariably linked to all of this is the likely weather you will encounter and this soon becomes a vital factor to consider when deciding on the best time to go. In Africa, for example, the climate extremes are significant and leaving from Europe to ride south across the continent means the heat of the Sahara Desert in the north needs to be avoided as well as the heavy rains across the equatorial region in the third quarter of each year (often at their heaviest from June to September). Bear these sorts of factors in mind when planning and research carefully to be certain that you consider the duration of the trip and the regions you are likely to be in at different times of the year.

CHECKLIST FOR AN ORGANISED TOUR GROUP

- **What training, if any, is offered?**
- **What back-up is provided en route?**
- **What is the expected level of experience?**
- **What is included and excluded from the fee being paid (eg freight, accommodation, guides, support vehicles, meals, flights, fuel, servicing, tolls, visas, carnets)?**
- **What level of insurance is required? Most operators will ask that you have comprehensive travel insurance designed to cover adventure travel**
- **What sort of deposit might be required to secure your place on the trip?**
- **Always carefully read and understand the general terms and conditions of any agreement you sign with the tour operator**

Africa

From the sands of the Sahara in the north, the Rift valley in the east, the jungles covering much of the central regions and the sheer beauty of the Cape, the African continent offers perhaps the most varied selection of terrain and sights you are likely to encounter on one continent and for many represents the ultimate adventure ride. Add to this the fact that several countries are regarded as politically unstable, the terrain is some of the toughest you will come across anywhere in the world and you are virtually guaranteed adventure of some description.

The ongoing political instability means the continent is constantly changing. Borders open and close without warning and tensions move to new areas overnight. This can be frustrating for those used to First World efficiencies but with the right approach and keeping up to date on the latest developments, traversing the continent is an unforgettable experience – just be prepared to modify your itinerary at short notice. A carnet is required for many African countries and a full set of jabs is recommended, as are water purification tablets.

If your time is limited, Morocco provides a fascinating introduction to the continent and is easily accessible from Europe. Anyone heading for Egypt should check the costs associated with importing bikes into the country – in 2007 these were running at 800 per cent of the value of the machine!

A full traverse of the continent in either direction is a fairly substantial undertaking (around two months and 7,800 miles) (12,500km) and timing is a significant factor given the diverse climatic regions you will be passing through. Anyone considering a full run, particularly first-timers, would be advised to use one of the two traditional trans-African routes which by and large attempt to circumnavigate the Sahara. For a north to south run, two options are:

- Commencing in Egypt and running the full length of the eastern coast of the continent through Egypt, Sudan, Ethiopia, Kenya, Tanzania, Malawi, Zambia, Zimbabwe, Namibia and/or Botswana before finally making it to South Africa; or
- A more westerly route starting in Morocco and then Mauritania running around the bulge of Africa. Some travellers choose to then ship their bikes to the east or south of the continent to avoid some of the unstable central areas. Those electing to make the run east need to negotiate the likes of Mali, Nigeria, Niger, and Chad before making it to Sudan from where the remainder of the easterly route makes for a reasonably straightforward run to Cape Town.

Alternatively, you could consider an adventure based solely in the south, taking in a combination of countries which offer a wonderful flavour of the continent: South Africa, Namibia, Botswana, Zimbabwe, Mozambique, Zambia, Lesotho and Swaziland. Ease of access and favourable exchange rates from the USA or Europe can help to offset the costs of shipping your bike to the region.

Riding solo has its advantages but isn't for everyone
📷 Robert Wicks

Asia

The Asian continent is as massive as it is diverse. Few continents include countries and regions as varied as Nepal, Japan and India which makes for wonderfully different biking adventures which could include a traverse along the old Silk Route, over the Khyber Pass to Pakistan, on to India, Thailand, Malaysia, Singapore and Indonesia before heading to Australia.

It's possibly best to look at the continent as three regions – South East Asia, the Indian Subcontinent and Asia-Pacific, all of which have striking cultural and economic differences.

The South East region offers tremendous value for money and includes countries such as Thailand, Laos, Vietnam, Cambodia, Malaysia, Singapore, and Indonesia. Travelling overland between countries is easy and expenses such as food and accommodation are very well priced. There is a huge amount to see in the region and if your ride isn't proving to be adventurous enough, there are some spectacular adventure sports to try including river rafting, jungle trekking and some of the best scuba diving in the world.

The Indian Subcontinent, home of the spectacular Himalayas, includes India, Nepal, Pakistan, Bangladesh and Sri Lanka. Most countries offer tremendous value for money and wonderful sights and sounds. Parts of the region, particularly India, can be as exciting as they are frustrating and the poverty, squalor, pollution and poor sanitation will take a lot of getting used to. That said the country is experiencing a tourist boom and going through a period of unprecedented growth which should hopefully facilitate various improvements along the way. The region includes large parts of the legendary Karakoram Highway – the highest paved international road in the world and a remarkable feat of engineering. The route extends more than 620 miles (1,000km) and connects China and Pakistan across the Karakoram mountain range at an altitude of 15,397ft (4,693m) – a must on any adventure ride in the region.

The final area is the Asia-Pacific region which includes China as well as Korea, Taiwan, Japan and Mongolia. Be sure to pick your routes carefully, be prepared to deal with language barriers in this region – particularly in rural areas – and check on the ever-easing regulations in China where use of your own machine outside of an organised tour group is still technically illegal.

⬇ **No matter where you are in the world, wonderful scenes such as this typify adventure motorcycling**
📷 Metal Mule

The Middle East

Tensions in the Middle East can make this region difficult to travel in but that said, it offers tremendous scope for the adventure traveller from the history and culture of Jerusalem to the ancient city of Petra in Jordan and diving one of the world's great reefs in the Red Sea. The most typical overland route starts in Istanbul and leads to Cairo, Syria, Jordan and then Israel, perhaps taking in Iran before heading further east. Various boats and ferries can be used to bridge overland travel. Bureaucracy is evident and your carnet will be essential for motorcycle travel. Be wary of travelling at night and avoid riding during the heat of the day as dehydration is a real issue. Be aware of dress customs and if you plan to visit Israel, try to make this the last stop on the journey as several Arab countries will not allow you entry should you have an Israeli stamp in your passport. It is also worth keeping a close eye on political developments as the region is in constant flux.

Australia

Like Africa, Australia offers a huge variety of geography, from desert and tropical rainforest to mountain ranges and exotic beaches. The sheer scale of the continent – Australia is almost as large as all of Europe put together – means distances between major centres are always going to be substantial.

These vast distances (an extended trip around the continent can cover more than 12,500 miles) (20,000km), together with an appreciation for the climate are perhaps your most important considerations when planning a trip in Australia.

Much of the country which extends beyond the Great Dividing Range (the country's most substantial mountain range stretching some 2,200 miles (3,500km) from the north-eastern tip of Queensland and running the entire length of the eastern coastline through New South Wales) is a fairly harsh desert environment, particularly in the summer. Secondary roads in the outback and in Central Australia are almost all unsealed. Heavy rainfall can make travel on unsurfaced roads hazardous. Finally, it is highly recommended that you avoid riding between sunset and sunrise, particularly at twilight given the likelihood of animals on the road.

↑ **Oman is the Middle East's adventure riding paradise**

📷 Robert Wicks

North America

Perhaps not as challenging as an African adventure, a trip around parts of North America will be rewarding for other reasons – it is a truly diverse region with so much to offer the adventure motorcyclist. The continent features some of the most breathtaking landscapes and varied terrain with everything from arid deserts to glaciers. Travelling in North America is not particularly difficult and the vast expanse that is Canada offers some of the most outstanding riding in the world. The wealth of national parks, forests and outdoor activities will certainly make for a great itinerary. General infrastructure and roads allow for any number of different routes. No carnet is needed and the low cost of fuel is a real bonus.

One way to see large parts of the USA would be to consider the 5,000 mile (8,000km) Trans-America Trail, a coast-to-coast, off-road motorcycle adventure. The route crosses the USA from west to east through at least 11 states using various dirt, forest and farm roads, dropping down into dried-up creek beds and riding atop abandoned railroad grades. See www.transamtrail.com for more details.

Central America

Each of the seven countries which make up the Central American region are unique and offer something special to the intrepid traveller.

Heading south from Mexico, the first stop is likely to be Guatemala where large areas of the interior are wholly undeveloped and will offer some challenging riding. El Salvador has put the tensions of conflict behind it and made great strides forward – it's the smallest country in the region but its geography, cuisine and friendly people make for a memorable journey. Honduras may present some bureaucratic difficulties and is still coming to terms with centuries of political instability. Nicaragua too has made great progress in recent years while its southerly neighbour, Costa Rica, is regarded by many as the gem of the region.

Panama signals the end of the road unless you are keen to put yourself through arguably some of the toughest terrain anywhere in the world – the notorious Darien Gap – a large area of undeveloped swampland, ravines and impenetrable jungle which effectively separates Panama in Central America from Colombia in South America.

It measures some 100 miles (160km) long and about

30 miles (50km) wide and should not be attempted without a thorough understanding of the physical challenges involved – there is no road to speak of and crossing the jungle will mean transporting your bike along river sections in dug out canoes. Given ongoing security issues in the region, most travellers elect to ship themselves and their bikes to avoid it.

South America

If you have travelled in Europe and/or North America, then a trip to South America is an excellent next step, offering some of the best scenery, some of the friendliest people and arguably some of the best adventure riding to be found anywhere in the world.

Main routes in countries such as Brazil, Chile and Argentina are well surfaced while roads in the more mountainous regions of Peru, Ecuador and Bolivia tend to be less forgiving. The continent is generally pretty safe and no carnet is required for travel which makes life a fair bit easier and cheaper.

Make sure you have a full set of inoculations before leaving and keep your malaria tablets handy. Don't underestimate the size of the continent – Chile's Atacama Desert extends some 620 miles (1,000km)

between the Andes mountains and the Pacific Ocean. Covering an area of some 70,000 square miles (182,000km^2), it is the driest place on Earth. Always keep abreast of political developments while you travel as these may have some impact on your routing. Undoubtedly one of the highlights has to be a trip to Ushuaia, the southernmost town on the continent.

⬇ **South America offers some of the most spectacular and varied terrain**
📷 Touratech

Trans Americas Motorcycle Expedition

GlobeBusters

Duration 19 weeks
Approximate distance 20,000 miles (32,000km)
Most miles in a day 475 miles (765km)
Days off the bike 42
Highest altitude 15,750ft (4,800m)
Start point Anchorage, Alaska
End point Buenos Aires, Argentina

Prudhoe Bay

Anchorage   Tok
                    Watson Lake
                    Prince George
                    Yellowstone
                    & Grand Teton
                    Grand Canyon
                    Tucson
                        Zacateras
            Palenque
                        Panama
                        City
                        Bogota

                    Cusco
            Lima
                Arica

        Santiago   Buenos Aires
        Bariloche

        Calafate
                Ushuaia

North to south
across the Americas
– the ride of a lifetime
GlobeBusters

Following their double Guinness World
Record success, for the Fastest Ride
Around the World and the Fastest Trans
Americas by Motorcycle, Kevin and Julia
Sanders founded GlobeBusters, now a
world leader in motorcycle expeditions across
the world.

Specialising in unique motorcycle journeys
for aspiring adventure riders, one of
GlobeBusters' most challenging is a ride of
epic proportions descending the Americas
along the Pan-American Highway from Alaska
to Argentina – otherwise known as the Trans
Americas Expedition.

The Pan-American Highway is an extensive
network of roads some 30,000 miles
(48,000km) in length and regarded as the
world's longest 'motorable road'. The most
northern point is Prudhoe Bay, Alaska and the
most southern point is Ruta 3 in Bahia
Lapataia, in Tierra del Fuego National
Park just outside of Ushuaia, the most
southern city in the world. Other than the
notorious Darien Gap, it's possible to ride the
whole length, from the top to the bottom of
the world!

This extraordinary route runs through
extremes of climate, culture and terrain –
tropical jungle in Central America, high
altitude mountain passes in the Andes in Peru,
the Atacama Desert in Chile, the Arctic
tundra in Alaska and the remote wilderness of
Patagonia. Some stretches of the highway are
passable only during the dry season, and in
many regions riding can be hazardous.

Riding this legendary route is an incredible
way to take in the diversity of North, Central
and South America in a single trip.

Route Notes – Morocco

DAY	DATE	START	END	ROUTE	DISTANCE
1	06.10.06	**OUARZAZATE** N30° 55.1' W06° 54.0'	**AKKA IRHEN** N29° 59.7' W07° 31.7'	P31, P32, Piste	190 miles (305km)
Ouarzazate ▯ Anezal 62 (62) ▯ Tazenacht 28 (90) ▯ Taliouine 85 (175) ▯ Akka Irhen 155 (330) 📷					
2	07.10.06	**AKKA IRHEN** N29° 59.7' W07° 31.7'	**FOUM ZGUID** N30° 04.0' W06° 52.0'	Piste	67 miles (108km)
Akka Irhen ▯ El-Mhamid 95 (95) ▯ Foum Zguid 10 (105) 📷					
3	08.10.06	**FOUM ZGUID** N30° 04.0' W06° 52.0'	**ZAGORA** N30° 19.7' W05° 50.3'	Piste	105 miles (169km)
Foum Zguid ▯ Bou Rbia 80 (80) ▯ Zagora 90 (170) 📷					
4	09.10.06	**ZAGORA** N30° 19.7' W05° 50.3'	**DRAA VALLEY / TAGOUNITE** N29° 59.0' W05° 35.0'	P39, 6958, 6965	78 miles (126km)
Zagora ▯ Draa Valley (Return to Zagora) 60 (60) ▯ Tamegroute 18 (78) ▯ Tagounite 48 (126) 📷					
5	10.10.06	**TAGOUNITE** N29° 59.0' W05° 35.0'	**TAMMASSINT** N31° 05.7' W04° 00.7'	Piste	103 miles (165km)
Tagounite ▯ Hassi Zguilma 85 (85) ▯ Hassi Iarine 25 (110) ▯ Tammassint 55 (165) 📷					
6	11.10.06	**TAMMASSINT** N31° 05.7' W04° 00.7'	**HASSI REMLIA** N30° 41.60' W04° 24.0'	Piste	43 miles (70km)
Tammassint ▯ Hassi Remlia 70 (70) 📷					
7	12.10.06	**HASSI REMLIA** N30° 41.60' W04° 24.0'	**MERZOUGA** N31° 05.7' W04° 00.7'	Piste	60 miles (97km)
Hassi Remlia ▯ Hassi Ouzina 32 (32) ▯ Taouz 35 (67) ▯ Merzouga 30 (97) 📷					
8	13.10.06	**MERZOUGA** N31° 05.7' W04° 00.7'	**TINERHIR** N31° 31.2' W05° 32.0'	3454, Piste	150 miles (241km)
Merzouga ▯ Erfoud 53 (53) ▯ Rissani 17 (70) ▯ Mecissi 55 (125) ▯ Alnif 48 (173) ▯ Tinerhir 📷					
9/10	14-15.10.06	**DADES GORGE / LAKE ISELI & TISLIT / TODRA GORGE LOOP** N31° 23.0' W05° 59.0'		P32, 56901, 56902	209 miles (336km)
▯ Tinerhir ▯ Boumalne Dades 53 (53) ▯ Dades Gorge to Msemrir 65 (118) ▯ Agoudal 50 (168) ▯ Imilchil 30 (198) ▯ Lake Iseli 18 (216) 📷 ▯ Agoudal 48 (264) ▯ Ait Hani 36 (300) ▯ Todra Gorge to Tinerhir 36 (336) 📷					
11	16.10.06	**TINERHIR** N31° 31.2' W05° 32.0'	**OUARZAZATE** N30° 55.1' W06° 54.0'	Piste, 6956, P31	159 miles (256km)
Tinerhir ▯ Iknioiuln 64 (64) ▯ Nekob 63 (127) ▯ Tansikht 38 (165) ▯ Agdz 29 (194) ▯ Ouarzazate 62 (256) 📷					

Route Notes

Once you have decided on your route it is useful to start drafting up a set of specific route notes. These are designed to draw together all the essential details of the route at a glance and supplement your other sources of information, acting much like a rally-style road book, only simpler in form. Your notes can take various forms but should ideally include major towns, GPS waypoints, road names and distances. Various publications and websites can help with GPS co-ordinates and in some cases, very thorough route information, so leaving a space to make further notes is also useful. The table opposite gives you an idea of some typical route notes for a journey in Morocco.

Budget

Adventure motorcycling often causes people to do irrational things – some sell their houses, others give up lucrative careers while many save every spare penny for years to undertake the ride of a lifetime.

Budgets for round-the-world trips can easily run into several thousand pounds while a short three-week adventure will come in at a fraction of that cost. Irrespective of how far you're going, being able to budget accurately from the outset of the planning stage is vital to give you at least a reasonable idea of what the trip should cost. Without a clear idea, you risk putting your trip in jeopardy (you may also compromise your financial security when you get back), particularly if it's a long haul venture

and you might find yourself having to bring in extra funds by working or borrowing money to keep travelling.

As a first step, use the Internet and guidebooks to research each of the countries you are going to visit so that you understand what a visa will cost, the price of fuel, ferry costs, potential accommodation options and other expenses. Also try and identify any additional costs specific to each of the countries such as special insurance or road taxes.

No budget can accurately provide for unexpected expenses, least of all a budget for an adventure motorcycling trip, so it is prudent to allow for at least some contingency provision. Having some money in reserve is vital for when things go wrong, but can also come in handy if you want to enjoy certain unplanned activities or additional routes. This provision, together with a decent level of research into the 'known' costs, should allow you to generate a relatively realistic budget to work towards.

Assuming you don't already have one parked in the garage, your single biggest expense is likely to be the motorcycle itself and, if applicable, the carnet which, for some countries, can push your budget to an unexpected level.

It may be tempting to spend significant amounts of money on a range of the latest accessories but remember that this can very quickly add up to a large sum in itself. Accessories often add a lot of unnecessary weight and many of them may not be essential, so choose wisely and allow your budget to go further on some of the more important elements.

➜ **On the road in Morocco – detailed route notes help with navigation and keep the end goal in sight**
📷 Robert Wicks

A high point on this round-the-world adventure

📷 Danny Burroughs

Certain continents are much cheaper than others. Travelling in Asia or Africa, for example, is considerably easier on the budget than say, Europe or North America particularly when you consider some of the basic day-to-day expenses like food, fuel and accommodation. As a guide, budget up to £50 per day for most countries in western and northern Europe, and around £35 per day for the rest of Europe, Canada and much of the USA for basic day-to-day costs. This would exclude any major costs such as servicing or freighting. On a budget, much of Central and South America can be achieved on £20. Africa and large parts of Asia can be done on £10 or less.

It is difficult to plan for unknown emergencies which can come in a variety of forms – unexpected repairs, getting specialist parts sent out to you, unforeseen medical expenses or an emergency flight home. A 'reasonable' ballpark figure would be to allow somewhere between 25-40 per cent of the total of your 'on the road' costs as a contingency provision.

A final consideration in planning your budget is to take into account any costs which might be ongoing at home while you are away on your travels. If you have sold up everything to take an extended round-the-world trip this may be less of an issue, but a three-month trip through Africa probably means the mortgage and utility bills still need to be paid so be sure to factor these costs into the equation and make provisions for payments to be made in your absence.

Sponsorship

The idea of getting your trip sponsored either in part or completely is a great idea but may end up being a far more onerous task than you first anticipate. Getting too caught up in this aspect of the trip can detract from valuable planning and preparation time but if you have the right contacts and/or a trip that is unique and likely to enjoy valuable media coverage, then it would be worth committing some time to this challenge.

Sponsors all have very different agendas and objectives – those of a large corporate entity will be poles apart from your local motorcycle shop that may provide you with some parts support and technical assistance.

BUDGETING CHECKLIST

Start-up Costs
- Bike Purchase Cost
- Research (maps and books)
- Training Course
- Visas
- Carnet (if applicable)
- Modifications
- Accessories
- Tools
- Riding Gear
- Equipment
- Freighting
- Ferries
- Insurance
- Inoculations
- Medical Kit

On the Road Expenses
- Fuel
- Tyres
- Maintenance
- Spares
- Servicing
- Accommodation
- Food
- Freighting and Ferries
- Communication
- Border Crossings
- Taxes

Other Costs
- Contingency Provision
- Ongoing 'Home' Expenses

Once you have an idea of the budget, keep a close eye on your spending and remember that your trip is more about mindset than money

The *Long Way Round* and *Long Way Down* expeditions enjoyed very good levels of sponsorship and showed what is possible at one end of the scale. Obviously the involvement of Hollywood superstar Ewan McGregor had a significant impact on the success of the project, and the marketing machine behind these two adventures was able to generate an extensive amount of press coverage. It would be extremely difficult for an individual to deliver the same kind of value, so these trips are best used as case studies of 'market potential' when talking to prospective sponsors.

Tips:

- Be clear about what it is you are offering and if you agree a deal, be sure to sign a contract so that you know your mutual obligations
- Make sure you can deliver what you promise – if you offer a sponsor certain 'image rights' from the trip, they will be expecting high resolution, quality photography and you need to be in a position to provide this
- Clearly show how your trip will return value (astute sponsors will want anything from two to five times of media and exposure value back from their initial investment made in your trip). If your expedition is not newsworthy, it is likely to fail at the first hurdle when talking to sponsors
- Do what you can to downplay the risk element associated with the trip – sponsors are often reluctant to engage with high-risk activities
- Demonstrate the commitment you have from media partners. This will put the sponsor at ease and leaves you not having to chase hard-to-find media opportunities once back home. Try to develop a relationship with a local or national magazine and send the editor regular updates via the Internet to provide readers with news and pictures – this gives sponsors a level of guaranteed regular exposure. For lengthy trips your own website, updated as you travel, is also a great idea to provide news to a wider audience and a good place to showcase the sponsor and their products
- Understand the sponsor's business and what your expedition could do for them – developing a tailored programme to meet their needs is a great first step
- Don't underestimate the value you hold – at the end of the trip you will come back having had great experiences which can often form the basis of an inspired talk to the sponsor's staff and clients, thereby returning further first-hand personal value.

Research

Once you have an idea of where you plan to travel, your research needs to start in earnest. As adventure motorcycling has grown in popularity, so have the number of potential information resources, from reference books and personal accounts to dedicated websites and discussion forums on the Internet.

Essentially you need to start gathering a file of information on all the different aspects of the trip – routes, maps, visas, carnets, health requirements, equipment and a host of other topics.

The Internet is without doubt the most useful tool available given the nature of the information available – remember that some of the areas you are likely to be travelling in may well be regarded as unstable or where borders open and close without warning, so it is vital to get the most current information. The Internet is also a useful tool to track the routes favoured by commercial operators and also to read other travellers' websites to gain insight into what kit they took, what worked and what didn't. Horizonsunlimited.com is a great starting point.

You also need to start sourcing the best possible maps available. Most travel bookshops should stock a good selection of current maps but for the widest selection both in store and online, the likes of Stanfords in London (www.stanfords.co.uk) is arguably the best in the business.

Other good sources of information

Motorcycle Publications – More and more monthly motorcycle magazines are dedicating space to adventure-related topics and these stories can often be useful for good advice, tips and a touch of inspiration.

Country Guidebooks and Travel Magazines – These invariably contain an 'off the beaten track' section or specifics relating to adventure travel and can be used to source particular information on the countries you plan to visit. They are useful for research at home but of limited use on the road. They don't tell you whether or not a hotel has safe parking for a motorcycle and by the time you get there the price guides are generally out of date. On the other hand, guidebooks do tell you in which area of town you will find cheap accommodation and give you an idea of what to see. Given how bulky they can be, consider guides that cover regions rather than countries.

Motoring Organisations – Your local or national motoring organisation is generally a good source of information relating to the official paperwork you are likely to need for the trip.

📷 Danny Wilkinson / ABR

Tour Operator Brochures and Videos – If you are interested in specific commercial tours, enquire about brochures and videos from the tour operator for an insight into what to expect.

Motorcycle Clubs – Joining a club may be of use particularly if some of the members have a specific interest in adventure motorcycling.

Other Travellers – Nothing beats talking to someone who has just returned from the place you are heading to because they are likely to be able to provide you with first-hand knowledge of conditions and what to expect, but always remember that to a certain extent, 'the unexpected' is the reason for going. Also remember once you're out on the road to be sure to glean as much information as possible from fellow travellers you meet, particularly if they have just completed a route you're about to tackle.

Travellers' Meetings – The growth in adventure motorcycling in recent years has seen a number of well organised and informative annual 'Travellers' Meetings'. Those run by Grant Johnson from Horizons Unlimited and Bernd Tesch's Globetrotter meetings are some of the best around and it is very worthwhile trying to attend at least one of these to get first-hand information from people who have 'been there and done it'. Normally held over a couple of days, the meetings consist of a series of presentations covering the major topics for aspiring adventure motorcyclists. The speakers are generally all highly experienced adventurers who are happy to share their insight.

Books – See a detailed list of publications and authors at the back of this book.

GRANT JOHNSON – FOUNDER OF HORIZONSUNLIMITED.COM

The motorcycle, since its invention, has appealed to the adventurous among us – it brings back the early days of adventuring on a horse, the single rider against the wind and the open country. Adventure motorcycling began with the first eager, curious rider on a bike rolling down a track he'd never seen before, wondering what was there, and if his new machine could take him there. Often it didn't but it was fun trying!

We did our own round-the-world trip over 11 years, leaving home in 1987 and finally returning, temporarily, in 1998. When we left home in 1987 we knew of only three people, Ted Simon, and Philip Funnell and his wife Hilary, who had ridden around the world before us. Before the Internet, information was very limited, and the few round-the-world bikers were disconnected, doing their own thing in their own individual way. Now with the Internet it's so easy to connect to other travellers that many of us have become part of a family, spread out across the globe, but connected, getting vital inspiration and information from each other at the click of a mouse. Now, we know that there were hundreds of round-the-world motorcycle travellers before us, and certainly thousands since.

The big, round-the-world dream of many, often kindled by Ted Simon and *Jupiter's Travels*, or more recently Ewan McGregor and Charley Boorman's *Long Way Round* and *Long Way Down* adventures, is becoming more and more often a reality.

We meet each other on the road, brief but often intense moments shared, we may travel together for a while, and then go our own way – but with new and strong friendships forged by a common bond, the road. Some travel for a few months, others for years, never really wanting to stop. Eventually for most, life on the road wears thin, and normal life (whatever that is) or perhaps a relationship, beckons. But it's only temporary – most of us head back to the road again and again.

Returning 11 years later in 1998, we were planning to write a book of our adventures on six continents, but it was the beginning of the Internet era, so instead we created a website, www.horizonsunlimited. com, which has since struck a chord among thousands of adventurous people. We are often encouraged by e-mails telling us how we made it seem possible, even easy, with all the information people could want in one place.

The information is out there – make of it what you will. But most importantly, do what you can, always, and with no regrets.

📷 Provided courtesy of *Long Way Round*

PREPARING FOR THE
LONG WAY ROUND

www.longwayround.com
www.longwaydown.com

Given the scale of the *Long Way Round* expedition, together with the commercial implications of a big-budget trip of this nature, the sponsors involved as well as the level of media attention, Ewan McGregor and Charley Boorman undertook a series of in-depth training courses and intensive route planning research to ensure they were fully prepared before their 20,000-mile (32,000km) journey. Key activities included:

Advanced First Aid Course – The pair learnt how to deal with medical emergencies when travelling unescorted through remote places without hospitals and medical facilities nearby. This included how to treat broken bones or sew their own wounds and provided them with the confidence required to carry out medical emergency assistance on each other if necessary.

Bush Craft and Survival Training – Focused on the natural threats of animals and plants. Learning how to light a fire without the aid of man-made substances was one of the most important skills they learnt.

Hostile Environment Training – The riders spent time learning how to deal with everything from rogue border officials to animal attacks and freezing temperatures.

Bike Maintenance – Specialists from BMW demonstrated the detailed mechanical functions of all aspects of the bikes and trained the pair intensively to make sure they were able to attend to basic maintenance and repair damage on the road.

Bike Familiarisation – The pair undertook a series of courses at the BMW off-road centre in Wales which gave them invaluable off-road training for the rough roads ahead.

GPS Training – The use of a GPS was a vital component in the success of the trip – getting lost would have cost them valuable hours and even days. It was equally important that the support team were able to pinpoint their exact location should they have required emergency assistance.

Personal Training – Riding motorbikes and surviving in the wilderness requires a tremendous amount of strength, energy and stamina. The pair enlisted the help of a personal trainer over a four-month period to get them as fit as possible and ready to go. This included a course in self-defence.

Nutrition – They took advice from a nutritionist who demonstrated how certain foods could complement the nutritional balance of others. This was to ensure they chose the best options from the limited availability of food during the trip.

Language/Culture – Given that over the course of their journey the language that was most commonly used after English was Russian, the pair undertook an intensive language course to enable them to communicate with locals and get by with everyday tasks.

Choice of Motorcycle

© Joe Pichler / KTM

n recent years, despite lagging sales in most sectors, the adventure segment of the market has been growing in leads and bounds with almost every major manufacturer launching a new machine in the category, some for the very first time. They clearly see a future in the burgeoning adventure market and have left aspiring adventurers spoilt for choice.

Much of the growth can be attributed to changing lifestyles as consumers opt for a motorcycle which allows them to commute but is also capable of allowing them to escape the city and confines of modern living to find a quiet corner of the world that maybe, just maybe, no one has seen before. Lured by the promise, or at least the possibility, of leaving all too familiar surroundings for the freedom of wide-open spaces, motorcyclists old and new are trading in their cruisers and sports bikes for something a little more versatile. With slightly knobby tires, improved ground clearance and a sense of adventure, the stage is set for, well, anything. Long road trips, detours into the wilderness, cross-continental tours – all are within reach.

Globally, the category is a broad one, with manufacturers adopting various naming conventions – 'adventure enduro', 'dual sport', 'rally touring' and 'adventure tourer' – to describe their particular model.

Some leading manufacturers have adopted an all-terrain approach with models such as the new KTM 1190 and successful 990, as well as the BMW R 1200 GS and F 800 GS, all of which are well equipped for all-terrain use and can comfortably cope with cross-continent expeditions with potentially very little modification required to the machine which rolls off the showroom floor. Other manufacturers have opted for models which, at first glance, exhibit "adventure" qualities, but underneath the skin are really road bikes with an adventure-oriented façade and this should always be borne in mind when making a purchasing decision.

The majority of machines in the sector tend to have large-capacity engines (600cc – 1200cc) intended for operating more than comfortably as a road tourer, but are equally adept on gravel tracks or even rougher terrain. For all their capacity and load-carrying ability, the biggest downside is weight which precludes them from coping well with extreme conditions. Never assume you can load the bike up excessively – the complete opposite applies – they are big bikes to start with and as a result you need as little additional weight as possible.

A smaller, lighter and more nimble off-road 'enduro' style machine (300cc–600cc) is best suited to dealing with arduous terrain but this too is a compromise as on-road ability is often reduced, load-carrying capacity is generally less, as is the bike's range unless kitted out with a long range fuel tank.

While this book generally tends to focus on the larger-capacity category (600cc–1200cc), there are a number of smaller machines including the Honda CRF 450 and Suzuki DRZ 400 that, with varying degrees of modification, are all capable and worth considering particularly if you're looking to keep weight to a minimum and possibly a low seat height.

Current Models

Key Factors

It is vital that before one makes a decision on the choice of bike, the intended application is clear. Knowing as much as possible about where you are headed and the type of terrain you face will greatly assist in the decision-making process.

There is no 'perfect' overland bike. What's good off road isn't necessarily good on road and what is right for one person is not necessarily right for another, so choose the bike that is the best compromise for you and the trip.

Be sure to research and test ride a range of alternatives before making your final decision. Key factors to look for include:

Budget – remember that a brand new, high-end all-conquering adventure bike may look like the best choice from the images of remote locations in the sales literature, but this is likely to come at a significant cost and will have a serious knock-on effect on the price of your carnet, which in turn can put a large dent in your overall budget. Explore second-hand options thoroughly but be sure you are getting value for money and a machine that is in good condition capable of the trip.

Timing and Availability – the sooner you get your bike the better. As an experienced motorcyclist you will already have a fair idea of how you want to customise it and as a novice, you will need as much time with your new best friend as possible, especially if you are planning on some off-road training which if possible, is best done on your own machine (though not essential). Furthermore, orders for certain parts you might want may take time to be fulfilled by aftermarket suppliers plus you can't complete much of the paperwork you need without a registration number.

Range and Consumption – consider the distances you will need to travel between points and understand if the bike's range is suitable. Fuel consumption is also important – a big 1,000cc engine, for example, can be a thirsty beast, particularly when working hard in the desert.

Load-carrying Ability – assess how much you need to carry and how the bike will cope with the load.

Terrain – research and understand the terrain you are going to be covering – some bikes are far better suited to certain types of terrain than others.

Spares and Reliability – ideally you want to choose a machine with a good track record and also one which is likely to have readily available spares which you can either buy on the road or source with relative ease from home.

Mechanical Knowledge – appreciate that you will need a level of mechanical competence to deal with technical issues that will arise from time to time. At the very least you should know how to carry out a basic service on the machine.

Handling and Weight – if possible before purchasing, try to ride a fully laden machine to appreciate what you are in for. A big 1,000cc off-road bike with fully loaded panniers and some additional gear can easily weigh in excess of 660lb (300kg).

Seat Height – ensure that the seat height allows you to reach the ground comfortably with at least one foot flat on the road surface. This does not sound that important but it is when riding at slow speeds, in traffic, on uneven road surfaces or in confined places that you will appreciate its relevance. Most bikes can be lowered a little so speak to your dealer. The more comfortable you can make yourself on the bike through further modifications the better.

Aprilia
Pegaso 650 Trail

Displacement	Power	Transmission	Suspension travel	Tyres	Seat height	Dry weight	Fuel capacity
660cc	50bhp @ 6,250rpm	Five-speed / Chain	Front: 170mm Rear: 170mm	Front: 100/90–19 Rear: 130/80–17	820mm	161kg	16 litres

An excellent long-range touring bike with a history dating back more than 12 years, thanks to superior comfort, an advanced new engine and a large number of innovations aimed at improving versatility. It boasts a modern, four-valve, dry sump engine with electronic fuel injection and a 44mm throttle body, a strong diamond-shaped steel frame and spoked wheels with medium-knobbly tyres for great handling on and off the road. The 70° steering angle provides agility while the comfortable seat and riding position add to its long-distance credentials. At 820mm the seat height makes it easy to get on and off for riders of all statures.

Aprilia
ETV 1000 Caponord

Displacement	Power	Transmission	Suspension travel	Tyres	Seat height	Dry weight	Fuel capacity
998cc	98bhp @ 8,500rpm	Six-speed / Chain	Front: 175mm Rear: 185mm	Front: 110/80–19 Rear: 150/70–17	820mm	215kg	25 litres

This bike has built up a considerable following since its introduction in 2005 and is a very capable all-purpose machine with advanced technology, a pace-setting aluminium frame and a highly acclaimed, powerful V-twin engine offering all-round touring versatility. The engine has been derived directly from that of the RSV, but has been thoroughly modified to make it perfect for touring, with overall bike design emphasis on ergonomics, rider and passenger comfort, and total wind protection. Its load-carrying capacity makes it highly versatile.

Benelli
Tre-K Amazonas

Displacement	Power	Transmission	Suspension travel	Tyres	Seat height	Dry weight	Fuel capacity
1,130cc	123bhp @ 9,000rpm	Six-speed / Chain	Front: 180mm Rear: 180mm	Front: 120/70–17 Rear: 180/55–17	850mm	205kg	22 litres

As Benelli's first foray into the adventure market, the Amazonas is something of an unknown quantity. The engine comes from Benelli's other 1,130cc motorcycles which has been packaged into the frame of an upright adventure tourer. On the plus side are the long-travel suspension, comfortable riding position and slim styling and good looks. On the downside, it's not designed to take a hard knock and the engine is prone to vibrate. It also lacks some real world adventure credibility so right now it's unlikely to rival the more established contenders in the market such as BMW and KTM.

BMW
R 1150 GS Adventure

Displacement	Power	Transmission	Suspension travel	Tyres	Seat height	Dry weight	Fuel capacity
1,130cc	85bhp @ 6,750rpm	Six-speed / Shaft drive	Front: 210mm Rear: 220mm	Front: 110/80–19 Rear: 150/70–17	860mm / 900mm	232kg	30 litres

This is essentially a BMW R 1150 GS with longer-travel suspension, a large 30-litre tank, taller screen and decent off-road tyres. Built by BMW between 2001 and 2005, the bike has won countless industry awards and was used by Ewan McGregor and Charley Boorman in their 'Long Way Round' adventure. Whether on gravel paths, sand tracks, rough terrain or over long distances, the chassis ensures optimum comfort and control – even when fully loaded. You'll need to get used to the weight and height but once you do, it's an imposing, durable and highly reliable ride.

BMW
R 1200 GS

Displacement	Power	Transmission	Suspension travel	Tyres	Seat height	Dry weight	Fuel capacity
1,170cc	105bhp @ 7,500rpm	Six-speed / Shaft drive	Front: 190mm Rear: 200mm	Front: 110/80–19 Rear: 150/70–17	850mm / 870mm	203kg	20 litres

The last air-cooled R 1200 GS features a revised boxer engine that sports dual overhead cams. It's allowed for an extra 500rpm, 5hp more and a better spread of torque throughout the rev range, making the bike more rideable in off-road conditions. The real benefit comes with the optimised power at low and medium engine speeds. Other new additions include an improved dash with bigger push buttons as well as adjustable handlebars that can be set for more comfortable road use or more aggressive off-road use when you're in the standing position.

BMW
R 1200 GS (air/water-cooled)

Displacement	Power	Transmission	Suspension travel	Tyres	Seat height	Dry weight	Fuel capacity
1,170cc	125bhp @ 7,750rpm	Six-speed / Shaft drive	Front: 190mm Rear: 200mm	Front: 110/80–19 Rear: 150/70–17	850mm / 870mm	205kg	20 litres

Now in its ninth year of production and with more than 170,000 units sold the BMW R 1200 GS remains the benchmark in adventure biking. With a change to the cooling system to a compact and efficient air/water combination for optimum heat management, the bike has a new lease on life, with improved power and performance. The familiar instrument cluster is also new and riders will like the ability to make height and tilt angle adjustments to the seat as well as the freely selectable riding modes for on- and off-road use. Ground clearance has also been increased by 8mm.

BMW
R 1200 GS Adventure

Displacement	Power	Transmission	Suspension travel	Tyres	Seat height	Dry weight	Fuel capacity
1,170cc	105bhp @ 7,500rpm	Six-speed / Shaft drive	Front: 210mm Rear: 220mm	Front: 110/80–19 Rear: 150/70–17	910mm / 890mm	223kg	33 litres

The GS Adventure has set the standard for the ultimate long-distance adventure motorcycle ever since its launch in 2005. It's the perfect synthesis of agility, touring ability and off-road capability delivered in the standard package. It is hugely forgiving and stable, infinitely reliable and comfortable and copes with any terrain – a real icon of modern-day adventure motorcycling. BMW continues to enhance and upgrade its top model given competition in the sector from the likes of Ducati's Multistrada and Yamaha's brand new shaft-driven 1,200cc Super Ténéré.

BMW
HP2 Enduro

Displacement	Power	Transmission	Suspension travel	Tyres	Seat height	Dry weight	Fuel capacity
1,130cc	105bhp @ 7,000rpm	Six-speed / Shaft drive	Front: 270mm Rear: 250mm	Front: 90/90–21 Rear: 140/80–17	920mm	175kg	13 litres

Unfortunately no longer in production, this model was based, in technical terms, on the R 1200 GS, but tailored to the needs of the enduro rider by providing supreme agility and easy control over tough terrain. This is not a bike for the meek – 'HP' stands for 'high performance' and the engine delivers 105bhp combined with lightweight construction, a low centre of gravity and innovative rear suspension making for a formidable machine. Rated by Touratech's Herbert Schwarz as 'the best adventure bike BMW has ever built', the entire drive-train is laid out specifically for off-road use.

BMW
F 650 GS (Single) / G 650 GS

Displacement	Power	Transmission	Suspension travel	Tyres	Seat height	Dry weight	Fuel capacity
652cc	50bhp @ 6,500rpm	Five-speed / Chain	Front: 170mm Rear: 165mm	Front: 100/90–19 Rear: 130/80–17	780mm	176kg	17.3 litres

Over an eight year period (1995–2003), BMW sold more than 110,000 F 650 machines, with a large proportion going to female buyers and new riders. Based on the 'enduro' concept, the bike features a relaxed, upright riding position that is the ideal compromise between on-road comfort and off-road control. To accommodate riders of different heights, several seat options are available including a high seat that provides taller riders with extra legroom. With a slender engine and under-seat fuel tank the bike's overall centre of gravity is reduced, making it feel both small and light. The old 650cc single was dusted off and given a facelift in 2011 – now available as the G 650 GS.

BMW
F 650 GS Dakar / G 650 GS Sertão

Displacement	Power	Transmission	Suspension travel	Tyres	Seat height	Dry weight	Fuel capacity
652cc	50bhp @ 6,500rpm	Five-speed / Chain	Front: 210mm Rear: 210mm	Front: 90/90–21 Rear: 130/80–17	870mm	177kg	17.3 litres

This is the competition version of the BMW F 650 GS, whose forerunners won the Dakar Rally on many occasions. It's a very capable machine and has been successfully tried and tested on many adventure rides the world over. Riders benefit from the longer suspension travel, large front wheel and enduro tyres. From the figures, weight looks like a concern, but once in motion it carries the weight well and doesn't feel heavy at all – it's a balanced, simple and well constructed package, with emphasis on reliability and durability. The Dakar was relaunched in 2012 as the Sertão following the success of the restyled G 650 GS.

BMW
F 650 GS (Twin) / F 700 GS

Displacement	Power	Transmission	Suspension travel	Tyres	Seat height	Dry weight	Fuel capacity
798cc	71bhp @ 7,000rpm	Six-speed / Chain	Front: 180mm Rear: 170mm	Front: 100/80–19 Rear: 140/80–17	820mm / 765mm	179kg	16 litres

Compact and lightweight, practical and well balanced, the F 650 GS (Twin) was used extensively in the making of sister publication *Adventure Riding Techniques* and proved to be an agile and capable machine over testing and varied terrain in Iceland. It's built around a punchy twin-cylinder engine, with a rigid steel tube trellis frame, double-sided swing arm, low seat height and narrow design. Cast aluminium wheels and telescopic forks make for a smooth ride. It needs a level of additional protection for any serious off-roading. The new F 700 GS is essentially the same bike but features twin front disc brakes with ABS as standard and 75bhp.

BMW
F 800 GS

Displacement	Power	Transmission	Suspension travel	Tyres	Seat height	Dry weight	Fuel capacity
798cc	85bhp @ 7,500rpm	Six-speed / Chain	Front: 230mm Rear: 215mm	Front: 90/90–21 Rear: 150/70–17	880mm / 850mm	178kg	16 litres

Unlike most large-capacity adventure bikes which can sometimes reach their limits because of excessive weight and design issues, the new F 800 GS delivers excellent off-road riding and excellent long-distance performance with a low dry weight of just 178kg. The overall package combines balance, power and weight, excellent ground clearance, long spring travel, precise wheel guidance and sophisticated ergonomics. The inline twin-cylinder engine comes from BMW's well-known F 800 model series. The accessories market expect this to be a popular model with a wide range of modifications and extra kit parts widely available.

BMW
G 650 X-Challenge

Displacement	Power	Transmission	Suspension travel	Tyres	Seat height	Dry weight	Fuel capacity
652cc	53bhp @ 7,000rpm	Five-speed / Chain	Front: 270mm Rear: 270mm	Front: 90/90–21 Rear: 140/80–18	950mm	144kg	9.5 litres

Described as 'the hard enduro for the off-road enthusiast', the BMW G 650 is a new departure for BMW and has a lot to offer, including long spring travel and no excess weight. The bike can be transformed into an extremely capable overland machine. Fairing components are both light and robust, while the 270mm suspension travel both front and rear means the X-Challenge copes very well off the beaten track. A long-range tank is a must if you're planning on covering big distances.

Cagiva
Elefant 900

Displacement	Power	Transmission	Suspension travel	Tyres	Seat height	Dry weight	Fuel capacity
904cc	68bhp @ 8,000rpm	Six-speed / Chain	Front: – Rear: –	Front: 100/90–19 Rear: 140/80–17	835mm	204kg	24 litres

This is a production version of the bike which triumphed in the Paris–Dakar Rally and uses an air and oil-cooled 90-degree V-twin motor (as used on countless Ducati road and race bikes) with a usable spread of torque. Suspension is excellent, with front Marzocchi forks and an Öhlins multi-adjustable rear shock. Its rally heritage is also evident in a large-capacity fuel tank, twin-headlamp fairing and high seat. Low gearing and the flexibility of the V-twin engine make it a very capable machine off-road but beware of overall build quality and high servicing costs.

Cagiva
Navigator

Displacement	Power	Transmission	Suspension travel	Tyres	Seat height	Dry weight	Fuel capacity
996cc	99bhp @ 8,500rpm	Six-speed / Chain	Front: 150mm Rear: 150mm	Front: 110/80–18 Rear: 150/70–17	850mm	210kg	20 litres

This bike is based on Cagiva's Gran Canyon trail bike, but utilises a detuned Suzuki TL1000 engine with modified cam profiles reconfigured for maximum torque. The engine configuration allows for a narrow chassis, complemented by 10-litre plastic tanks on either side of the frame. The tanks are joined by a pipe across the frame so that fuel is evenly drawn from both sides. The soft suspension and strong brakes just about keep up with the engine. A good bike if you can find one; spare parts are also hard to find.

Ducati
Multistrada 1200 S

Displacement	Power	Transmission	Suspension travel	Tyres	Seat height	Dry weight	Fuel capacity
1,198cc	150bhp @ 9,250rpm	Six-speed / Chain	Front: 170mm Rear: 170mm	Front: 120/70–17 Rear: 190/55–17	850mm	189kg	20 litres

In this new machine, Ducati claim to have produced a bike 'to tackle any kind of journey and road surface', using technology from their race bikes. A single button changes the fundamental characteristics of the bike – power, torque delivery, suspension settings and traction control can all be set on the move, enabling the bike to adapt to the needs of the rider and the terrain. Spares aren't exactly going to be in abundance in remote parts of the world and Ducati does not have much in the way of an off-road pedigree just yet, but the thinking behind this new model might just change that.

Honda
Crosstourer 1200

Displacement	Power	Transmission	Suspension travel	Tyres	Seat height	Dry weight	Fuel capacity
1,237cc	127bhp	Six-speed, shaft drive	Front: 180mm Rear: 180mm	Front: 110/80–19 Rear: 150/70–17	850mm	275kg	21.5 litres

This is Honda's latest offering in the big trail bike sector, defined and ruled by the BMW GS for the past decade. Honda enjoyed much success with the beloved Africa Twin in years gone by and fans will be pleased to see the Japanese brand competing again. Adventure credentials include a half-fairing and GS-like beak up front. Accessories include crash bars wrapping around the fairing and a taller windscreen, as well as panniers and top case. The chassis comprises a twin-spar aluminum frame with a single-sided swing arm incorporating the left-side shaft final drive.

Honda
NX650 Dominator

Displacement	Power	Transmission	Suspension travel	Tyres	Seat height	Dry weight	Fuel capacity
644cc	44bhp @ 6,000rpm	Five-speed / Chain	Front: 220mm Rear: 195mm	Front: 90/90–21 Rear: 120/90–17	880mm	167kg	16 litres

The Dominator was first launched in 1988 as a middleweight dual-purpose bike, with an air-cooled single-cylinder engine in a simple, trail bike chassis. Don't expect significant off-road ability – it's less capable off-road than its styling might suggest. It does offer long-travel suspension and trail-type wheels and tyres but as a package, it's better suited to poorly surfaced roads rather than proper off-road riding. The engine is rather dated now – its four-valve design is unchanged since 1988, and while there is torque in abundance, it struggles at speeds in excess of 70mph (115km/h).

Honda
XL1000V Varadero

Displacement	Power	Transmission	Suspension travel	Tyres	Seat height	Dry weight	Fuel capacity
996cc	93bhp @ 8,000rpm	Six-speed / Chain	Front: 155mm Rear: 145mm	Front: 110/80–19 Rear: 150/70–17	838mm	241.5kg	25 litres

This is a bike for riders who want long-term comfort twinned with power, ability, and good handling. The Varadero first came into production in Europe in 1999 and was an instant hit. The chassis is comprised of a steel tube cantilever frame, aluminium swing arm and conventional front forks. Bear in mind that the adventure bike styling belies the more road-orientated engineering underneath and the long travel suspension is the only real 'off-road' characteristic of the Varadero. More recent models have a sturdy aluminium sump guard to protect lower engine components.

Honda
XL 650V Transalp

Displacement	Power	Transmission	Suspension travel	Tyres	Seat height	Dry weight	Fuel capacity
647cc	55bhp @ 7,500rpm	Five-speed / Chain	Front: 200mm Rear: 170mm	Front: 90/90–21 Rear: 120/90–17	843mm	191kg	19 litres

This has been a stalwart in Honda's line-up for 20 years and was given a major makeover in 2001 when the 583cc engine was bored out to a larger 647cc version, and the bodywork heavily restyled. This is a good bike for riders seeking off-road confidence as the chassis tends to offer safe, predictable handling while the long-travel suspension gives a plush ride. The engine copes well and it's only when you hit motorway speeds it begins to feel the strain. The brakes are not a strong point and suspension offers limited adjustment.

Honda
XL 700V Transalp

Displacement	Power	Transmission	Suspension travel	Tyres	Seat height	Dry weight	Fuel capacity
680cc	59bhp @ 7,500rpm	Five-speed / Chain	Front: 177mm Rear: 173mm	Front: 100/90–19 Rear: 130/80–17	841mm	191kg	17.5 litres

Upgraded from the former XL 650, this remains a versatile machine that handles well-travelled highways and off-road tracks with equal ease and enjoyment. The low-profile seat version lets smaller riders take full advantage of a lighter and more responsive machine. The new model's fuel tank is smaller (down from 19 to 17.5 litres), but the improved fuel consumption of the new fuel-injected engine actually extends the overall range. The bike is equipped with the Honda Ignition Security System (HISS) – a fail-safe electronic interlock to prevent the engine from being started by anything other than the machine's two original keys.

Honda
XRV750 Africa Twin

Displacement	Power	Transmission	Suspension travel	Tyres	Seat height	Dry weight	Fuel capacity
742cc	60bhp @ 7,500rpm	Five-speed / Chain	Front: 220mm Rear: 214mm	Front: 90/90–18 Rear: 140/80–17	860mm	207kg	23 litres

With more than ten years of production history, the Africa Twin has become something of a favourite in the off-road community. It's certainly getting on a little now, but still a hugely capable machine offering reliability and range. Supple suspension, a commanding riding position and good ground clearance make you appreciate that this bike was designed to travel a long, long way. This is further supported by the large fuel tank, heavy-duty sump guard, wide handlebars and good fuel economy. Concerns to be aware of are its overall weight and uncomfortable seat.

Kawasaki
Versys 1000

Displacement	Power	Transmission	Suspension travel	Tyres	Seat height	Dry weight	Fuel capacity
1,043cc	116bhp	Six-speed, sealed chain	Front: 150mm Rear: 150mm	Front: 120/70–17 Rear: 180/55–17	845mm	239kg	21 litres

Not a true adventure bike but styled to at least create the impression, Kawasaki's new Versys joins the brand's 'dual-purpose' category. The bike is based extensively on the Z1000, with long-travel suspension, a large tank and comfy seat. Not nearly enough for hard-core adventuring, this bike is a capable on-road machine with very good torque in the lower rev range and gearing that has been changed to suit the application. All in all the Versys combines the comfort of a tourer with the forward view of an adventure-style bike but it hasn't been engineered for anything vaguely challenging.

Kawasaki
KLE 500

Displacement	Power	Transmission	Suspension travel	Tyres	Seat height	Dry weight	Fuel capacity
498cc	44bhp @ 8,300rpm	Six-speed / Chain	Front: 220mm Rear: 200mm	Front: 90/90–21 Rear: 130/80–17	850mm	181kg	15 litres

First introduced in 1991, the KLE is a great dual-purpose bike. Its strongest point is price, offering excellent value for money. You also get smooth power delivery from the reliable parallel-twin engine, while the chassis ensures good all-round handling, performance and versatility for the compromise needed between road and trail. It's a good bike to start out on but beware of the soft suspension and lack of delivery on the throttle. The oversize sump guard almost seems at odds with the rest of the design and may lead you into thinking it's more off-road capable than it is.

Kawasaki
KLR 650

Displacement	Power	Transmission	Suspension travel	Tyres	Seat height	Dry weight	Fuel capacity
651cc	44bhp @ 6,000rpm	Five-speed / Chain	Front: 231mm Rear: 231mm	Front: 90/90–21 Rear: 130/80–17	889mm	153kg	27 litres

First introduced in 1987, this big-bore dual-purpose bike is suitable for all skill levels and provides riders with amazing versatility. Light, durable, immensely off-road capable, its huge fuel tank and thick seat let you keep going longer than you'd ever have thought possible. A big plus is the low-end grunt but also the bike's composure at motorway speeds, making long distance travel a pleasure. It's been ridden to the Arctic, across North and South America, and throughout Europe, Africa, and Asia, as well as on full global circumnavigation rides.

KTM
990 Adventure

Displacement	Power	Transmission	Suspension travel	Tyres	Seat height	Dry weight	Fuel capacity
999cc	104bhp @ 8,500rpm	Six-speed / Chain	Front: 210mm Rear: 210mm	Front: 90/90–21 Rear: 150/70–18	860mm	209kg	19.5 litres

The popular 990 Adventure is a revised version of the successful 950 Adventure featuring greater displacement, electronic fuel injection and a regulated catalytic converter. It is a touch lower than the companion S model and features improved safety factors with its ABS with the quality WP suspension offering a plush ride. Strong torque is perfect for off-road riding and load/pillion carrying alike. The twin fuel tanks require filling individually, which is a minor inconvenience but helps keep the bike slimline by tucking fuel storage into nooks and crannies.

KTM
990 Adventure R

Displacement	Power	Transmission	Suspension travel	Tyres	Seat height	Dry weight	Fuel capacity
999cc	113bhp @ 8,500rpm	Six-speed / Chain	Front: 265mm Rear: 265mm	Front: 90/90–21 Rear: 150/70–18	915mm	209kg	19.5 litres

This impressive machine spearheads KTM's adventure family. The reworked engine delivers a 20% increase in power for top-class performance. Apart from being more powerful (some novice riders may find the power intimidating), the R model is also 2kg lighter than the standard version and features a higher seat for taller and more experienced riders. The suspension has 55mm extra travel to give it extra off-road capability. ABS is not available on the R model but overall it's a very capable machine with a new cockpit and modified front storage compartment.

KTM
1190 Adventure R

Displacement	Power	Transmission	Suspension travel	Tyres	Seat height	Dry weight	Fuel capacity
1,195cc	147bhp @ 9,500rpm	Six-speed / Chain	Front: 210mm Rear: 220mm	Front: 90/90–21 Rear: 150/70–18	890mm	217kg	23 litres

First unveiled in October 2012, the latest addition to KTM's impressive adventure line-up comes in two versions, the Adventure and the Adventure R. The bike represents a significant step on from the 990 and represents one of the most technologically advanced KTM models to date. Some say it is too tarmac focused but the R dispels that myth with its bigger wheels and longer travel suspension making it perfect for riders who don't like to take the beaten path. There are multiple adjustments for rider position, unmatched power and weight figures in its class and a huge range of accessories.

KTM
640 Adventure

Displacement	Power	Transmission	Suspension travel	Tyres	Seat height	Dry weight	Fuel capacity
625cc	127bhp	Six-speed, shaft drive	Front: 180mm* Rear: 180mm*	Front: 110/80–19 Rear: 150/70–17	850mm	275kg	21.5 litres

Directly descended from successful rally racing bikes, the 640 Adventure is characterised by its low weight, tough exterior, agile chassis with long suspension travel and a robust LC4 engine. Some pre-2004 machines suffered from main bearing failure so make sure the official fix has been completed if you're buying second-hand. Get used to the vibrations – they're evident from the moment you set off and know that the electrics can be fickle. On the plus side you get tremendous handling, good braking and sophisticated WP suspension. Aftermarket suppliers stock a vast array of goodies, including lighting, panniers, protection and cockpit conversions.

Moto Guzzi
Stelvio NTX

Displacement	Power	Transmission	Suspension travel	Tyres	Seat height	Dry weight	Fuel capacity
1,151cc	104bhp @ 7,500rpm	Six-speed / Shaft drive	Front: 170mm Rear: 155mm	Front: 110/90–19 Rear: 180/55–17	840mm	214kg	18 litres

The iconic Italian manufacturer has taken some of the key ingredients from their other machines – a big, air-cooled twin-cylinder engine, shaft drive and a single-sided swing arm and mixed them into an off-road styled chassis to create the Stelvio to take on BMW's class domination. The seat height is a fair bit lower than the 1200 GS and the Stelvio is marginally lighter too (by 5kg), but at this stage of its development it's not an accomplished off-roader. Perhaps worth a look if you're after something a little different.

	Displacement	Power	Transmission	Suspension travel	Tyres	Seat height	Dry weight	Fuel capacity

Moto Morini
Granpasso

Displacement	Power	Transmission	Suspension travel	Tyres	Seat height	Dry weight	Fuel capacity
1,187cc	118hp @ 8,500rpm	Six-speed / Chain	Front: 190mm Rear: 200mm	Front: 110/80–19 Rear: 150/70–17	830mm	198kg	25 litres

Performance and versatility are the main attributes of this new machine. An extra-large fuel tank, twin headlights and aluminium sump guard give it an adventurous demeanour, enhanced by a wire-spoked 19-inch front wheel. The seat height will prove challenging for shorter riders who may also struggle with a machine that is wide. Some comfort will come from the fact that it's over 10bhp more powerful than rivals such as BMW's R 1200 GS and Moto Guzzi's Stelvio. Öhlins rear suspension and front Marzocchi forks complement the package.

Suzuki
V-Strom DL 650X

Displacement	Power	Transmission	Suspension travel	Tyres	Seat height	Dry weight	Fuel capacity
645cc	87bhp @ 8,800rpm	Six-speed / Chain	Front: 150mm Rear: 150mm	Front: 110/80–19 Rear: 150/70–17	820mm	199kg	22 litres

This new model offers a step-up in off-road credentials from the earlier dual-purpose DL 650 V-Strom. The new DL 650X is based on the non-ABS version of the V-Strom 650 and comes with an alloy bash plate, hand guards, steel engine protection bars and a decent screen. It's aimed at riders who intend to use the bike's off-road ability which has received mixed reviews and many Suzuki fans would like to see the Japanese manufacturer go one step further to lift the model's off-road credentials to a more acceptable level.

Suzuki
V-Strom DL 1000

Displacement	Power	Transmission	Suspension travel	Tyres	Seat height	Dry weight	Fuel capacity
996cc	96bhp @ 7,600rpm	Six-speed / Chain	Front: 150mm Rear: 160mm	Front: 110/80–19 Rear: 150/70–17	840mm	208kg	22 litres

Surprisingly no longer part of the Suzuki range given EU emissions ratings, this bike delivers comfort, convenience and a good range from the tank. It's not as off-road capable as the market leading heavyweights and needs a fair bit of modification for even moderate off-road use but a smooth throttle response of the fuel injection's Dual Throttle Valve system ensures easy riding. Although the rear shock offers preload and rebound adjustability, this is not a bike for heavy off-road work but is certainly capable enough on wide trails where the surface is smooth.

Suzuki
DR 350

Displacement	Power	Transmission	Suspension travel	Tyres	Seat height	Dry weight	Fuel capacity
349cc	30bhp @ 7,600rpm	Six-speed / Chain	Front: 280mm Rear: 255mm	Front: 80/100–21 Rear: 110/90–18	890mm	130kg	9 litres

This is a small and affordable trail bike with a single cylinder four-stroke engine. It's rugged, easy to ride and simple to maintain. Negatives to consider are a poor finish and modest power output (some may see this as a plus), but generally speaking it's an endearing machine. If you're buying a Suzuki DR 350, make sure you get a post-1995 electric start version and pay attention to the suspension – by now most Suzuki DR 350s will have thinned fork oil and a tired shock – replacing or refreshing these will make a huge difference to the handling.

Suzuki
DR 650

Displacement	Power	Transmission	Suspension travel	Tyres	Seat height	Dry weight	Fuel capacity
644cc	43bhp @ 6,400rpm	Five-speed / Chain	Front: 260mm Rear: 260mm	Front: 90/90–21 Rear: 120/90–17	885mm	147kg	17 litres

A long-standing model in Suzuki's range, the DR 650 was first introduced in 1990 as a replacement for the DR 600 model. This is a lightweight single cylinder and a very popular model for adventure riders. It is easy to handle and highly reliable, with a good power to weight ratio. A major plus is the compact and lightweight four-stroke engine which has been tuned for strong low- and mid-range power and fuel efficiency. The seat height can be lowered 40mm and the tyres come with an on/off road tread pattern fitted to 21 inch front and 17 inch rear wheels.

Suzuki
DR-Z400S

Displacement	Power	Transmission	Suspension travel	Tyres	Seat height	Dry weight	Fuel capacity
398cc	40bhp @ 8,500rpm	Five-speed / Chain	Front: 295mm Rear: 295mm	Front: 80/100–21 Rear: 120/90–18	935mm	132kg	10 litres

The Suzuki DR-Z400S was launched in 2000 both as a commuter and as a veritable off-roader and the bike performs both functions well. Models from 2002 onwards have an electric starter. Power and torque of the water-cooled 398cc single-cylinder, DOHC, four-valve engine were gradually improved in later models. It's reliable and has very few known issues. Biggest concerns are the small tank and narrow motocross-style seat. Plus points are strong low-rpm power, a fully adjustable rear shock absorber and multiple function digital display.

Triumph
Tiger 800XC

Displacement	Power	Transmission	Suspension travel	Tyres	Seat height	Dry weight	Fuel capacity
799cc	94bhp	Six-speed / Chain	Front: 220mm Rear: 215mm	Front: 90/90–21 Rear: 150/70–17	843mm	215kg	19 litres

This is Triumph's entry into the relatively crowded middleweight adventure sector – there is the standard 800 and then the XC aimed more toward dirt than the street. The bike delivers smooth power across the rev range and its ergonomics work well on-road and in the dirt. Another plus is the bike's suspension, though it lacks the adjustment options found on its rivals. On the downside, weight is quite high by comparison to its rivals and there have been complaints about the amount of engine heat channelled onto the rider's legs. The Triumph's touring capabilities are bolstered by excellent fuel efficiency. All in all, a punchy and respectable middleweight in the class.

Triumph
Explorer 1200

Displacement	Power	Transmission	Suspension travel	Tyres	Seat height	Dry weight	Fuel capacity
1,215cc	135bhp	Six-speed / Shaft drive	Front: 190mm Rear: 194mm	Front: 100/90–19 Rear: 150/70 – 17	837 – 857mm	259kg	20 litres

This is a brand-new Triumph and the impressive three-cylinder engine shares no parts with any other in the current range. Key features are 0,000-mile service intervals, a 950W generator and shaft final drive. There is emphasis on simplicity wherever possible, comfort, ease of use, durability and reliability. Comes as standard with traction control, ABS, cruise control and heated grips. It's lighter than the Crosstourer but heavier than the GS. The seat height is adjustable but you're going to need some strength to deal with the weight. The engine is smooth and responsive, with excellent torque delivery. Full off-road credentials are still to be confirmed, but early signs are good.

Yamaha
1200 Super Ténéré

Displacement	Power	Transmission	Suspension travel	Tyres	Seat height	Dry weight	Fuel capacity
1,199cc	108bhp @ 7,250rpm	Six-speed / Shaft drive	Front: 190mm Rear: 190mm	Front: 110/80–19 Rear: 150/70–17	845mm / 870mm	233kg	23 litres

This model signifies Yamaha is serious about regaining the high ground of the adventure market it enjoyed in the late 1980s with its XTZ 750 Super Ténéré which went on to win six Dakar Rallies. Key features include a good size 23-litre tank for reasonable range, seat adjustment from 845–870mm to suit different rider heights, a sleek shaft drive requiring no running maintenance, a powerful electronics package for different engine settings, tubeless rims and a sturdy aluminium sump guard. The limited first production run will also come with panniers as standard. Expect to see many of these on your travels.

Yamaha
XT 660 R

Displacement	Power	Transmission	Suspension travel	Tyres	Seat height	Dry weight	Fuel capacity
660cc	47.3bhp @ 6,000rpm	Five-speed / Chain	Front: 225mm Rear: 200mm	Front: 90/90–21 Rear: 130/80–17	865mm	165kg	15 litres

This is an all-rounder that is light and slim, with a fuel-injected 660cc single-cylinder water-cooled engine. A new electronic fuel injection system together with twin catalytic converters offer strong green credentials. The bike is tall with reasonable suspension but the low-slung exhaust pipes are vulnerable and need protection. The bodywork seems to favour style over functionality. These touches together with the engine's claimed 48hp match it up against Suzuki's V-Strom 650 or BMW's F 650, though the XT probably edges out both of these competitors as somewhat more capable off-road.

Yamaha
XT 660 Z Ténéré

Displacement	Power	Transmission	Suspension travel	Tyres	Seat height	Dry weight	Fuel capacity
660cc	48bhp @ 6,000rpm	Five-speed / Chain	Front: 210mm Rear: 200mm	Front: 90/90–21 Rear: 130/80–17	895mm	183kg	22 litres

This is the bike which resurrected Yamaha's legendary XT model. Powering the new XT 660 Z Ténéré is a 660cc liquid-cooled 4-stroke single cylinder SOHC engine which delivers strong low- to mid-range power. It's equipped with an all-new chassis whose rugged, go-anywhere character perfectly complements the big-single engine. Its off-road credentials are enhanced by the long-travel forks which give 210mm of front wheel movement, complemented by a lightweight aluminium swinging arm with 200mm of rear wheel movement. A large-capacity 22-litre fuel tank underlines the machine's serious long-distance potential.

Yamaha
TTR250

Displacement	Power	Transmission	Suspension travel	Tyres	Seat height	Dry weight	Fuel capacity
249cc	19bhp @ 8,500rpm	Six-speed / Chain	Front: 280mm Rear: 280mm	Front: 80/100–21 Rear: 100/100–18	914mm	113kg	12 litres

This bike once won the national enduro championship so it's certainly a capable machine. An air-cooled, four-stroke, four-valve, DOHC single engine with electric start, six-speed gearbox and disc brakes front and rear, the TTR also features plush long-travel suspension and nimble handling. Other plus points include a comfortable seat, excellent reliability and light weight. The low seat height and forgiving ride make this an ideal bike for those starting out on trail riding. This is the bike used by Lois Pryce on her trans-Africa trip.

Bike Preparation

Touratech

ertain bikes currently available could probably stand up to a reasonably arduous journey with little need for many modifications, but there are very few riders who are likely to head off without making at least some changes to the bike to customise and personalise it to suit the journey that lies ahead.

Some riders will under-prepare, others will over-prepare. Ultimately, the extent of changes you make to the bike will be determined by your budget and the nature of the trip you have planned. In the end you need to find a balance between what you can afford and what you feel is essential for your trip.

The range of modifications is extensive (for example, just look at the latest Touratech catalogue – www.touratech.com) and it is not difficult to spend in excess of the value of a new bike on accessories alone!

The sooner you can get your hands on the bike you've decided on the better. In order to get everything modified and prepared for a round-the-world ride, including a decent shakedown test, you would ideally not want to have the bike for any less than a year before your intended departure date. Shorter trips may require fewer modifications and therefore less time, but the reality is that irrespective of the type of journey, the more time you have with the bike before you leave, the better you'll know it and how it works. You will have time to test it thoroughly, understand its weak points and modify it to the point where you feel happy it can do the job required. What follows is by no means a definitive list but certainly provides a basic outline of the key areas that should be considered.

Anatomy of an adventure bike

Basic modifications are essentially undertaken to reduce risk, enhance comfort and make for a better all-round riding experience. They form an important part of your pre-trip preparation and should be initiated as soon as possible.

Some modifications may be purely cosmetic (be careful of the additional weight these can add), while others may be considered necessities so choose wisely to keep the weight down. It's also useful to establish what modifications other people have made to the same model and the reasons these were made.

Finally, ensure you test the modifications thoroughly (most will need some degree of 'tweaking' to get them just right) and most importantly, understand how they are assembled and how they function, particularly if they have been fitted or made by someone else, in case they need disassembling, replacing or repairing.

Typical modifications can include:

FUEL TANK Depending on the range required, you may want to fit a long-range tank or make provision to carry reserve fuel separately. The standard KTM 990 Adventure tank is 22 litres (4.8gal), while the BMW R 1200 GS Adventure offers a larger 33 litre (7.3gal) tank as standard which is a fair bit bigger, but also a fair bit heavier. That said, fitting a larger tank is almost certainly preferable to carrying two jerry cans of spare fuel – the bigger tank will keep the additional weight close to the bike's centre of gravity while separating the fuel out can potentially unbalance the bike.

WATER STORAGE For long-distance desert travel, you will need to carry spare water and the same principle applies as for fuel – the lower you can keep it and the closer to the bike's centre of gravity, the less impact it will have on handling.

SEAT Make sure your seat is as comfortable as possible. Seat foam should be replaced if old, while the addition of a sheepskin cover can help those long days on the road. Gel padded seats are another option for added comfort.

SUSPENSION Any modification to the suspension is primarily required to improve the chassis response of the bike under loaded conditions. Depending on the bike, fitting stiffer fork springs may improve handling when fully loaded, offering a more progressive feel and preventing the bike from bottoming out. Rear shock should be sprung and re-valved to suit the load. Fit fork sliders to protect the fork stanchions from stone chips and mud.

FOOT PEGS Consider foot pegs with a wider base making for a more comfortable ride particularly if you're likely to be standing up for long periods of time. Big, wide foot pegs make a huge difference when riding standing up on a technical trail by providing added stability.

WINDSCREEN SPOILER This raises the windscreen height and is designed to reduce the air flow behind the windscreen as well as the noise level when riding at high speed (very useful when communicating via radio). There are different versions available but one which can be clamped on and easily removed is best.

NAVIGATION EQUIPMENT If you're taking a **GPS**, this will typically need a mounting bracket attached to the handlebars and a power lead.

CRASH PROTECTION If not already fitted as standard, it is worth investing in some basic, low-speed crash protection, including crash bars and handlebar protectors which will help to protect the engine casing and brake and clutch levers respectively in the event of a fall. A useful tip when riding off-road is to ever so slightly loosen the clamp holding the clutch and brake levers to the handlebars. Even with handlebar protectors it's possible to break a lever, but in the event of a spill there's a good chance the clamp will simply turn on the bar thus saving the lever.

HEADLIGHT PROTECTORS Usually made from transparent polycarbonate or in the form of a powder-coated wire mesh, these give your headlights excellent protection even from large stones.

ADDITIONAL HEADLIGHTS Offer increased visibility and safety when riding by illuminating further down the road. The bulb is also designed to produce a more natural light colour. A fog light can also be useful.

SUMP GUARD A bash plate protects the engine casing by distributing the impact of any knock from rocks or when crossing uneven terrain.

KICKSTAND EXTENSION Allows the bike to stand more firmly on softer ground.

Motorcycle News (MCN)

→ **Full off-road tyres made riding the KTM Rally Replica a lot easier in the sands of Oman**
📷 Robert Wicks

Tyres

Making sure of the right tyre choice is essential and in the first instance requires you to have a relatively good understanding of your route and the sort of terrain you are likely to be travelling across. Ultimately, tyre choice is always a compromise between the ability to grip the road and longevity. The softer the rubber compound the better it grips but it will not last as long as a harder tyre. The harder the compound, the less it grips but the longer it will last.

Assuming you have a good idea of what the route is likely to be like, the key points to consider are:

- Running with tubed or tubeless tyres
- Tyre tread choice – either a dual purpose tyre or a knobbly tyre

It may be that you start with dual purpose tyres and carry more serious off-road rubber with you for use over tougher terrain.

If your route takes you over reasonably easy off-road terrain and sealed roads, then an intermediate (dual purpose) tyre is probably best. Most of the leading manufacturers produce tyres in this category which tend to feature a chunky tread pattern which delivers

impressive traction on dirt roads. This together with the choice of compound allows for a combination of both on- and off-road use.

Popular brand names include the Avon Distanzia, Bridgestone's Battle Wings, the Metzeler Tourance, Pirelli Scorpion, Dunlop Rally Raid and Michelin Anakee and Desert variants.

The choice of whether to run with tubed or tubeless tyres is essentially dictated by the construction of the wheel rims in the first place, the tyre itself in the second and the nature of the riding you plan to do. Rims with wire spokes that go right through the middle of the rim need tubes while alloy rims that are cast as a single unit can accept tubeless tyres. Rims with spokes that attach to the rim on the side rather than the middle, can be used with or without tubes. Tubed tyres and their associated spoked rims are hardier and offer more flexibility (eg one can deflate the tyre to a greater extent when travelling over thick desert sand). They can also tackle tough off-road conditions with stones, rocks and potholes as the spoked wheels can handle this type of abuse better than alloy wheels.

Tubed tyres tend to generate more heat than their tubeless counterparts and in the event of a sudden puncture, can be more dangerous as the tyre can

⬇ **Most manufacturers offer a full range of road, intermediate and full off-road tyres. Michelin's Desert brand (below right) are some of the toughest off-road variants available and have won countless rally raid events in recent years. Always be aware of travelling at high speed on off-road tyres however – they generate a lot of heat and can become unstable so keep your speed and distances to a reasonable level**
📷 Michelin

come adrift from the rim (unlike tubeless).

Tubeless tyres and their light alloy rims are not always that well suited to tough conditions as they could lose their shape following an impact which would result in the tyre no longer sealing itself against the rim. However, one of the big advantages of tubeless tyres is the ease of repair when one has a puncture as the tyre can usually stay on the rim during the repair process (large side wall punctures are the exception of course). The tyre also fits more tightly onto the rim meaning that a sudden puncture is less of a threat, plus they tend to be safer at high speeds.

This benefit comes at the expense of having a far tougher job of removing the tyre from the rim (so called 'breaking the bead') in the first place. It is also worth bearing in mind that badly punctured tubeless tyres can accept a tube in an emergency.

When deciding on tyre choice, explore the following key points in detail with your dealer:

- Manufacturer's recommended tyre size
- Will the tyre fit your particular rim?
- Can the width of the tyre be accommodated by your motorcycle frame?
- What is the maximum speed rating for the tyre?
- What is the maximum load for the tyre?
- What is the recommended and maximum tyre pressure?
- How does the tread width and tread depth compare with comparable tyres by other manufacturers?
- Is the tyre essentially a soft or hard rubber compound?

Finally, remember that motorcycle tyres come in pairs – each particular model has a front wheel version and a partner rear wheel version. Both tyres have the same characteristic profile. Generally, one will wear out two rear tyres to every front tyre but this does depend to a large extent on your style of riding, the terrain and the weight being carried.

Fuel Tanks

One of the most important possible modifications you can make to your motorcycle is the addition of a long-range fuel tank. This may not be necessary if you are confident of the distances between fuel stops on the route you are taking and the availability of fuel supplies at these points.

Some manufacturers can save you the trouble of fitting an aftermarket product. For example, BMW offer the standard R 1200 GS with a 20 litre (4.4gal) tank but they also offer the R 1200 GS Adventure with a massive 33 litre (7.3gal) capacity.

Employing a long-range tank means not having to carry additional jerry cans or at least reducing this requirement considerably if you are planning a significant expedition. The bigger tank will obviously increase the weight of your motorcycle but is likely to offer better weight distribution and balance compared to carrying additional fuel containers which may need to be located in various positions on the bike. The larger tank should also prove to be a stronger unit, capable of taking a few more 'knocks' than the original standard tank.

Assuming you decide to make this modification, there is a good selection of custom-designed aftermarket fuel tanks available for most models. There are some important points to bear in mind when considering a long-range tank:

Choice – Make sure you purchase the model required for your specific motorcycle (there may be small differences for each model variant that aren't immediately apparent)

Capacity – Check the stated capacity to make sure it meets your needs. A decent long-range tank should take in the region of 30–35 litres (7.9–9.2 gal), giving the ability to complete lengthy runs without refuelling

Parts – It is useful to check if items such as the fuel cap and fuel pump on the long-range tank are interchangeable with those same standard items which may be easier to source

Design – Good tanks are aerodynamically designed for improved air flow and offer some protection for the rider

Space – Risers may need to be fitted to provide adequate clearance for the handlebars above the modified tank

Weight – Though larger, a modified tank often made of some form of high-tech composite material can weigh less than the standard aluminium tank and this is worth checking together with the shape to ensure it lowers the centre of gravity.

⬇ **This immaculate BMW F 650 GS Dakar features an extended long-range tank giving the bike significant additional range over the standard tank**
📷 Robert Wicks

↑ **Sometimes you have to plan for an unexpected load**

📷 Walter Colebatch

Luggage

Successfully carrying your gear during an adventure trip requires some careful decisions early on in the planning stages. Almost irrespective of the type of trip you have planned you will essentially need a combination of luggage options to cover:

Secure storage – This is a major issue when touring on a motorcycle and having peace of mind to leave your luggage mounted to the bike is vital

Convenient storage – For essential items that you need quick, regular access to like money, maps or your camera

Cool storage – This can be handy for items like medication, batteries and camera film

Protective storage – Motorcycles vibrate even on excellent roads – now add a poor surface like gravel, add dust, add rain and you have a very hard environment for your camera, video camera and GPS. Too much dust and/or vibration and you may just find your equipment failing in the middle of a once-in-a-lifetime tour. Special protective equipment bags and boxes are available that offer moisture, vibration and dust protection

Bulk storage – To carry items that simply don't fit in your other luggage like clothing, sleeping mat, bike spares and a tent. Whatever you choose make sure it is waterproof.

The principal choice for your secure and protective storage is to decide on using either a soft luggage option or to opt for hard aluminium cases.

The popularity of hard luggage has grown significantly in recent years and a number of solutions are available from suppliers all over the world. Many manufacturers offer their own ranges of hard luggage and this too can be a consideration although the bespoke aluminium 'boxes' from specialist aftermarket suppliers would seem to be the most popular choice today. Hard luggage offers you a reasonable level of security and excellent load-carrying capacity. This does, however, often come with a higher price and some people simply find them too bulky. Soft luggage comes in various forms and is generally lighter and more manageable but is at the mercy of the elements and is nowhere near as robust as aluminium panniers.

The second point to consider is the size of the load

you plan to carry. A typical aluminium pannier can carry 30–40 litres but just because your bike has a load-carrying capacity of 'x', don't take that as a licence to load it up to the hilt. Always assess the load you are placing on the bike and judge how this will affect its handling, particularly over rough terrain. Maintaining the weight as centrally and as low as possible will allow you a far better degree of control, balance and manoeuvrability.

The third choice is the mounting kit – ie a racking system which allows the luggage system to be attached to the subframe of the bike. Unless you are confident of coming up with a rack design to carry your load, you understand how different stresses will impact on the design and are sufficiently skilled in the art of welding, it is probably best not to attempt your own racking system and to rather opt for one of the many systems available through the main aftermarket suppliers. The rack you choose should be sufficiently robust and rigid to carry the anticipated load and also make mounting and dismounting of the luggage a simple process. Some racks in fact offer the option of variable positions (different heights and angles) for the luggage which can be useful if your load changes en route or for when you carry a passenger.

Aluminium panniers should have the following key features:

- Strong – remember, if the bike falls over the panniers will often take the brunt of the fall
- Waterproof
- Dustproof
- Secure – they need to lock and be locked onto the bike
- Give the option to secure additional luggage on top
- Offer easy access to the contents
- Easy to remove from the bike – some systems can be over-complicated and very fiddly
- Useful if they have a carrying handle for getting them up stairs and general moving about
- Avoid panniers that are too wide. While they offer a bigger payload they can complicate your life in congested traffic or on narrow tracks
- For serious touring the best material is undoubtedly aluminium. Besides offering security they are easily repaired en route. Plastic panniers are used by some riders, but are simply not as robust and can be tricky to repair

Soft luggage is sometimes a more appropriate solution but offers little by way of security
📷 KTM

An interesting option with hard panniers is a 'pannier liner bag'. This is a soft bag that fits exactly into the shape and size of the hard case. The idea is to pack the soft bag and then fit it into the hard case. On arrival at your destination the panniers stay on the bike and you take the soft bag into your accommodation.

Whatever system you decide on, place your order as early as possible as there can sometimes be a long lead time in sourcing panniers as many manufacturers 'make to order'.

A tank bag acts as convenient storage and sits astride your petrol tank. It is ideal for holding essential items to which you may need quick and regular access such as key documents, your cash or a camera. One of their most endearing features is a clear plastic sleeve into which you can slip your map thus having it visible at all times. Some bags can expand and contract in size depending on your needs.

It is important to ensure a secure fit to your bike

before you purchase as tanks and tank bags come in different shapes and sizes. Bags can be attached by using magnets or straps. The latter is the preferred choice given the uneven terrain likely on an adventure ride and these are essential for modern plastic tanks.

For an extended trip, many riders also carry a 'roll bag' or 'pack sack' which are very robust, waterproof bags made from PVC and designed to offer a flexible storage system for bulky items. They come in a variety of sizes with carrying capacity ranging from 20–100 litres.

To attach a roll bag to your motorcycle you need a flat surface of some kind behind the pillion seat. Alternatively, the bag can run across the top of the pillion seat and rest on your panniers, but this can hinder access to the panniers themselves and goes against the principle of keeping the weight as low as possible. Many riders resort to a home-made carrier frame solution as few commercial products seem to be available.

While security is a problem with soft luggage in

TANK BAG Tank bags are great for carrying all the gear you need to access quickly and easily, such as a camera, snacks and maps

PANNIERS Factory-fitted panniers provide secure storage for bulky or heavy items like tools, food and water

📷 KTM

general, these types of bags offer a large payload. Do not use elastic cords to secure your bag but nylon tie-downs or ropes instead. If you intend to camp then your tent will either need to fit inside your roll bag or be lashed next to it. Some more specialised bags have special compression straps making their overall size a lot smaller when fully compressed.

It will take several attempts to get your packing right and as you spend more time on the road, you will get it down to a fine art and have easy access to all your most important gear when needed. Remember to test the system before you leave so there are no nasty surprises once out on the road. Deciding on your luggage system is really a personal choice that will be determined by your budget and the load you plan to carry. Research all the suppliers and products carefully to ensure you make the best possible choice.

When it finally comes to packing, apply the rule of mass centralisation – keep the load light and as close as possible to the centre of gravity. Put heavier items in the panniers rather than in a top box or tank bag as these are located too far away from the bike's centre

of gravity. The extra inertia above the centre of gravity has a direct impact on your bike's handling, making it slower to lean and turn at speed. Additional weight behind the rear axle will lighten the front end of the bike, further upsetting the machine's balance.

↑ **Consider lining your panniers to ensure the contents keep dry no matter where you ride**

📷 Touratech

Freighting

Depending on the scale of the trip you have planned, freighting of your motorcycle may be something you need to undertake either at the start, at some point during the journey, or once at your final destination to get it back home. Freighting may be necessary to get your motorcycle to the intended start point, it may be needed to bypass a particular country or region through which you cannot pass, you may need to return home midway through the trip as a result of injury or for personal reasons, or perhaps you are limited by time and once reaching your destination, the plan is to simply freight the bike home and then jump on a plane yourself. Certainly for anyone planning a round-the-world trip, freighting will have to be undertaken a couple of times and there are a number of important considerations.

Sea freight tends to be more geared towards larger forms of cargo and not dealing with relatively small items such as motorcycles. Consequently, the general consensus would seem to be that air freight rather than sea freight is the preferred choice. That said, the single biggest drawback of air freight is, unsurprisingly, the cost, which can vary dramatically depending on factors such as location, choice of agent and the physical volume to be transported. Despite this downside, there are several good reasons to consider the air freight option:

- Shorter time
- More options (other flights) if it goes wrong
- More reliable (many travellers using sea freight have reported long waiting times – ie getting to their start points only to find the bike(s) are still on the way). This can cause massive disruption to plans and the implications can be significant if on a limited time budget

If you are considering sea freight, try to get an estimate of what the fees and additional charges are likely to be ahead of time so that this can be factored into your budget. You may even find that they are a fair bit higher than expected and any potential saving by using sea freight rather than air freight is negated. If that is the case and the numbers look right, then it's time to seriously consider the air freight options.

Excessive weight will drive up air freight costs, so where possible, travel with your gear to the start point, keeping costs to a minimum.

Costs

Shipping costs are generally calculated on a weight per volume basis. If the weight is over x/cubic foot then you pay the weight, if under you pay based on volume. As motorcycles are bulky, plus you have to think about all your luggage, spares and other equipment, it is essential to try and reduce the volume down to the minimum in order to pay the weight-based price.

Using an Agent

Getting everything together that you need to ship your bike can seem like an arduous task, and this is often the case, especially if you have not had the experience before. Appointing an agent can be useful in this case, with the major benefit of them taking care of all the relevant paperwork to ensure the shipment meets all the requirements of the carrier and the country it is being sent to. Entry requirements differ from country to country and employing a company with local knowledge can be very beneficial, particularly if there are translations involved. Generally speaking, they should also ensure the goods are packaged correctly (or at the very least provide you with detailed information on how to do it yourself to the required standard) and will prepare a 'hazardous goods certificate' which is likely to be required when freighting by air. There are literally hundreds of handling agents and shippers willing to freight your bike but it pays dividends to carefully research the market and compare costs before making what amounts to a very important decision. Try to use an agent that has experience in shipping bikes – agents who are unfamiliar with this type of cargo will invariably take longer to process things and the risk of a delay is far greater.

⬆ **Freighting over, it's time to get on the road and take in the view**
📷 Robert Wicks

FREIGHTING COSTS

- **Collection of the bike (unless you transport it directly to the shipper)**
- **Actual shipping or freight charges determined in volume (cubic metres) or weight terms for sea freight or on a rate per kilogram format for air freight**
- **Crating and packaging (if you don't do it yourself)**
- **Temporary import charges, bond payment or evidence of a carnet in countries where this might apply**
- **Transit insurance – determined as a percentage of the declared value of the motorcycle – it is recommended that you take specific advice on this to ensure you are covered sufficiently in the event of a claim**
- **A range of miscellaneous fees which need to be identified and clarified in advance to avoid any nasty surprises at the other end, including terminal handling, inspection fees, customs presentation, customs clearance, port security fees, handling, VAT (or local equivalent), fumigation, trucking to the shipping agent or to other final destinations, customs and bill of landing**

Packaging/Crating

Making your motorcycle fit into the smallest possible box will undoubtedly make a difference to costs. Consider going past your local dealership to see what they might have in the way of crates – this can help to reduce time and cost. Remember to allow clearance below the crate should it need to be picked up by a forklift. Once you have built or arranged the crate, undertake the following:

- Make sure the bike is as clean as possible – customs offices in many countries will insist on this to prevent migration of insect, animal or plant pests
- Lower the suspension – it is important not to fully compress the forks – tie the bike down on its suspension ensuring the forks are compressed sufficiently so that any unexpected knocks or jolts to the crate will not loosen the straps by the shock compressing and rebounding
- Lower the tyre pressures
- Remove the screen
- Remove the side mirrors
- Remove the front wheel (replace the front axle once done though) and front mudguard to help reduce the volume
- Pack your panniers and place them alongside the motorcycle (remember you may want to take some heavy items on your own flight as personal baggage which can potentially reduce the freight bill in the process)
- Ideally the bike should be free-standing and secured only by tie-down straps without making use of the centre or side stand
- Use a minimum of six straps to secure the bike in place
- Disconnect the battery and tape up any ends. If you are planning on air freighting the bike, the shipping company may insist that you remove the battery altogether, potentially requiring you to purchase a new one on arrival
- Drain any excess fuel from the tank (and check on availability of fuel at your arrival port)

Step One

A clean bike will avoid complications with customs officials

Step Two

Make use of the available space for bulky items such as spare tyres

PACKING TIPS

- Keep a track of website forums where you might come across someone heading to the same location at the same time and you can look to share costs
- Make sure to get a copy of the way bill or 'bill of lading' which will be the principal document used to track your bike
- Know who you are dealing with at both ends of the operation and get as much detail as possible
- Always keep at least three–five full spare copies of all your paperwork relating to the shipment, together with a copy at home with someone you can reach in case of emergencies

- Try to determine what assistance, if any, the agent will provide once the bike gets to the destination. For example, check what storage options are available and/or included in the price quoted. It can be useful to have a week of storage available while you get everything else arranged
- At the end of the day balance peace of mind against budget considerations and make the best possible choice in terms of how to freight your bike.

Step Three

Wrap the screen and other components once removed and secure them before closing the lid

Step Four

Write your name and contact details in large letters on the outside of the crate and make sure you tip the local help

Nik Boseley

Gear

dopting a common sense approach when deciding on the gear you will take is the best method. There are certain things you definitely need and a lot of things that could be considered 'nice to have' on a long adventure ride, the deciding factor more often than not being the space available. One way is getting everything together that you would like to take and then halving it. This may seem like a crazy idea at the time, but you will be astonished at just how little you need to survive.

The emphasis should generally always be on taking robust kit (a simple functional watch, for example) which is suited to the task at hand.

It's also imperative to buy the best gear you can afford, particularly a good helmet and protective riding gear. If you are planning a lengthy trip your gear will take a lot of punishment by being exposed to the elements on a daily basis and washed less frequently than normal.

In addition to space constraints, a lot of what you carry will also be determined by the route you intend taking. If you can afford to stay in hotels and eat out, then a tent, sleeping bag and cooking set are probably superfluous to requirements. Think carefully about your route and plan your kit accordingly.

↑ **If you can fit all you need into two panniers without the need for a roll bag, the bike will be easier to handle across tough terrain**
📷 Greg Baker

The Checklist

From early on in the planning stages one of the most important things to do is to start formulating a checklist of all the items you need. This can take various forms, but keeping it on a computer-based spreadsheet is possibly the most convenient. In this way it can easily be updated or amended and can be sent via e-mail to your riding partner(s) if needed.

It's best to divide the checklist up into different sections to cover the following key areas:

- Documents & Finance
- Clothing
- Riding Equipment
- Bike Spares & Tools
- Navigation & Communication
- Toiletries
- Medical Supplies
- Cooking
- Camping and Sleeping
- Miscellaneous

Some of these things you may already have so get them together and tick them off the list. Then put a plan in place to start acquiring everything else. Don't be surprised if you find yourself making several trips back to the same stores to get everything you need.

Assuming you are planning on riding in a group, always make sure you discuss what everyone else is taking to ensure the level of duplication is minimised – it's pointless everyone taking exactly the same kit as much of it will not be used and you need to make the best possible use of the limited space you have available. Study your route carefully and unless you are planning an entirely remote excursion, there will undoubtedly be opportunities to replenish certain things like batteries, medical supplies or other similar items.

Keep the list as up to date as possible as you plan the trip. Get yourself a large plastic container or cardboard box and keep everything together during the planning months. That way you can avoid any last-minute panics about where you put some of the essential items.

Be meticulous when you start the final packing session. Whether you are riding out from home, packing everything into a trailer and hauling it to the start point, or freighting your bike and equipment to a different location, it is imperative that you are very thorough and ensure that everything on your list gets packed. If you are indeed crating your bike ahead of the ride, make sure you know which items are going in the crate with the bike and which items you plan to take with you on the flight. Finally, it's a really useful idea to take a copy of the checklist with you on the trip.

Documents & Finances

Of everything that you will be carrying, most care needs to be taken with your paperwork and documents – these are essential to a successful trip and should be looked after vigilantly at all times.

Depending on where you are headed, the duration of your trip, how you plan to travel and exactly when you plan to go will determine the paperwork you need to prepare and take with you. Section 2 of this book addresses the most important documents in some detail such as visas, carnets and international driving permits.

A list of the typical paperwork you might need is as follows:

- Passport
- Birth Certificate
- Travel Insurance Documents
- Other Travel Tickets
- Green Card and/or Third Party Insurance
- Carnet
- Registration and/or Ownership Documents
- Permission Letter (if using a bike not registered in your name)
- Driving Licence
- International Driving Permit
- Vaccination Certificates
- Copy of Marriage Certificate (if travelling as a couple)
- Spare Passport Photos
- Cash and Travellers' Cheques
- Credit/Debit Cards
- Certified copies of all relevant documents

Clothing

In addition to your riding kit, you are going to need at least some casual clothing, preferably lightweight cotton where possible. This should be chosen for the climates you will find yourself in but don't overdo it – clothing is bulky and can occupy much-needed space in your panniers or roll bag. Another consideration is to dress in accordance with the social customs prevalent in the country you are visiting – this applies in particular to women travellers in Muslim countries.

At most, take one or two spare sets of casual gear and wash items regularly. Casual clothing should be both practical and functional, allowing you to blend in to your environment to at least some extent. Riding around a Third World country, you're likely to stick out like a sore thumb so use your clothing to help keep a low profile – this will also assist in making you less of a target for petty crime. Your casual clothing should consist of:

- T-Shirts
- Long Sleeve Sweatshirt
- Shorts
- Trousers/Dress/Skirts
- Socks and Underwear
- Belt
- Sun Hat
- Casual Shoes/Sandals

⬇ It's possible to survive on very little by keeping things simple
📷 Touratech

Consider a spare pair of gloves, especially on long trips
📷 KLIM

↑ With an open face helmet you'll need goggles
📷 KLIM

⬇ For some adventure biking is the chance to stop watching the clock; for others, a good timepiece is an essential piece of kit
📷 Robert Wicks

Riding Equipment

Leaving home with the right riding kit is essential – it will need to protect you from the elements and in the event of an accident. Hopefully, by the time departure beckons you will have had the opportunity to wear and test all of your essential gear. There is little point in throwing a new pair of boots on as you head off on the adventure of a lifetime only to find they are half a size too small. Your gear may need some adjustments and subtle modifications can make all the difference on a long ride.

A pair of durable, high quality riding boots is essential and don't for a moment think that a pair of hiking boots will do the job and help save on space. Your feet need all the protection they can get – they will invariably get dragged under your panniers as you negotiate tough

sections of terrain and if you fall off, your lower legs and feet can easily get trapped underneath the bike. Many manufacturers now make a range of intermediate boots offering high levels of protection (much like a motocross boot with a quick release system) but with equally good levels of comfort (that you might find in a touring boot) and waterproofing.

Comfort off the bike is also important (remember you will no doubt be walking around doing some sightseeing wearing your boots) so this sort of intermediate product is often the best possible compromise. The Dainese 'Virunga' and Alpinestars 'Vector' boots are good examples to consider.

A proper riding suit comprising pants and a jacket with suitable body armour is worth the investment. With advances in fabric and armour technology, a textile suit is probably the best route to go. If possible, buy a suit which allows the jacket and pants to zip together – this offers added warmth if needed and also better protection by not exposing any skin in the event of a crash. Another key consideration is making sure your suit is breathable – keeping the rain out while allowing sweat to escape. Don't just try the suit on before you buy it, sit on a bike and make sure it's comfortable when riding. High quality zips are essential as are pockets but make sure they seal properly. Finally, make sure the armour is sufficient (knees, elbows, shoulders and back) and that it all stays in place when you move around. Supplement the suit with a decent kidney belt for added comfort and protection of your lower back.

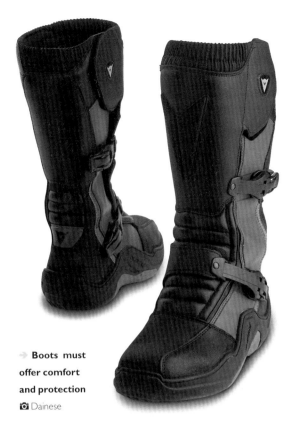

→ **Boots must offer comfort and protection**
📷 Dainese

A good quality helmet is another essential piece of kit and it's worth purchasing the best you can afford. The most popular helmets for adventure riding tend to be motocross in style – light and comfortable, worn either with a pair of goggles or with an in-built visor. An alternative to this is a helmet with a face that flips up and open. These can be very useful when stopping to ask for directions as they reveal your face and allow you to be clearly heard – important when you're asking for vital directions. It's also less intimidating and more personal for the person you are talking to. Try a range of different helmets on before deciding and also make sure the one you choose has good ventilation especially if travelling to hot climates.

To further assist with 'climate control', use base layer clothing made of 'wicking' fabrics which allow perspiration to escape in the heat but retain body warmth in cooler temperatures.

Finally, you may want to consider a neck brace for extra protection. This is a relatively new concept developed initially for the off-road race market and they come in various guises. One version, introduced by KTM in collaboration with BMW, is made of carbon fibre and fibreglass reinforced nylon.

A detailed list of riding equipment is as follows:

- Riding Boots
- Jacket
- Pants
- Helmet
- Gloves
- Balaclava and/or Scarf
- Goggles
- Ear Plugs
- Kidney Belt
- Neck Brace

Anatomy of a Riding Suit

In almost every other pastime that involves people being exposed to a wide range of temperatures and elemental conditions there is a known clothing formula that enables the body's core temperature to be kept at optimum levels for maximum comfort and performance. It's known as the three-layer system – and the same rules should apply when it comes to adventure motorcycling.

A single wicking base layer (layer 1) is used to remove sweat from the body by passing it outwards towards a waterproof/breathable and protective outer layer (layer 3). This outer layer allows sweat to escape, but it does not allow water in. These features help to keep a rider warm and dry in almost any conditions, and if it gets really cold you simply add a warm mid-layer to combat the conditions (layer 2).

Using this information, taking into account the most effective way the human body cools (by evaporating sweat off the skin) and also considering the specific needs of adventure motorcycling a clear checklist of requirements emerges with which all good riding suits should comply:

- It must be an excellent fit, comfortable and as light as possible. If, at the end of a hard day's riding you didn't think about your riding suit once, it's perfect.
- The external shell must be waterproof . Wet bodies and moving air cause wind chill, which can be deadly.
- It must be breathable to allow your own sweat to escape – the human body can easily produce 2 litres of sweat an hour, and that's no good on the inside of your jacket!
- It must be abrasion resistant – the ability to remain intact after time spent in contact with tarmac or the ground is vital.
- It must provide impact resistance – most of us will hit the ground at some point during our riding career, so having high-quality CE-rated armour that is properly fixed in place is vital.
- It must allow evaporative cooling to take place – it needs vents which allow air to flow through the suit over your body; it is not enough simply to have randomly placed holes.
- It must have suitably placed storage space for important documents and equipment.
- Its design must be fit for purpose – e.g. if you intend to ride off-road you will probably be riding with an MX-style boot. Your suit pants must work with this style of boot. If you are riding an off-road style of bike you will need ome protection on the pants to stop the exhaust burning your legs.
- It should have some way of enhancing rider visibility in poor light.

CASE STUDY: Klim Badlands Pro riding suit

Four huge vents in the jacket and four more in the pants allow a full flow of air over the body hotspots to take full advantage of evaporative cooling.

D30 CE 1621 type approved position-adjustable armour, including a level 2 viper back protector held in place with a kidney belt.

GORE-TEX Proshell Armacor Kevlar fabric to high abrasion areas.

Numerous pockets internally and externally.

Anatomical cut, stretch panels, kidney belt, single layer.

GORE-TEX – the only breathable material technology 'Guaranteed to keep you dry'.

3M Scotchlite reflective strips.

Pants designed for use with knee braces and MX-style boots. Leather internal patches to the lower leg and knees are vital for heat and abrasion resistance.

→ **Try to buy the best suit you can afford – the Klim Badlands Pro suit sets the benchmark when it comes to adventure riding**
📷 KLIM

To sum up, look for a highly comfortable single-layered suit made from an abrasion-resistant, breathable and waterproof material. It should have high quality CE rated armour (fitted as tightly as possible to your body). There should be a simple venting system that allows evaporative cooling to your body and legs, and all of this should be designed in a way that allows safe and secure storage of the equipment you need to carry. Finally, you should make sure that any necessary riding-style specific functionality is included.

DAVE LOMAX - ADVENTURE SPEC

Humans have been riding motorcycles for the last 100 years, and in our Western world that riding has mainly been for pleasure. Some people choose to ride for the thrill of speed; some to try and ride over seemingly impassable obstacles. However, there has always been a third group of people who ride for a very different reason. They ride because riding gives them the freedom to explore. It doesn't matter whether that is places, cultures or even their own limits.

At Adventure Spec we believe that with the right bike, the right kit and a little bit of knowledge almost anyone can become one of these riders and see things that will fundamentally change the way they view life.

We are committed (and also addicted) adventure riders who have been consistently exploring as far as our finances and families will let us for longer than we can remember. In the Adventure Spec team we've got ten Dakar rallies under our belts and we've ridden on every continent (yep, when we couldn't ride bikes we turned to Ski-Doos in Antarctica!). We've explored jungles, deserts, mountains, swamps, plains and just about anywhere you can get a motorbike – and some places you can't! We've even spent our life savings making films to tell the world about how great adventure motorcycling is. In short, we're hooked.

Our mission at Adventure Spec is twofold. First, we want to spread the word about the greatest pastime in the world, and second, we're keen to let you know how easy it is. Remember what we said above – a bike, some kit and some knowledge? This is what we have learned that really matters:

- Don't be fooled by motorcycle manufacturers' marketing. Sometimes the best adventures happen on the smallest bikes. Any bike will do
- The only equipment you really need for an adventure (in addition to your bike) is fuel
- A great adventure can take anywhere from five minutes to a lifetime. There is no set formula: next time you're out on a ride, turn off the GPS and make a random left turn. Who knows what might happen!
- It doesn't matter if you have one week's holiday or a year because it's not the time you have, it's what you do with it

- Ideas, ideas, ideas. Sometimes we all need a little inspiration. Check out the greatest adventure motorcycle travel website in the world once in a while www.horizons-unlimited.com (and wish you had 20 years for a holiday!)
- The less you take, the better the adventure you will have. Overweight is underprepared…
- Of course you'll also need a little knowledge to take with you, so be reassured that adventure motorcyclists are the most enthusiastic, friendly and approachable bunch of people in the world. We might all be different nationalities, sizes and religions but we all speak the same language when it comes to our bikes, so don't be afraid to ask!
- Every journey starts with a simple step – just put a date in the diary for your next adventure now

Finally, at some point in your wanderings through the world of adventure motorcycling you might come across a small website called adventure-spec.com. Rest assured that whatever information or products you find in there, it/they will have been lovingly and obsessively designed, chosen, made or bought for one purpose and one purpose only – they will be 'Adventure-Spec'!

Ride safely!

Dave Lomax and the Adventure Spec Team
For more information log on to:
www.adventure-spec.com

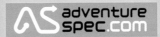

One way of remembering your adventure is to create a notable design on your helmet. "Preparing the helmet for painting is the key to a good result," says graphic artist and helmet specialist Steve Hatt, who prepared author Robert Wicks's Arai lid. In this case the helmet was white to start with so there was no need for primer, just a good key with fine sandpaper to dull the surface.

To maintain the integrity of the helmet it is not disassembled, apart from the visor and peak. All the rubbers and seals are carefully masked right from the start and the masking left until the helmet is finished completely. Again, so as not to damage the helmet, all the paints used are water based because solvents would eat into the helmet and could soften the structure.

"The base colour Rob decided on was orange, so the entire helmet was given two coats and then left for a day to harden. The paint was then keyed again with fine sandpaper," adds Steve.

Starting with the top, the area for the flag and the spot where the map was to go, these parts were masked and given a base coat of white. Then the 'ripples' were added, with dark grey to give the wavy effect. The map was done in a similar way but using harder lines and sepia paint to give an antique map effect. Transparent colours were then added over the flag, allowing the ripples already painted to accent the 3D effect.

Once these two areas were dry they were given a sealer coat and then masked off from the rest of the helmet.

Next the areas where the desert was to appear were marked out and carefully removed. The areas were given a coat of desert-sand colour and then, using the sepia again, a subtle desert

effect was added along with the camels. "At this stage I added a fairly heavy shadow around the edge to give the effect of the areas being cut out from the orange and giving an overall 3D design," says Steve. The same method was used around the chin area, while Rob's name and blood group were also masked and sprayed white.

On the rear of the helmet the 'evolution logo' was drawn out, and then carefully cut from masking film and applied to the already masked-off area. This was a fairly simple task as it was only one colour. The mask, however, takes around half an hour to create but less than a minute to spray!

Steve concludes: "Once all the masks were removed, a few subtle shadows and highlights were added freehand and then the helmet was left to harden for two days before finally being given two clear coats to bring it to life. With this done the helmet was ready to have the primary masking from the rubbers removed and the visor and peak refitted."

The whole process takes around two weeks to complete from initial design to finished helmet.

For more information and to see other examples of Steve's work, log on to: graffixunlimited.co.uk

Bike Spares & Tools

It's impossible to know exactly which tools and spares you are going to need on an adventure ride and even less certain is what might be available to you en route. Ultimately it will boil down to a selection of the key items you are most likely to need as it would be physically impossible to carry a full array of spares with you – there simply isn't the space or the need.

Knowing as much as possible about your motorcycle from a technical perspective, particularly any weaknesses the bike may have, will enable you to carry out at least a degree of routine maintenance and simple repairs on the road when necessary. Also, leaving home with the bike in good condition in the first place and then ensuring that it is looked after on the road will go a long way to reducing potential technical issues.

It's also important to have a good contact back at home who can source particular parts from your local dealer and arrange to get them shipped out to you if needed. For long-distance trips make sure you have all the tools needed to strip and rebuild the bike. Garages in remote areas may have some heavy tooling but not necessarily all the basic hand tools you need to work on your specific bike.

Finally, always ensure you carry a good range of consumables such as duct tape and cable ties – these will invariably be put to use on even the shortest of trips in a variety of different applications.

What follows is a reasonably comprehensive list designed to cater for a long trip:

Be sure to carry the bike's tool set with you
📷 KTM

General
- Spare keys
- Motorcycle repair manual
- Actual tool kit supplied with the motorcycle

Wheels and Tyres
- Puncture repair kit
- Tyre levers
- Spare rear tyre
- Spare front tyre
- Heavy-duty inner tubes
- Spoke key

Bike Spares
- Air filter (washable/reusable variety)
- Fuel filter
- Brake, throttle and clutch cables
- Brake and clutch levers
- Length of fuel hose
- Selection of electrical spares – bulbs, fuses and connectors
- Selection of bolts, nuts and washers

Toolkit
- Spanners
- Set of Allen keys

- Screwdrivers
- Extension tube to allow high torque fastening of wheel nuts etc
- Pliers
- Mole grips
- File
- 3/8'' drive ratchet and sockets
- Small hacksaw and spare blades

Other
- Engine oil
- Coolant fluid
- Small 12-volt compressor
- Surgical gloves

Consumables
- WD40 or equivalent water displacement spray
- Wire
- Scotchlok electrical connectors
- Duct tape
- Electrical tape
- Selection of cable ties in various sizes
- Superglue
- Araldite
- Metal putty
- Small tub of grease

Navigation & Communication

Many riders have completed global rides without a GPS, a mobile phone and a laptop. What you finally end up taking is really a personal choice – you may want, or need to keep in touch with developments back home, or alternatively you might want to be as far away from modern conveniences as possible.

A GPS is certainly recommended but take the time to understand how it works and how to get the best out of it well before you leave. Upload waypoints and routes and use its other features such as sunrise and sunset times and average speed to plan and monitor your progress. The subject of GPSs is discussed in greater detail under 'Navigation' in section 2. Remember to factor into your budget the costs of a suitable bracket which will attach the unit securely to the bike. It needs to be securely fastened on and easily removed.

Another task to complete well ahead of departure is purchasing the maps you need – a vital ingredient to any adventure ride. A trip to a good map and travel book shop like Stanfords in London (www.stanfords.co.uk) should be enough to get you excited about the trip. Maps can generally be purchased en route, often at much less than you would pay at home.

Even for an extended round-the-world trip, a laptop remains a luxury but is a useful piece of kit for accessing e-mail (though you will find Internet cafés in most places these days), burning precious photos from the trip to CD and perhaps updating your website with the latest news so friends and family back home can keep in touch with your adventure. Size is critical, as is protecting the laptop from the elements. Placing it in a hard Tupperware box inside one of your panniers is one option. An alternative is a watertight protective case (like the ones made by Pelican) – this is a bulky solution but offers the best possible protection. The case could be modified to carry some of your photographic equipment too.

If you are planning on bike-to-bike communications, take the time to carefully install the headset and microphone boom into your helmet and test the system

thoroughly to make sure it works before heading off. It's best if the system is hard wired so that it runs off the bike's electrical system.

Costs for satellite phones have reduced quite considerably of late and this can be considered as an emergency communications device. That said, with extensive mobile phone network coverage in many areas, taking a satellite phone should not be considered a priority unless travelling to extremely remote areas.

Navigation and communication equipment:

- GPS
- Maps
- Compass
- Radio System
- Radio Spares
- Small Binoculars
- Mobile Phone
- Phone Charger

- Satellite Phone
- 12-volt Inverter (150W)
- Laptop
- Laptop Power Cord
- Blank CDs
- Guidebooks
- Route Notes

TIPS

- **Try to ensure you get the latest editions of whichever maps you buy**
- **Always check the scale and the amount of detail available**
- **Two maps of the same country from different cartographers can be very useful to cross-check information such as approximate distances between villages**
- **Purchase your maps as soon as possible to start familiarising yourself with possible routes and the country or region in general**
- **Consider laminating your maps with a thin clear adhesive film to keep them dry and stop them from tearing**
- **Don't be surprised if the terrain you cross varies quite considerably from what the map indicates – particularly in places like Africa where in some areas roads are rapidly deteriorating while in others construction is underway to renew ailing road networks**
- **Finally, consider making use of online mapping resources such as Google Earth (http://earth.google.com) to get a sense of the geography of the regions you are going to be travelling through. Though not all areas are available to view in high resolution, you can get a good feel for where you're headed**

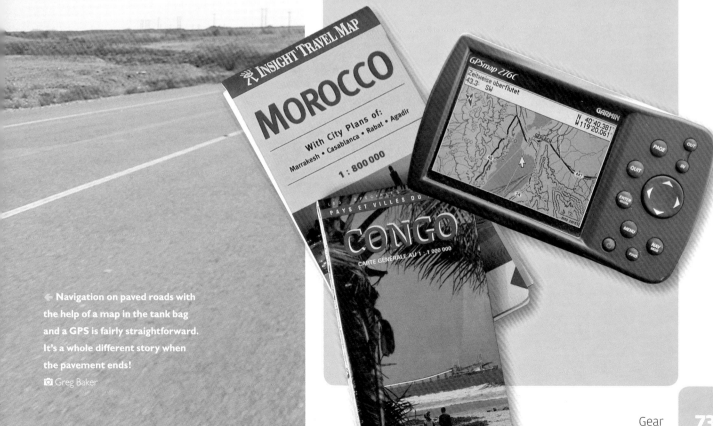

← **Navigation on paved roads with the help of a map in the tank bag and a GPS is fairly straightforward. It's a whole different story when the pavement ends!**
📷 Greg Baker

Toiletries

Keep your toiletries to the minimum – remember you can find toothpaste just about anywhere and be prepared to improvise when necessary. You'll more than likely go for a couple of days without a shower or bath so make sure you have a good bar of soap on hand to make the most of the experience when it does come about. A handful of baby wipes will give a surprisingly effective clean-up if no shower or water is available!

- Toilet Paper
- Soap
- Toothbrush
- Toothpaste
- Baby Wipes
- Shaving Cream
- Razor
- Small Towel

Medical Supplies

Staying healthy while on the road is essential and having a comprehensive medical kit with you at all times can prove invaluable in this respect. It's easy to go overboard and take the makings of a portable clinic with you, but a practical approach when planning your first aid kit is best. You should be able to replenish certain items on the road and ensure that you consult your doctor about any existing ailments before departure. A pre-emptive trip to the dentist is also highly advisable. Not everything on the following list needs to be taken with you but discuss your needs with a doctor or travel clinic and also with others in your group to minimise duplication – not everyone needs an identical kit. Put your kit to good use when needed and don't ignore minor injuries or ailments – deal with them quickly to avoid further complications which could impact on the trip at a later stage.

- Sunscreen
- Insect Repellent
- Pain Medication
- Broad-based Antibiotic
- Cold and Flu Medication
- Anti-inflammatory Tablets
- Malaria Prophylaxis
- Anti-fungal Ointment
- Latex Gloves
- Plasters
- Tweezers
- Thermometer
- Bandages and Tape
- Antiseptic Cream
- Treatment for Burns
- Eye Drops and Eye Wash Glass
- Set of Needles and Syringes
- Diarrhoea Tablets
- Water Purification Tablets
- Re-hydration Sachets
- Any Personal Prescription Medication

Camping

The need for camping equipment will depend largely on the sort of trip you have planned but don't take camping equipment if you have no intention of making use of it as it's very bulky kit.

Spend wisely to get the best balance between performance, price, weight and size for items such as tents, sleeping bags and mattresses. Though on the pricey

🎥 Robert Wicks

side, one of the latest self-inflating mattresses is worth considering – they are tremendously compact (about half the size of a conventional roll mat) but when inflated, offer far higher levels of comfort – something you will want after a long day in the saddle.

If you are travelling to a malaria area, make sure you take your own mosquito net even if you are not camping – not all places supply them and often they are not in good condition at the places that do offer them.

- Tent
- Tent Accessories
- Ground Sheet
- Roll Mat or Self-inflating Mattress
- Sleeping Bag
- Inflatable Pillow
- Mosquito Net
- Spare Nylon Rope

Cooking

Any good camping shop will stock everything you might need to cook successfully on the road but it is advisable to keep utensils to a minimum – though not particularly heavy, they can be bulky. A couple of robust plastic bottles for water are always handy and make sure to give your utensils a good wash with hot water whenever you have the opportunity.

Stoves come in a variety of shapes and sizes and it is worth spending some time to choose the one that will work best for you. A model which can work on more than one type of fuel (some stoves can burn paraffin, white gas, aviation fuel or petrol) can be useful particularly when you don't know what the next fuel source might be. Remember to allow space for bulky self-sealing gas canisters or fuel bottles and also for a few basic spares for the stove.

- Food
- Cooker/Stove
- Fuel/Canisters
- Cooking Pot(s)
- Plate
- Cup
- Cutlery
- Drying Towel
- Pot Scourer
- Dishwashing Soap
- Water Containers
- Water Purifier
- Water Purification Tablets

📷 Cotswold Outdoor

Miscellaneous

The range of potential 'miscellaneous items' is endless and one has to draw the line somewhere. The list shown here covers most key items though it's unlikely anyone would take every item listed – there simply wouldn't be the space.

An important consideration is what photographic gear to take. Cameras and lenses are heavy and bulky – just what you are not looking for. A small, simple compact digital camera is the ideal choice but for those with more serious photographic ambitions, a robust film or digital SLR can be considered. Given the subject matter, a good wide angle lens and another which offers some flexibility (in the 20–200mm range) is about all you are going to be likely to accommodate. Whatever you end up taking, consider that it will need to be protected from dust, rain, vibrations and heat, making a cleaning kit essential. A bespoke hard case is the ideal way to transport photographic gear or other 'critical' items. This will need to be secured to the bike but may add unwanted weight.

A good quality multi-tool is a must have – some models offer as many as 25 different functions, from wire cutting and stripping to a serrated blade and multiple bit drivers.

Another useful item to consider is a hydration system (such as those made by CamelBak). Popular with endurance athletes and outdoor enthusiasts, it lets you carry a good amount of water (usually two or three litres) with a convenient valve to drink from whenever you like – essential to keep you hydrated when travelling in hot climates.

Finally, some small gifts from your home country can go a long way and often come in very handy. Some people take pens, sweets or postcards – whatever you take, keep it sensible and don't overdo it.

- Glasses
- Sunglasses
- Money Bag
- Sewing Kit
- Small Calculator
- Large Plastic Bags
- Multi-purpose Tool
- Washing Powder
- Bungee Cords
- Pen and Notebook
- Fluorescent Marker
- Batteries
- Torch
- Watch
- Bum Bag
- Hydration Pack
- Lighter or Matches
- Wallet
- Roll or Stuff Bag
- Bike Lock
- Small Gifts
- Straps
- Rope
- Tank Bag
- Camera
- Camera Batteries
- Battery Charger
- Camera Cleaning Kit
- Memory Cards or Film

Riding Techniques

f you are a competent off-road rider then there probably isn't much need to attend a training school but if you've had little or no off-road experience, a few days with an instructor is sure to be money well spent. Riding a motorcycle off-road takes practice and an understanding of how the machine handles across varying types of terrain from dusty gravel back roads and deep sand, to steep inclines and declines, mud and rocky tracks. A good training school will give you the confidence to negotiate your heavily laden motorcycle competently across these different terrain types.

Most schools are focused on basic off-road riding skills and very few will offer you the opportunity to practise riding a fully loaded adventure bike, but the experience should give you a good insight into the key off-road riding techniques.

Each course varies and offers something a little different for participants so choose carefully and decide which one will offer you what you feel you need. Only a few schools allow you to use your own motorcycle so it's a good idea to enquire as to what motorcycles are available on the course. If they provide the same bike you are planning to take on your trip, this could be very beneficial as you will get some first-hand experience of how the bike performs and it will feel more familiar when you set off.

Terrain will vary greatly once you hit the road and the remainder of this chapter is dedicated to explaining the various riding techniques needed for crossing gravel roads, sand, ascents and descents, rivers and mud. It's imperative that you are comfortable with each of these skills and able to tackle the variety of terrain that comes your way. The chapter also highlights the importance of undertaking a shakedown run – the first chance to test both you and the bike under reasonably testing conditions.

↑ **A few days at a training school will give you some idea of your off-road riding ability and how to improve your skills**

📷 Robert Wicks

Training Schools

Most off-road schools offer courses over a one- or two-day period at a bespoke training facility. If you haven't purchased all your riding equipment by the time you go training, most schools tend to offer gear either as part of the course or for hire. It is recommended that you have as much of your own equipment as possible so that you can start to feel more comfortable with what you are going to be using on the trip.

At BMW's off-road skills course in Wales, for example, instructors teach participants the essentials of off-road riding with the objectives of increased confidence and machine control, together with improved riding skills and ultimate enjoyment when riding off-road. Key lessons include:

Being able to lift, balance and manoeuvre a motorcycle in awkward situations – This is particularly relevant given the variable terrain you are likely to cross.

Slow-speed manoeuvring and control – This is vital should you cross hazardous, rocky terrain and can even prove useful when negotiating your way through traffic in a bustling town.

Balance and control – An essential given the weight you are likely to be carrying, the terrain that will be covered and places and spaces which you will have to negotiate with the bike.

Throttle and clutch control – As vital off-road as it is for anyone riding on the road. Proper throttle and clutch control makes a tremendous difference to how to handle the bike and how to cope in difficult situations.

Enhanced braking ability – Hazards on the roads are far more prevalent the further you move away from built-up areas and your ability to brake hard and in a controlled manner off-road on a bike carrying considerable momentum is a fine art.

Ascending and descending hills – This can be intimidating at first but being able to cope with these confidently is an essential skill which should be mastered particularly if you are headed into unknown terrain.

Several schools will offer an advanced off-road riding course which may be worth considering in the event that you feel you need further tuition.

Techniques & Terrain

Riding off-road requires carefully honed skills which allow you to deal with unpredictable terrain and conditions. Each type of surface requires a certain technique, but in general, six basic tips are:

- Look up – look ahead, beyond your front tyre
- Keep the throttle open
- Lean forward – arms relaxed and bent
- Keep the bike perpendicular to the road surface
- Use the back brake and stopping power of the gearbox
- Expect the unexpected – traffic, pedestrians, animals, potholes and changes in the road surface

Gravel Roads & Tracks

A lot of time will be spent on gravel roads and you need to try and make use of that part of the track which offers the best traction, largely free from loose stones and sharp edges. This will not always be possible, with many roads covered entirely in loose sand and small stones. Always apply the basic rule – look up and look ahead for patches that offer better traction, keep the throttle open and ride towards them, standing up when necessary.

By always looking ahead you can usually see a bad patch before you actually have to ride over it. This is your cue to slow down. That way you have room to gently accelerate through the bad section without starting to go too fast. If you find the bike moves around a bit, accelerate a little more and the bike will steady up. As the road surface becomes more radical, push down harder on the foot pegs, allowing the bike to bounce around freely beneath you as it moves over the uneven surface with knees gripping the bike lightly, legs bent and your upper body moving freely.

When the surface changes to larger rocks, reduce speed and try to pick the path of least resistance, always keeping in mind the need to protect your tyres and rims. Tricky as it may be, make sure you ride within your limits and try to stay relaxed – this will help you to manoeuvre the bike and conserve your energy. On long stretches in the desert (without fuel stations) always try to ride at a steady speed (around 50mph) to conserve fuel.

⬇ Riding on this type of track is great...if you're in front!
📷 Joe Pichler

Sand

Although disconcerting, riding in loose sand is not that difficult once you get the motorcycle moving. It is also comforting to know that should you come off your landing will be somewhat softer.

If you know you are about to ride through miles of deep desert or beach sand you will require a bit of preparation. First you will need to reduce your tyre pressure significantly, at the same time being conscious that this may cause the rear tyre to slip on the wheel rim unless you have a rim lock fitted.

Slow down and as you move onto loose sand gently tap into the power. Ride steadily with your elbows away from your body and allow the bike to move around beneath you. If necessary, speed up a little if the bike moves around too much.

Should the sand become really deep, try your best not to stop. It is very important to keep moving, even if you have to paddle with your feet or jump off the bike and run beside it for a short stretch. Digging bikes out of the sand is an energy sapping exercise and the heavier your bike, the greater the chance of getting stuck.

If you do get bogged down, don't abuse your clutch by trying to power the bike out. Instead turn the engine off and lie the bike down on its side. Fill the holes left by the wheels with sand and try to compact the sand with your feet. Pick up the bike, start it and get it moving before you jump aboard.

Steep Ascents & Descents

Before you commit yourself to a climb, you have to be sure that a combination of your skill, bike, power, tyres and surface leave the odds in your favour! Getting halfway up with the bike stalling and falling down on top of you is not a place you want to be! You also need to know something about the terrain at the top. Making a steep climb only to reach the top and find there is no place to turn the bike or there is a steep drop off on the other side is worth avoiding. If you power up over the lip you will have little chance of stopping if there is a huge drop on the other side – something which can be quite common when riding in sand dunes.

Getting up a steep incline successfully depends on the preparation you make before starting out. If you are entirely happy with the decision, you need to be fully focused and totally committed.

Choose a line up the incline, choose a suitable gear, increase the revs and move into the power band. The bike will accelerate but moderate it to a suitable speed. Move your weight forward over the front wheel. For a quick short incline you can remain seated but for a longer climb it's best to stand up on the foot pegs and move your weight as far forward on the bike as possible. Be careful not to rest your weight down onto the handlebars as this can prevent you from steering effectively.

↘ **A steep climb needs focus and commitment from the outset**
📷 Thorvaldur Orn Kristmundsson

Keep the revs a little below the power band. Ease off the throttle if you have to and if the bike's revs begin to drop, ease the throttle open. You do not want the back wheel to spin and lose traction and if the revs continue to drop, change to a lower gear.

If you find you have miscalculated and the terrain in front of you becomes too steep, aim your front tyre for a ledge, boulder or pothole and 'hook' your front tyre over/into it and anchor it there with the front brake. Lay the motorbike down on its side and move it down to a safer area before attempting to ride it back down again.

If you cannot get out of the situation and you see that you are going to stall on a section that is too steep, it is probably time for you to part company with the bike. Jump – ideally sideways as far as you can. Allow the motorcycle to fall down and away from you – a controlled fall is always better than an uncontrolled one.

On steep descents, the entire manoeuvre takes commitment, confidence and belief that the bike can get you down in one piece. To retain steering control, the front brake should be applied gently without locking the wheel. Similarly, it is easy to lock-up the rear brake and thereby lose any stopping power as you trundle down the hill. The motorcycle will 'plunge' down the first few metres but quite quickly the bike's speed will level out as engine braking takes effect. It's unlikely you will move out of first gear, though this is largely dependent on the gradient and how comfortable you feel. Navigate your way down, arms easy and relaxed, gripping the bike with your knees when the need arises.

If you need to slow down, gently squeeze the front brake lever with one finger. As most of the weight (and therefore downward pressure) is on the front of the bike it is unlikely to lock-up unless the surface is very loose. In this case, use the front brake intermittently on firmer ground and run through the loose parts of the descent. Despite moving slowly and not applying the throttle, the bike should not stall unless you stop.

Trust the bike on a steep descent and use engine braking to see you down safely

📷 Thorvaldur Orn Kristmundsson

↑ Take nothing for granted when crossing rivers
📷 Touratech

Crossing rivers

Never plunge into a river without investigating the river bed first. Sight on a spot on the opposite bank and walk straight towards it. If it is good, return for your motorbike and ride it through along the identical route.

Crossing a river is about balance and smoothness. Use the momentum of the bike (and your body) to easily and smoothly move forward. If the bike bucks, blip the gas smartly to keep the bike upright and moving.

If the river bed is uneven and the river crossing challenging, remove your panniers, top box and other bags.

A slowly moving motorcycle that is bucking around needs to be as light as possible.

Know where the air intake manifold is on your bike. If the water is close to the height of the manifold, you must turn the engine off and push it through (or fit a snorkel to the manifold opening).

If your bike takes in water (or falls over during the crossing) it will stop, no problem, but do not try to restart it. Attempting to restart the engine will cause damage to the starter-motor subsystem and an expensive repair bill. On the other bank remove the plugs and crank the engine

Step One

Be sure to check the river before attempting to cross. A close visual inspection is essential

Step Two

If you're uncertain, consider walking across with the bike. You could also consider removing your panniers to lighten the load

Step Three

If you're happy with the conditions, mount up and cross to the other side using the throttle to maintain your momentum

Step Four

Be conscious of the depth at all times and 'paddle through' in the seated position if it starts to get deep

📷 Greg Baker

to clear any water that may have been drawn into the cylinders. Spray WD40 liberally into each cylinder, replace the plugs and start as normal.

If the river is not too deep but is flowing strongly, don't stand up and try to ride your motorbike through. Stay seated and using your legs, paddle your bike across. Depending on the strength of the river, get a friend to walk through with you.

Generally a river bed offers a hard surface (otherwise the river would become a swamp) so don't worry about thick mud at the bottom. You may, however, find some

mud right next to the river banks so gently power through these areas. River beds are also generally made up of stones with smooth edges. Therefore you can deflate your tyres by 50 per cent for a wide and difficult crossing.

And finally, look up, body relaxed, arms easy, body balanced, legs bent. Gently power towards a spot on the opposite bank making a small bow wave with the front wheel. If the bow wave starts to wet your upper body then you are going too fast and you will fall off should the bike hit an awkward spot. Don't look into the dark murky depths unless you want to investigate it up-close and personal!

Mud

There are no secrets or easy answers for a rider wanting to move a heavily laden adventure bike through mud. This is a slow process often involving a lot of paddling with your feet as you move forward. If the mud is not too deep and you can still stand up, move your weight off the front wheel, thereby preventing it from digging in. A gung-ho approach of blasting through a long patch of bad mud at speed seldom works for bigger bikes. Instead commit, look up and look ahead, and aggressively keep the bike moving at a brisk walking speed.

Your bike may also overheat during a period of slow riding and higher than normal revs so check the radiator to ensure that it is not caked with mud.

The Shakedown

With the training out of the way and your bike starting to take shape, a first shakedown run is a good idea. Some people may be using the bike for their daily commuting routine, others may be using the bike exclusively for the adventure ride. Irrespective of how well you think you know your bike, life is about to change. Fully loaded with all the kit and equipment you need and a full tank of fuel, your motorcycle is a different beast altogether.

And this is why the shakedown runs are so important. It is imperative that you are comfortable on the bike and the modifications you have made work as intended. Does the tank bag with the all-important map sit in the right place and not move around? Does the seat feel comfortable enough and does the GPS bracket need adjusting? Does the bike-to-bike communications system work and what is the maximum range of the radios?

There are so many little things that need checking and the more that work properly in advance, the more sleep you will have the night before you leave!

Riding across off-road terrain for long periods with a heavy payload puts a lot of stress on even the best adventure bikes, so test, not just on the road, but ideally on the sort of terrain you're likely to be covering on the trip. Load up with everything you plan to carry to make this as accurate a simulation as possible.

Time permitting, try to do a fairly long run so you have an idea of what it is like doing longer distances on the bike. Make notes of the things that cannot be fixed immediately and make them priorities when you get back from the test. If there were several things that needed attention after the first test, a second run is probably a good idea, giving you a further opportunity to test individual items and be comfortable that they work as planned.

Give yourself enough time to test the bike and make further modifications. There is little point in heading off on a test run the day before you're set to leave. If you come across a serious mechanical issue or decide to make a significant change to one of your modifications, you will need time to do this and it would be madness to jeopardise the start of your trip for the sake of not conducting the test run in good time.

If you are travelling with someone, try to conduct the shakedown test together. In that way you have help in finding solutions to what are often small, but niggling issues. At the same time you get to see how your colleague has dealt with certain issues and also if there are any major issues with his/her bike which you might need to be aware of.

Finally, the shakedown test is also a good opportunity to start thinking about some of the items you might need on the trip in order to implement some running repairs. Cable (zip) ties, elastic bands, tape, wire and superglue are just some of the things that come to mind. Make notes and add items to your checklist before packing.

↑ **A good shakedown run will offer a taste of things to come**
📷 Yamaha

Documentation

Mihai Barbu

ealing with the paperwork both before and during an adventure ride is, for many people, one of the least exciting elements but it should be considered a vital ingredient to making sure the trip is successful. As with the ride itself, there are no guarantees but careful preparation ahead of departure and then looking after your documents while riding will go a long way to making life on the road considerably easier.

As a general rule, make sure that you commence with securing all the relevant paperwork needed as soon as you have committed to the trip – whatever you do, don't leave this part of your planning to the last minute as it will undoubtedly jeopardise your departure date.

Managing your Paperwork

As soon as you know you are going to be heading off, start getting all your paperwork together. Make a list of all the vital documents you either have or need to get, including visas, international driving permit, carnet, personal, bike, travel and medical insurance, green card and bike registration papers. This can be time consuming but it is time well spent.

As you start to gather the various documents, ensure the addresses all tally up to avoid any confusion once on the road. An old address on one document and a current address on another will only serve to perplex a pedantic border official.

Your passport should be valid for at least six months, or longer if you are planning an extended trip. If this is the case, then it may also be worth investing in a passport with multiple pages to accommodate the numerous stamps.

Leave copies of all your important documents at home with someone that you can contact directly. In the event of losing all your paperwork or having it stolen, appreciate that it will take a lot of effort to get things replaced. Without a passport, driver's licence or relevant papers for the bike, your options will be very limited so make sure someone back home can e-mail or fax copies of the paperwork to you.

On the road keep a copy of all relevant documents in a watertight plastic bag and hide this somewhere on the bike. In the event of losing your originals, you have access to a set of the most important documents. It may be worthwhile making colour copies of your passport, driver's licence and registration documents and laminating them in plastic for extra protection. Getting copies certified at a relevant authority may help in certain countries. A final tip is to scan all your paperwork (including a copy of vital documents such as your passport) in an easily readable PDF format and e-mail it to yourself. Also keep the same files on a portable USB flash memory stick in your pocket or round your neck.

Visas

Arranging your visas and understanding the conditions which apply to each one of them is a crucial and time consuming part of planning a trip. In essence, a visa issued by a particular country grants you permission to formally request entrance to the country during a given period of time and for certain purposes. They are generally added into your passport (stamped or glued) or sometimes issued separately.

Some visas can be granted on arrival in a certain country or by prior application at the country's embassy or consulate if you are short on time. It is worth considering making use of specialised travel agencies who are experienced and know how to minimise red tape to facilitate getting visas issued.

For visas which can be issued ahead of departure, get the process under way as soon as possible. For those visas which need to be acquired en route, regard this as part of the 'challenge' of the trip as the process can be anything from straightforward to downright laborious. Opening hours for many embassies are limited which can often add to the frustration. Be prepared by having all your documentation to hand and it's a good idea to have a good supply of passport photos. Get these done before leaving and keep them somewhere safe. Finally, try to be as clear as possible about your planned route and the towns you plan to visit. This adds credibility to your application and can certainly assist in progressing the application.

The most important considerations to bear in mind with visas are:

- Research the costs and factor these into your budget as they vary considerably between countries
- Always check exactly how long the visa is valid for once stamped on entry into the country. If you plan to return back through the same country, try to obtain a multiple-entry visa
- Remember that visa regulations change quite frequently so getting the most up-to-date information from the relevant embassy or consulate is vital
- Establish the length of time you have got between the date of issue and when it must be presented (at a border). Some visas start from the date of issue. Others give you six months from the date of issue in which to present it at a border. This is a vital consideration when planning your route and time spent in each country
- Some countries may require you to obtain an exit visa in order to be allowed to leave the country – make sure you do this if stated

VISA EXPERIENCES

During their round-the-world expedition, Adam Lewis and Danny Burroughs put a lot of work into ensuring their visa planning worked well. Their efforts paid off and this summarises their experience thus far from London to Laos:

Western Europe – Not applicable (both travelling on UK passports)

Eastern Europe – Visas available at the borders

Syria – Available from the Syrian embassy in Istanbul. You need a 'Letter of Recommendation' from the British embassy, costing around £40; normally available in 24 hours

Iran – This visa was the key to their trip. They were careful not to apply to the Iranian embassy in London but used an agency in Iran to facilitate the visa. They followed the agency's instructions, e-mailed them any questions and specified 'Istanbul' as the consulate from which they wanted to collect their visas. They also established that if Iranian visas were not being issued at the time, an alternative was to go via Kyrgyzstan and China to the top of the Karakoram Highway, though this was fraught with bureaucratic red tape and additional costs – around three months of paperwork to get permission and a bill for £75 per day for a compulsory guide

Pakistan – Collected from the Pakistani embassy in London before they departed; same day service

India – Picked up their visas in Islamabad, but took a week to secure

Nepal – Available at the border

Thailand – Thirty day visas available at the border but no longer extendable. Sixty day visas are available at the Thai embassy in Kathmandu

Cambodia – Available at the border

Laos – Dependent on the border – not available on Cambodian border so they secured them from the Laos embassy in Phnom Penn in 24 hours

- Your own nationality affects all of the visa issuing information you ever read or are given – this includes availability, conditions and price. Other factors are also considered before a visa is issued, including the intended duration of your stay and the activities that you will be undertaking in the country.

International Driving Permit

For adventure motorcyclists, the International Driving Permit (IDP) is a useful document to accompany the standard driving licence. IDPs are valid in more than 150 countries and function as an official translation of your driver's licence into ten foreign languages – it simply confirms that you are the holder of a valid licence in your home country. These licences are not intended to replace valid (national) licences and should only be used as a supplement to a valid licence. You will normally be asked to present the two documents together. IDPs are not valid in an individual's country of residence. Before departure, you can obtain one from an automobile association. This is a straightforward process and should not take more than two weeks to be arranged. It generally requires you to submit your driving licence and passport photo as well as a nominal fee. IDPs are usually valid for a period of 12 months from the date of issue.

COUNTRY-SPECIFIC IDP REQUIREMENTS

Afghanistan	IDP required
Albania	IDP required
Algeria	IDP required
Angola	IDP required if licence does not incorporate photo
Argentina	IDP required
Armenia	IDP required
Australia	IDP recommended
Bahrain	Specific IDP conditions
Bangladesh	IDP recommended
Belarus	Specific IDP conditions
Benin	IDP required
Bhutan	IDP required
Bolivia	IDP required
Bosnia	IDP recommended
Botswana	IDP recommended
Brazil	Specific IDP conditions
Brunei	IDP required
Bulgaria	IDP required
Burkina Faso	IDP recommended
Cambodia	IDP required
Canada	IDP recommended
Cape Verde	IDP recommended
Cayman Islands	IDP required
Central African Rep.	IDP required
Chad	IDP required
Chile	IDP required
China	IDP not recognised. Riders recommended to do their own research
Colombia	IDP required
Comoros	IDP required
Congo (DRC)	IDP required
Congo (Republic of)	IDP recommended
Côte d'Ivoire	IDP required if licence does not incorporate photo
Czech Republic	IDP required if licence does not incorporate photo
Dominican Republic	IDP required if licence does not incorporate photo
Ecuador	IDP recommended
Egypt	IDP required
Equatorial Guinea	IDP recommended
Eritrea	IDP recommended
Gabon	IDP required if licence does not incorporate photo
Georgia	IDP required if licence does not incorporate photo
Ghana	IDP recommended
Guam	IDP required
Guinea Bissau	IDP recommended
Guinea Republic	IDP recommended
Haiti	IDP recommended
Hong Kong	IDP recommended
Hungary	Specific IDP conditions
Iceland	Specific IDP conditions
India	IDP required
Indonesia	Specific IDP conditions
Iran	IDP required
Iraq	IDP required
Israel	IDP required for car hire
Italy	Specific IDP conditions
Japan	IDP required
Jordan	IDP required
Kenya	IDP recommended
Korea (South)	IDP required
Kuwait	IDP required
Kazakhstan	IDP recommended
Kyrgyzstan	IDP recommended
Laos	IDP recommended
Lebanon	IDP recommended
Lesotho	IDP recommended
Macao (Macau)	IDP required
Malaysia	IDP recommended
Mexico	IDP recommended
Montenegro	IDP recommended
Mozambique	IDP recommended
Myanmar (Burma)	Specific IDP conditions
Namibia	IDP recommended
Nepal	Specific IDP conditions
Niger	IDP recommended
Nigeria	IDP required
Oman	IDP required
Pakistan	IDP required
Peru	IDP required for stays longer than 30 days
Philippines	Required for car hire
Portugal	Specific IDP conditions
Qatar	IDP required
Romania	Specific IDP conditions
Russian Federation	IDP required
Rwanda	Specific IDP conditions
Sao Tome & Principe	IDP recommended
Saudi Arabia	IDP recommended (women not permitted to drive)
Serbia	IDP recommended
Senegal	Specific IDP conditions
Seychelles	IDP recommended
Sierra Leone	IDP required
Slovakia	Required for car hire
Slovenia	Specific IDP conditions
Somalia	IDP required
South Africa	Specific IDP conditions
Spain	Specific IDP conditions
Sri Lanka	Specific IDP conditions
Sudan	IDP recommended
Surinam	IDP required
Swaziland	IDP required if licence does not incorporate photo
Syria	IDP required
Taiwan	IDP required
Tanzania	IDP recommended
Thailand	IDP required
Togo	IDP required
Tunisia	IDP required if licence does not incorporate photo
Turkey	IDP required for stays longer than 90 days
Ukraine	IDP required
UAE	IDP required
USA	IDP recommended
Vietnam	Specific IDP conditions
Yemen	IDP required for car hire
Zambia	IDP recommended
Zimbabwe	Specific IDP conditions

Carnets

The carnet (known officially as a 'Carnet de Passage en Douane') is an internationally recognised customs document which allows you to temporarily import your motorcycle into a particular country without having to leave a cash deposit at the border. In essence, it acts as an international guarantee to cover the payment of any taxes or duties owed to the government of that particular country in the event that the bike is not re-exported.

A carnet is not required for Europe or North America, though it is required for many countries in Africa, Asia, and the Middle East as well as Australia and New Zealand. It is also recommended for travel in South America.

To obtain a carnet, you are required to provide security based on the age and reasonable market value of the motorcycle, as well as the countries to be visited. In the UK, for example, this security can take one of three different forms:

- Cash Deposit – this is paid to the issuing authority and refunded once the carnet is discharged
- Bank Guarantee – calculated as the highest possible duty payable in each of the countries to be visited. Each country has its own duty which can range from 100 per cent to 800 per cent of the value of the motorcycle. The guarantor effectively agrees to pay any duties up to the limit of the guarantee. Bear in mind that banks will almost always charge a fee for arranging the guarantee

- Insurance Indemnity – arranged through an insurance company either nominated or recommended by the issuing authority. A percentage of the premium is refunded once the carnet is discharged, typically around 50 per cent but check this with the issuing authority.

The amount required depends on the rates of customs duty and taxes in the countries visited but is always a multiple of the value of the motorcycle as illustrated below:

Jeffrey Polnaja

Robert Wicks

SECURITY RATES

Country	Multiple	Example 1: 2007 KTM 990 Adventure worth £9,000	Example 2: 2004 BMW R 1150 GS worth £5,500
Egypt	800%	£72,000	£44,000
Iran, India, Pakistan, Nepal	500%	£45,000	£27,500
Kenya, Nigeria, Libya, Middle East and Far East (incl. Singapore, Malaysia and Sri Lanka)	200%	£18,000	£11,000
South America	300%	£27,000	£16,500
Africa (excluding Kenya, Nigeria, Libya), Japan, New Zealand, Australia	150%	£13,500	£8,250

Information kindly provided by RAC Carnets

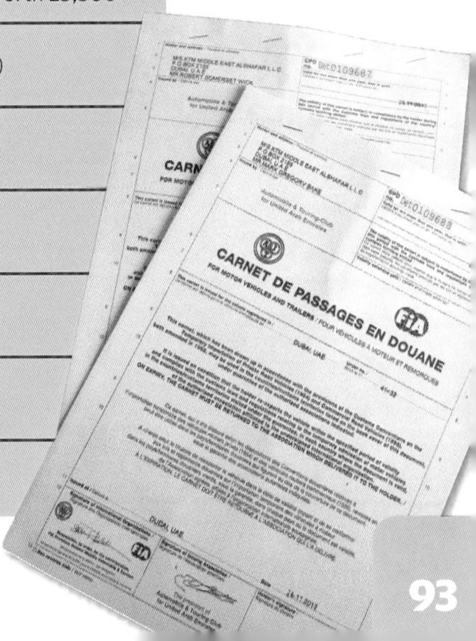

These security rates are correct at the time of going to press, but it is advisable to get updates from the relevant national motoring authority in your country as they do tend to fluctuate.

National motoring associations are generally the only issuing authorities for carnets. At all times, the carnet actually remains the property of the issuer and consequently should be kept safely with your other essential documents. Once issued, the motoring authority becomes directly responsible for the payment of customs duties and taxes if regulations concerning the temporary importation of your motorcycle are infringed. When applying you will generally be asked to supply details of your insurance indemnity form (if applicable), a copy of your passport, a copy of the vehicle registration document and an accurate list of the countries you intend visiting. The issuing authority estimates the value of your bike and then generates a quotation based on the highest duty rate levied by the countries on your list to ensure there is sufficient 'cover' before issuing the carnet.

There are several steps in the process of getting a carnet issued but it should typically take no more than a month to arrange. Carnet booklets are generally made up of five,

ten or 25 pages. This means that a five-page carnet will allow you to temporarily import your motorcycle into five countries or on five different occasions. Each page is divided up into three sections – the lower section is removed by customs on entry into a country; the middle section is removed on exit; the top, counter-foil section is used to reconcile your bike's movements and is stamped once on entry and once on exit.

At the end of your journey, the carnet should have an entry and exit stamp for every foreign country visited. Once home, the carnet will be endorsed proving that the vehicle is not subject to any claims made by foreign customs. This then allows your financial guarantee to be released. If your bike is stolen or written-off in an accident, make sure you obtain a copy of the police report as well as some form of acknowledgement from the local customs authority otherwise you will almost certainly be held liable for certain duties.

Carnets are generally valid for a full year from the date of issue and can only be extended with the prior agreement of the local customs authority and the local motoring authority so bear this in mind if undertaking a lengthy journey.

Motorcycle Insurance & Green Cards

Obtaining comprehensive insurance for your motorcycle for an overland expedition is difficult to achieve at the best of times and generally only obtainable from specialist brokers willing to consider your planned exploits. As with other forms of insurance you consider for the trip (of the personal, travel and medical variety), you need to be entirely clear with the broker about what it is you plan to do and exactly where you plan to travel. An accurate description of this alone may well deter certain brokers, though there are some specialists that will consider meeting your needs.

Third party insurance will generally need to be bought locally as you progress on your trip. Don't however count on this having much value in Third World countries. Rather take a prudent and sensible approach when riding to minimise potential risks.

A Green Card (otherwise known as an International Motor Insurance Certificate) is an internationally recognised document particular to certain countries that serves as evidence that you have the minimum insurance cover required by law in the country you are visiting.

Without a Green Card you will be required to purchase insurance at the border of the relevant country which means unwanted additional bureaucracy and expense so it is advisable to have one with you. It provides no insurance cover in itself but instead serves as easily recognisable proof of your third party insurance – very useful in the event of an accident for example.

Insurers do not normally charge a fee for a Green Card, though an insurance broker may elect to levy an administration fee for arranging it on your behalf. If for some reason you do not take a Green Card with you on the trip, you should instead carry your official Certificate of Insurance. Don't let your insurance company fob you off about not needing a hard copy of your insurance document – you do. Adam Lewis and Danny Burroughs learnt the hard way during the Eastern European leg of their round-the-world trip: at the Montenegrin, Albanian and Macedonian borders they had to buy insurance because they could not produce a Green Card.

Request the card well in advance of your trip and make sure you receive all the relevant documentation before you go. It is not necessary to have one when travelling to the EU and certain other European countries. Those that currently do require a Green Card are: Albania, Andorra, Bosnia-Herzegovina, Bulgaria, Cyprus, Estonia, Iran, Israel, Latvia, Macedonia, Moldavia, Morocco, Poland, Romania, Serbia-Montenegro, Tunisia, Turkey and Ukraine.

No driving permit needed here...
📷 Joe Pichler

Personal & Medical Insurance

Personal and medical insurance can sometimes be seen as a minefield with many different considerations. Traditional insurers are unlikely to be in a position to help but with the growth in adventure travel in recent years, there is now a competitive market for insurance to cover expeditions and overland trips. Some initial research on the Internet is a good place to start and the key considerations when deciding on insurance cover are as follows:

- Be honest and open about the trip you are doing – there is no point in trying to get reduced rates for your cover by not disclosing vital information about your trip – in the long run it will only serve to render the policy invalid
- Some policies don't cater for activity undertaken on larger capacity motorcycles
- Check if you are covered when travelling through countries which are considered high risk. Cover is generally not available in countries regarded as so-called 'no-go areas' or 'hot spots'
- Check if you can extend your cover and at what additional cost if your trip goes on for longer than anticipated
- Read the small print for any specific exclusions
- Make sure to take your policy document with you together with all the relevant contact details in the event of having to make a claim. Understand the procedures to be followed in an emergency
- Finally, remember to factor these costs into your budget when planning for the trip
- Read the small print again!

Typical Policy Benefits

A comprehensive travel policy could include the following typical range of benefits. Each insurer tries to offer something unique so shop around for the best deal. Make sure you establish the extent of cover provided for each of the individual elements of cover.

Cancellation – Should cover you for loss of travel, accommodation expenses and related fees as a result of certain circumstances – determine what these are.

Curtailment – Offers you cover for the value of the portion of your travel and accommodation expenses calculated from the date of your return to your home, which have not been used. You should also be covered for reasonable additional travelling expenses (likely to be an economy class ticket) to return home earlier than

planned due to particular circumstances such as injury or serious illness .

Loss of Passport/Travel Documents – This is certainly worth taking as it is likely to cover you for reasonable additional travel accommodation expenses you have to pay whilst abroad, as a result of you needing to replace a lost or stolen passport and other important travel documents.

Baggage & Personal Belongings – This could provide you with cover for the value of or repair to any of your personal baggage, which is lost, stolen, damaged or destroyed. There is typically a maximum value associated with any one item – be sure to specify high value items separately if the policy allows.

Personal Liability – This provides cover for personal legal liability claims made against you resulting from your negligence during your trip. Certain exclusions apply in this case and quite often the policy will not include cover whilst using motorcycles. It is worth exploring this in some detail with your insurer to understand the position clearly.

Medical Insurance – Good medical insurance is absolutely essential – don't leave home without it. In terms of an actual medical policy, you should look to be covered for all emergency medical and surgical treatment and hospital charges.

Remember that any policy you take out is unlikely to cover any claims that are a result of pre-existing medical conditions.

If for medical reasons you need to be transported back to your home country, the cost of a private air ambulance, or for a block of seats large enough to accommodate a stretcher and medical equipment on a commercial flight, plus a medical attendant to accompany you can cost upwards of £30,000 so ensure that your policy includes the all-important evacuation or repatriation clause – this ensures that if it is deemed to be 'medically necessary', there is sufficient cover to get you flown back home.

Finally, it is worth enquiring if the policy you intend to take includes at least some level of emergency dental cover.

Money

Carrying your funds for the journey safely and securely is a key issue and can be done in a variety of ways to minimise the risks involved.

Essentially you should balance the amount of hard currency you are willing to carry with other forms of funding such as credit cards and travellers' cheques. Money can also be wired to you from home, but this can, depending on your location, take some time to be received.

Cash – A good idea is to separate your cash into two parts, one small amount which is easily accessible and can be used for everyday expenses, with the bulk of the cash you're carrying hidden away on your person. Opening up a fat wallet in a local market is simply asking for trouble. Understand which currencies are best for the different countries you will visit. In Africa for example, the US Dollar is still king but don't make the mistake of taking small denominations – US$20 notes are best and be cautious with US$100 bills as some banks may not be willing to change them given counterfeit concerns. A mixture of bills in different denominations tends to work best. Riding from Cairo, a traveller recently took one thousand US$1 bills with him and still had them with him when he got to Cape Town six weeks later!

Credit Cards – A credit card is a really useful and compact way of carrying funds with you. Its use will be limited in remote areas (some countries in Africa won't even entertain the idea) but it will be extremely handy on certain occasions. Keep tabs on the amount you are spending and ensure you have the necessary funds back home to cover your expenses as the trip progresses.

Travellers' Cheques – Travellers' cheques are one of the safest and most convenient ways to carry your money on an overland trip but also have some downsides to consider. They are generally available in all major international currencies and offer a number of benefits over other forms of currency – they are easy to use, refundable and accepted worldwide, though you may have difficulty using them in remote locations as the facility to cash them simply doesn't exist.

Some agents may charge a small fee when you buy your travellers' cheques, whilst others will offer them without any fee being applied. Remember to safeguard your cheques as you would your cash and always carry them with you. When cashing cheques take your passport with you and enquire first whether there is a tax on imported cheques that might be applied in the country you are visiting.

Keep track of the numbers of the travellers' cheques as you cash them during your trip. Make a point of keeping this record separate from the remaining cheques.

ESSENTIAL MONEY TIPS

- Check if your bank allows for free withdrawals and transactions abroad
- For a lengthy trip consider changing the address on all your bank accounts and credit cards to someone at home you can trust. If you have any problems, credit card companies will cancel your card and issue a new one to the cardholder's address only
- Make sure you can do all your banking online – managing your finances back home remotely can be very handy, particularly if you are on a long trip and need to move funds about or make payments. With Internet cafés in most locations, this is certainly achievable. If this is not possible, then have someone at home that can help to transfer funds
- One option is to set up current and credit card accounts. Use the current account card only for cash withdrawals and the credit card for everything else. Arrange for the full balance of the credit card to be paid from the current account and then it doesn't matter if you're somewhere you can't get access to pay it
- Almost every border control point has someone willing to change money with you – find out what the going rate of exchange is before you 'open negotiations' and don't be afraid to barter to get the best possible deal.

BMW Motorrad

In an increasingly commercial world, good quality photographs can not only generate some income to offset the costs of your trip but will also keep sponsors pleased and offer you the opportunity to share your adventure with friends and family. One of the advantages of adventure motorcycling is the fact that we generally get to travel well off the beaten track and, as a result, have the opportunity to take some rather special photographs that not only serve as a record of the journey but can also be an inspiration to others. Most of the images in this book are intended to do just that – to inspire others to set out on two wheels.

The good news is that digital technology continues to improve at a rapid rate, with cameras becoming smaller, lighter and cheaper all the time. Once you're over the issue of price, your biggest enemy is weight and storage of the gear on board the bike. If you can afford it, then spend some money on a decent polarising filter – you'll be amazed at the difference it makes.

In addition to your main camera it is very useful to carry a small compact camera for when you want to capture a scene but haven't the time to take out the SLR, or if using it might perhaps be intrusive. It will fit neatly into a jacket pocket and you'll be amazed how often it comes in handy.

Don't forget all the other necessary items such as batteries, chargers, memory cards, external flash unit, cleaning equipment and a lightweight tripod. (The alternative to the latter is Joby's 'Gorillapod' – infinitely more flexible than a traditional tripod and easier to carry.)

Camera gear needs to be accessible so it's best stored in your tank bag, together with your other essential items. This bag should be waterproof or at least have a waterproof cover. Always take time at the end of each day to care for your camera and lenses by getting rid of dust – and always make a point of carrying your full memory cards with you. As the saying goes, memory is cheap, memories aren't.

Essential for any photographer is a checklist of everything you will need for the trip. Check that all your gear is covered by insurance and that it is up to date. Take proof that you purchased your equipment at home and not abroad so you won't get landed with customs duty on your return.

Equipment

If you're serious about your photography then you'll probably have a good idea of the gear you want to take, but if you're new to this world then the best piece of advice is to spend as much as you can afford on a good digital SLR body and a couple of lenses. You will want a decent combination of lenses to capture landscapes, portraits and everything in between, so consider something like a wide-angle lens starting at 20mm, as well as an 80–200mm zoom lens extending to 300mm for added flexibility.

◄ **A space-saving
flexible tripod**

⬇ **Compact digital
cameras are a favourite
amongst adventure riders
given their size and ever-
increasing features**
📷 Canon

Use your images to tell the story of your adventure

Research

Good travel photography undoubtedly starts at home before you depart, so time spent researching where you are headed will be very worthwhile. Having an idea of what is there and the subjects you might want to cover will provide an excellent starting point – a good travel guide will give you a sense of what to expect – so begin thinking about ideas early on. It's also important to appreciate the local customs and traditions of where you are headed as the last thing you want to do is offend someone by pointing your camera at them. Some basic phrases in the local language will go a long way towards assisting you in communicating with people when photographing them.

Content

Every place has its own particular look, character and ambience. If you want photographs from your trip to be memorable and lasting they should capture all of these qualities, and say as much about a place as giving the literal look of it. Your photographs need to bring these and other sensations back, to trigger your memories and enable you to communicate how you felt to others.

Your aim should be to convey not only the places and scenes you have witnessed but also the feelings and emotions associated with the locations. The unexpected is always around the corner when you travel, and with some careful preparation and a keen photographic eye you can produce some great results.

Always be aware of your first impressions. As *National Geographic* photographer Robert Caputo puts it: "First impressions are invaluable sparks to creative interpretation, and by definition are not repeatable. You've seen the place in pictures, you've read about it. Now you're there, and all your senses can partake."

Adventure travel opens up a whole new world of photographic opportunities

Types of Shots

Landscapes

One of the shots you will almost certainly be taking is the landscape shot – mountain passes, forests, open plains, sandy deserts, swamps, lakes, rivers and beaches. Each has its own characteristics and you need to think carefully about what qualities and emotions you want to convey through the photography. A small tripod will be useful, together with a wide-angle lens. Remember that not every shot needs to show your bike!

Cities and Towns

Like landscapes, each city and town has its own look and feel, whether that's a distinctive setting, its architecture, the skyline, a famous local site or a particular kind of food or dress. There's always at least one thing that is unique. When covering a town or city, even a small village, you need to do three basic things at a minimum: capture a sense of place, which is usually a wide shot that shows the setting, skyline or other view that gives a feeling for the whole; show landmarks for which the place is famous; and document the life of its inhabitants. For the cityscapes and wide shots, as well as for the landmarks, it's a good idea to check out the postcard racks in your hotel lobby or at kiosks. They will quickly give you an idea of where the best views are and what is considered well known enough to warrant a postcard.

Buildings

When you are photographing buildings, statues or other monuments, think about what they represent before you shoot. As an example, there's a large statue of Vulcan outside Birmingham, Alabama. You could make a perfectly nice image of him standing on his hill on a sunny day, but such a picture would not say a lot about whom Vulcan is. A photograph on a stormy evening, with perhaps lightning in the background, would convey much more. Cannons on a historical battlefield might look better in fog than in bright sunlight, for instance. Get the idea of the subject, then think of the weather, light or angle that would best communicate it.

Portraits of Friends and Strangers

We often travel with people we know and it is important to use this to your advantage by making your photographs more effective. Robert Caputo says: "Try to strike a balance between a picture of them and a picture of the place. A friend of mine once made a close-up portrait of me in China.

It's often an unusual
angle that makes for
a great photo

It wasn't a great portrait, but more importantly, it could have been made in my backyard – there was nothing of the place in the frame."

As a general rule it is always best to ask permission if you want to photograph someone. Translate "Please can I take a photograph of you?" into the local language and you will be surprised how well this request works. Respect people when they decline, but at the same time don't be surprised if people ask for money to be photographed. Caputo adds: "You cannot always ask permission, of course. If you are shooting a street scene or taking a wide shot of a market, you can't run up to everyone and ask if it's okay. In general, people do not mind this sort of photography – it's only when they're singled out that they get uncomfortable, so be sensitive to the scene in your viewfinder. If people are getting nervous, ask permission or move on."

If you've had a positive response, it is always a nice touch to show people the image (assuming you're shooting digitally, of course) .

The Bike(s)

Think about unusual angles when photographing a bike by getting low down and including detail of the terrain to tell more of a story. Detail shots of specific components also make for interesting images and help to convey a sense of the place you've travelled to.

GENERAL PHOTOGRAPHY TIPS

- Get out there and off the beaten track – in fact, try to get lost. Even if you find yourself in a small village, don't stick to the main street – set off on foot and explore the back streets because it is there that you will find the best images, away from the crowds. The only way to discover the rhythm of life is to experience it. Time spent discovering a place will enrich your experience
- Think about when to set out – early morning and late afternoon, when the light is softer, are often the best times of day for photography
- Always have your camera at the ready to capture what is going on around you. As one photographer puts it, "Serendipity plays an enormously important role in travel photography"
- It is vital to make time for your photography and this needs to be factored into the riding plan for the day. Taking good photographs requires a commitment of time and energy and you will be very disappointed with the results if it's a rushed effort
- Don't procrastinate – if there is a chance to get out and shoot, make use of the time as the weather may prevent you from shooting the very next day
- Take more than one shot of a subject by trying different angles and distances so that you have options when it comes to the editing process. You can never take too many images
- Spend time looking for detail, which will add significantly to your portfolio. Detail shots are everywhere to be found – in markets, architecture, vehicles, fruit, clothing, even in animals. A macro or telephoto lens is great for this type of shot
- Use a wide-angle lens to capture portraits of local people in their environments and use a longer lens to shoot unposed images from further away. In this way the subject remains natural without the pressure to pose
- There is little point in returning home with the same images that appear in the guidebooks, so always try to find viewpoints that are not traditionally used for photos
- Try to capture the essence of local daily life – this is undoubtedly more interesting than the tired old tourist track
- Apply various creative filters (available through Photoshop and Apps such as Snapseed on an iPad) to create more captivating images
- Get yourself into some of the photos rather than spending the entire trip behind the lens
- Above all, take pictures with a view to telling the story of your adventure.

Section 2

On The Road

Living on the Road

Krzysztof Samborski

Y ou've taken the plunge, committed the time and money and ridden off into the sunset and now the real fun begins. And that 'fun' can come to a rather abrupt halt if you do not follow some fairly basic guidelines for 'living on the road'. You will have to develop new routines and ways of doing things and will have to deal with a range of key issues, from simple health and personal safety to dealing with food and water as well as the more complex issues of border crossings and adapting to life in a foreign country.

On your journey, whether it is a short excursion or a more substantial expedition, you will be exposed to various health hazards. It's always best to follow a common sense approach and to be as prepared as possible so that you are in the best position to deal with the unexpected. Some basic preventative measures go a long way, as does having at least one person in your group who is competent at first aid.

You will also have to be equipped to deal with common ailments, and before you leave make sure you are up to date with your inoculations. This chapter can only scratch the surface of what is an enormous topic and you are advised to undertake as much research as possible and get up-to-date information for each of the countries you plan to visit in order to understand the key health and personal safety issues you are likely to encounter.

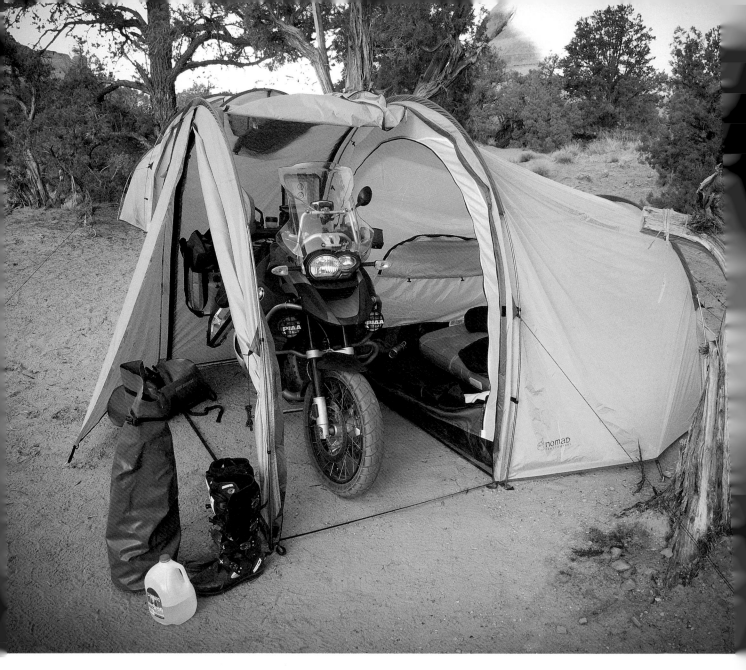

↑ **The innovative**

Nomad tent –

beats the hell out

of doing a repair

in the rain

📷 Redverz Gear

Europe

Staying Healthy

Staying healthy on the road can be difficult given the range of different risks to which you will be exposed. There are some fairly common ailments which could just as easily occur at home, a range of rather nasty diseases which you need to be inoculated against as well as a number of other health related issues – such as altitude sickness – which can have an impact.

Common Ailments

At some point on your journey you are likely to suffer from at least one if not more of the following common ailments – a cold, exhaustion, diarrhoea, allergies and almost certainly sunburn. Always adopt a common sense approach and make sure your first aid kit is sufficient to provide you with at least a degree of relief from any of these ailments.

Inoculations

The extent of the inoculations you need will largely depend on where you intend travelling and hence it is worth investing in some professional medical advice. Some services can provide you with all of your travel vaccines and immunisations plus expert, up-to-date advice on travel health issues and information specific to the countries you plan to visit. Be sure to understand the time frames for the different vaccinations – some may be needed a few months before your departure while some may require a follow-up jab just before departure. The following section should help you to understand a little bit about each disease so you can be on the look-out for potential symptoms and have the necessary inoculations before heading off:

Tetanus – Infection generally occurs through wound contamination, and often involves a cut or deep puncture wound. As the infection progresses, muscle spasms in the jaw develop. This is followed by difficulty swallowing and general muscle stiffness and spasms in other parts of the body.

Hepatitis A – An acute infectious liver disease transmitted, for example, through contaminated food.

Hepatitis B – Another liver disease, symptoms of which include liver inflammation, vomiting, jaundice and, rarely, death.

Rabies – A preventable viral disease that causes acute encephalitis (inflammation of the brain). The virus exists in the saliva of mammals and is transmitted from animal to animal or from animal to human by biting and/or scratching. The virus can also be spread by licking, when infected saliva makes contact with open cuts or wounds, and with the mouth, eyes, and nose. If left untreated it can be fatal. Be wary of stray dogs and other animals.

Yellow Fever – An acute viral disease. In several countries you will be asked to produce proof of having had the vaccination.

Typhoid – Common worldwide, typhoid is transmitted by ingestion of food or water contaminated with faeces from an infected person.

Meningitis – Is the inflammation of the protective membranes covering the central nervous system. Most cases of meningitis are caused by micro-organisms, such as viruses, bacteria, fungi, or parasites that spread into the blood. If you suspect you may have meningitis ensure you seek prompt medical evaluation.

Polio – An acute viral infectious disease which attacks the nervous system. It is spread from person to person by coughing and sneezing or by ingesting food or drink containing faeces of the contaminated person.

Diphtheria – An upper respiratory tract illness characterised by sore throat and fever. A milder form of diphtheria can be restricted to the skin. It is highly contagious.

Malaria – A mosquito-borne disease, it is one of the most common infectious diseases. Each year some 350–500 million cases of malaria occur worldwide, and over one million people die, most of them young children in sub-Saharan Africa. Symptoms include fever, chills, and flu-like illness. Left untreated, it can result in severe complications and death. Mosquito nets around your bed or tent, keeping your skin covered to avoid getting bitten, use of creams and/or sprays and obviously the use of anti-malarial drugs are effective tools if you are travelling to a malaria region.

OTHER HEALTH ISSUES

HIV/Aids – HIV infection in humans is now classed as pandemic and AIDS has killed more than 25 million people since it was first recognised in 1981. At least a third of deaths are in sub-Saharan Africa. Screening of blood products for HIV in the developed world has largely eliminated transmission through blood transfusions or infected blood products in these countries, but in Third World countries you need to be extremely vigilant. This is needed more as a result of a lack of resources than ignorant hospital staff. Carry latex gloves and your own sterile kit. Be extra careful if helping out at the scene of an accident if there is blood involved. In the event of needing a locally performed blood transfusion, do everything possible to ensure a safe blood source and make sure you know your own blood group before leaving home. Always practise safe sex.

Dental Issues – A thorough check-up at the dentist is the best possible preventative measure. In the event of a dental emergency, try to get the problem seen to in a large town or city where the quality of the treatment is likely to be better than in the more rural areas (this is not necessarily true for all countries but a good rule to follow in most instances).

Altitude Sickness – Whether it's a trip to Morocco and an 11,500ft (3,500m) pass over the High Atlas mountains or up to 18,380ft (5,600m) traversing the world's highest motorable road at Khardung La in India, you need to understand altitude sickness and how to deal with it. Different people have different susceptibilities and for some otherwise healthy people, the early signs of Acute Mountain Sickness (AMS) can appear at around 6,500ft (2,000m) above sea level. Although it's unlikely that you will be at high altitude for long periods of time be aware of the early symptoms which tend to manifest themselves within six to ten hours. Symptoms include: headaches with fatigue, an upset stomach, dizziness and disturbed sleep. Exertion will normally aggravate the symptoms which are generally only temporary and subside in a day or two as you begin to acclimatise. Altitude sickness usually occurs following a rapid ascent and can usually be prevented by ascending slowly.

General Safety

Adventure motorcyclists have an advantage over their four-by-four counterparts in that the bike is perceived as far less of a symbol of wealth than the large four-wheel equivalent. Use this to your advantage but always adopt a common sense approach to safety related issues. Your personal safety is paramount so always be vigilant and adopt the right approach in tricky situations – you should be willing to cut your losses and run if needed. More often than not you will be pleasantly surprised by the hospitality and kindness offered by local people but as a general rule, don't at any point place convenience over your personal security. Note the following key points:

Bike – Your number one consideration when staying at a guest house or hotel is safe parking for your bike. Many places that don't have obvious secure parking will let you park inside the lobby – simply ask the manager. Irrespective of where you park consider making use of a bike cover – it is by far one of the best security devices – you will be amazed by how 'invisible' it makes your bike. In most countries theft is not an issue but 'fiddlers' are and a couple of fully loaded adventure bikes rolling into a small town is hardly likely to go unnoticed.

Riding Gear and Equipment – Other than lugging your riding gear with you when not on the bike, one of the best security options is to make use of an adjustable, lockable wire mesh net which can either fit over the outside of a backpack or simply as a 'hold-all' for storing your riding gear when stopping at a tourist attraction. You can fit your riding kit (including boots and helmet) into it, lock it to your bike and put the cover over whilst you walk around in more casual gear. Another useful investment is a spiral cable lock. It can be used to secure your helmet and

jacket by threading the cable through the arms and helmet visor and then to a secure point on the bike. With your bulky gear securely fastened to the bike, you can take a walk or do some shopping without having to worry.

Be vigilant about your other equipment, in particular high value items such as cameras and other electronic goods.

Accidents – Wherever possible, report any accident or incident to the police straight after it has happened and insist they provide you with a report – this can be difficult in certain countries but will be extremely useful in the event of an insurance claim.

Communications – This doesn't sound like a security consideration but if you are travelling in a group of two or more it is one of the best security devices you can invest in. When reading a map and trying to navigate through an overcrowded city with no discernible directions, you aren't always able to keep an eye out for the rest of your group,

making it easy to get split up. Having a second pair of eyes to warn you about what's approaching from behind can also be very useful.

Money – Experienced travellers suggest a dummy wallet while the bulk of your valuables is stored somewhere else. Keep money and credit cards hidden – ideally in a money belt pouch and be discreet when paying for goods, especially on the roadside. Be aware of pickpockets in markets and crowded streets, if using public transport or anywhere else you might feel vulnerable.

Systems – Develop systems and routines to make your life on the road simple. For example, always keep your keys in the same place when not in the bike and keep your panniers organised, thereby making it easier to find things. Routines make unfamiliar environments seem a little more familiar which in turn means you are less likely to forget something or expose yourself to some sort of unnecessary risk.

First Aid

A good understanding of basic first aid skills will allow you to administer treatment in the event of injury and may go a long way to saving someone's life before medical help arrives. Being out in the middle of nowhere means you need to be prepared for the unexpected at any time so it's a good idea to have at least one person in your group with basic first aid skills, including CPR (cardiopulmonary resuscitation).

If you have any doubt whatsoever about an injury, make sure you see a doctor as soon as possible. Even a small puncture wound can quickly lead to an infection if left untreated. Only move the injured person when necessary. Never move an injured person unless there is an immediate danger (such as a fire). Moving can potentially make the injury worse, which is especially true with spinal cord injuries. In general, you should be competent and able to recognise the symptoms and apply treatment accordingly for the following:

- Basic Life Saving Procedures
- Fractures
- Bleeding
- Shock
- Head Injuries
- Burns
- Heat Exhaustion
- Frostbite and Hypothermia
- Dealing with Poisons, Bites and Stings

Food

On the road your diet is likely to be rather different to what you might traditionally eat at home but it is vital that you get enough of the right sort of food given the physical nature of the trip and the need to be mentally aware at all times. Diet plays a major role in this respect and the right sort of nutrition will also assist in combating illness and make you less susceptible to infection.

Depending on the length and nature of your journey it is probably best to take certain food items from home and purchase additional items en route from village markets, street vendors and supermarkets. Also take the time to enjoy local cuisine – each region will undoubtedly have its own delicacies that are worth trying as part of the travel experience.

Food can generally be taken in tin cans, dehydrated foil bags and some in its natural state repackaged in an appropriate container. Tins come ready to eat but do weigh a lot and can take up a lot of space. Dehydrated packs are lighter and easier to pack, but make use of a lot of water when rehydrated.

Some useful food tips:

- Vary your intake of food to include a mixture of carbohydrates, proteins, fat, vitamins and minerals
- On extended trips it is worth considering taking a course of multi-vitamins and mineral supplements to ensure your body is getting what it needs, particularly if your diet may be limited or cannot easily be varied
- Heating food sufficiently will kill bacteria
- Avoid raw seafood and meat and also be wary of salads which are difficult to clean and are easily contaminated
- Always try to have a stock of 'snacks' which can be eaten during rest breaks such as dried fruit, nuts, energy bars, chocolate, boiled sweets, biscuits and crackers
- Follow basic hygiene rules when preparing food and always wash your hands before eating
- Fruit and vegetables should be reasonably safe if peeled or cooked
- Always check the 'sell by' date on tins of food before purchasing

Water

Some level of dehydration is a given on any ride and an overland journey in hot desert conditions will only exacerbate the extent to which water is lost from the body through sweating and urination. These lost fluids must be replaced as failing to do so will result in a series of increasingly serious health issues. In a hot and arid climate it is quite possible to become heavily dehydrated in a matter of hours and the human body can only survive for a limited period of about five days without water in a moderate climate. You will therefore need a regular supply of water primarily for drinking, but also for washing and cooking. The most important points to consider are where to find it, how best to purify it and how to carry it.

■ **Be wary of using water from wells such as this one in a remote Moroccan village**
📷 Robert Wicks

Finding Water

Staying healthy on the road requires you to be ultra-vigilant about the water you drink. This includes being cautious of ice which might be added to a drink at a hotel or restaurant. Today bottled water is widely available in many remote locations, but you should always check the bottle is sealed and has not been tampered with (ie refilled with tap water before being sold). Any water which comes from the wild or is purchased on the roadside definitely needs to be filtered and purified.

Purifying Water

Water purification is needed to remove contaminants from drinking water so that it is pure enough for human consumption. It involves getting rid of parasites, bacteria, algae, viruses, fungi, potentially toxic minerals and man-made chemical pollutants.

A water purification system is probably not necessary unless you are travelling to really remote areas and taking water from streams or wells.

If you are travelling without access to reliable water sources, then any water should first be filtered to remove particles and then purified to remove any harmful organisms. There are a number of different methods to consider:

Boiling	Once sufficiently filtered, water should be boiled for at least five minutes to remove harmful organisms
Chemicals	Alternatively, chemicals such as iodine, potassium permanganate or a chlorine-based tablet can be added. This can leave the water with an unpleasant taste
Manual filters	These handy pumps can purify and sterilise impure water and are ideal for long trips when access to reliable water is limited

Carrying Water

Water is reasonably heavy and can take up a lot of space but it's a resource that you cannot go without. Basic water bottles or steel fuel bottles from your local camping store will suffice. Be sure to keep them clean and, much like fuel for your motorcycle, fill up at every available opportunity. Bottles are best located inside your panniers but if you need to store them externally on the bike, make sure they are fastened securely and check on them regularly.

A lightweight hydration system (such as those made by Camelbak) is a very useful item particularly when travelling in hot climates. They come in different sizes and the water is easily accessible through an over-the-shoulder valve. Consider a pack which has some additional storage space as this can be used to carry essential items when heading out on day trips.

> **TIP**
>
> **In an emergency, use a sock or a handkerchief as a filter to get rid of at least some contaminants before boiling.**

Accommodation

Deciding on your intended accommodation is a fairly important decision as it is likely to have a big impact on three things: your budget, your lifestyle on the road and the load you need to carry.

If you plan to make use of hotels and other forms of fixed accommodation there is little need for a tent and other camping equipment. While you might be living in some 'luxury', this option will come at a cost and also, if you have pre-booked your accommodation, you need to be sure you can make it to each of the locations on the chosen dates. This allows little flexibility, particularly if something should go wrong and you are delayed. If you plan to travel remotely for long stretches this may not be a realistic option anyway.

Camping on the other hand is considerably cheaper and arguably more in keeping with the spirit of adventure

travel. It does mean carrying additional gear in the form of a tent, roll mat or mattress, sleeping bag and cooking paraphernalia – none of which is particularly heavy, but all are rather bulky items which will take up valuable space.

Life on the road can certainly be a little easier if you spend some nights in local hotels, hostels or bed and breakfast style accommodation. You should generally get a good night's sleep and have the use of a bath or shower. Camping gets you out under the stars and makes the reality of the journey and the experience in general that much more worthwhile.

Depending on the nature of the trip you have planned, what tends to work well is using a combination of fixed lodgings and tented accommodation. This gives you flexibility, some potential budget savings and a good balance in terms of lifestyle on the road.

⬆ **Always keep your bike in mind when finding somewhere for the night, particularly in built-up areas**
📷 Adam Lewis and Danny Burroughs

Border Crossings

Travelling through foreign countries and particularly those in the Third World can result in some of the most frustrating situations and significant levels of bureaucracy compared to what you may be used to at home. Remember that someone rolling up at a forgotten border post on an adventure bike quite out of the blue is not an everyday occurrence.

First and foremost it's important to try and have the most-up-to date info available as the status of border crossings can change at very short notice, particularly in places like Africa. It's well worth trying to ascertain specific information before getting to the border if you have any doubt about its status. Visit the local police station or authority and also talk to travellers heading in the opposite direction for the latest news.

Next up, make sure all your documents are readily available and in order, together with copies if needed. A stock of passport photographs will come in very handy at this point.

With the information to hand and papers at the ready it's then worth following the advice of Erwin Thoma who in 2000 travelled for six months on a BMW R 1100 GS through Central America – from Mexico to Guatemala, Honduras, Nicaragua, Costa Rica, Panama and to Colombia:

BORDER CROSSING TIPS

- **Avoid weekends and public holidays – sometimes this can take longer, extra fees may be levied and it may be harder to get photocopies done at the borders**
- **Arrive early in the morning or shortly after the lunch break or show up shortly before they close the border – check your guidebook concerning the opening times of the border post**
- **Dress respectably – it tends to get a better reaction**
- **Be polite – bureaucracy is seldom based on logic and you need the officer's stamp of approval to continue with the journey**
- **Always visit the migration office before the customs office**
- **Try to park your bike in such a position that you can keep an eye on it**
- **Most borders have guides to 'help' you through the process. It may help to speed up the process by using a guide but make sure you clarify the costs first before accepting any assistance**
- **Be patient and allow at least an hour to get through**
- **If you are told that something you ask for is not possible, try to find out why and if there is a good reason. Ask to talk to a supervisor if necessary – sometimes meeting the chief of the border post or customs office can work in your favour and an exception granted but don't count on this happening every time**

- **Never offer money without being asked for it. If you are asked for money, ask for a receipt and the reason why you are being asked to pay. Keep all receipts as long as you stay in the country. If you have to bribe someone, remember the date, the time, the amount of money and if possible the name of the officer and write to the embassy of the country and the tourist office**
- **Try to have some money of the country you are heading for with you. Small denomination bills can be useful**
- **Change currency with other travellers and try to know the exchange rate before you arrive at the border. There tend to be locals willing to do a deal at nearly every border crossing**
- **Your passport, driving licence and bike registration papers are the three most common documents asked for by border officials – at most of the borders you will need photocopies of the aforementioned documents. Always make sure your documents have been stamped in the correct way to avoid problems further down the road**
- **Even if you are not asked for them, it is wise to have copies of all important documents. Most borders have photocopy shops available, but it is best to have the copies ready in advance**
- **I never queue up with a motorcycle. I always pass the waiting line of cars, buses and trucks and get in behind the second or third car in line.**

Provided courtesy of Erwin Thoma and www.horizonsunlimited.com.

Adapting to New Countries

There is no magic formula to ease the transition into a new country but there are a couple of things you can do which will help:

Firstly, some research into the country you are visiting will help tremendously. Being aware of basic cultural and religious differences and making an effort to learn even a little of the local language will make a tremendous difference. This will give you not only a head start on arrival, but also immediate respect – if you show an interest in the other person's language and culture they will show an interest in you and this can help to get things done more efficiently.

Secondly, always head off with an open mind and a willingness to learn – it's important to try and look beyond the stereotypes and misinformation that often exists about certain countries. Also don't expect things to be done in the same way they are at home and only once you have spent a period of time in one particular country can you start to make judgements of any sort.

It's also important to be conscious of local rules – in Sudan, for example, you need to report to a police station within three days of your arrival to confirm you are in the country. Following this procedure is important and shows that you respect the rules of the country.

Particularly on long journeys always be prepared to spend a few days in some of the major cities. This may provide for some real culture shocks in terms of driving habits, food, bureaucracy and culture. Approach this with an open mind as not only will it allow you time to secure visas, carry out repairs to the bike, change money into local currency, check e-mails and replenish both spares and essentials like food and water, but it will offer you the chance to experience a very different way of life and to see things from a different perspective. The pace in Third World countries is generally much slower and the sooner you get used to this way of working, the better. Use the opportunity to attempt to cross the bridge into a new and exciting culture – in the vast majority of cases it will be the most rewarding of experiences.

↑ **Make sure your personal paperwork and documents for the bike are all in order before trying to cross an international border**
📷 GlobeBusters

↓ **Keep an open mind and stick together**
📷 Johan Engelbrecht

↑ Julia Sanders fills up in South America with an armed guard for comfort

📷 GlobeBusters

Advice for Women Travellers

Women travellers are often at risk but there are a number of things which can be done to reduce the likelihood of a nasty situation developing. Always remember that your chosen mode of transport and apparent adventurous spirit will automatically ensure that people perceive you differently to a more 'traditional' female tourist. In addition to this, it's vital to use common sense, be prepared and always trust your instincts. The following tips should prove useful:

Being Prepared

- Make sure you know as much as possible about the country you are visiting and what you want to see – acquainting yourself with the culture and customs can certainly help you to avoid potentially dangerous situations
- Always keep your valuables concealed

- Never display expensive jewellery
- When walking around local towns, always be certain of your location and try to stick to main roads
- Wearing a wedding band and referring to your 'husband', even if you are not married, can sometimes come in handy, especially in Africa

Personal Safety

- Don't be shy to raise the alarm and alert others around you
- Avoid isolated places when sightseeing
- Hitch-hiking should be regarded as a high risk and should only be undertaken in the event of an emergency
- If you feel at all unsure or uneasy, try to look like you are part of a larger group
- Choose your accommodation carefully and always ask to see the room before staying somewhere; check the door and the lock that goes with it

Dress Code

- Appreciate that in some countries or cultures, dress standards are stricter than those which you may be accustomed to at home
- The way you dress will have a direct effect on the way people react to you. To help avoid unwanted attention, always be sensitive to local dress standards, some of which are considerably modest by Western standards. In some cultures, for example, bare arms and legs are regarded as unacceptable

Attitude

- Be confident but not to the point that it appears arrogant
- Always try to retain your composure and ideally remove yourself from a difficult situation as quickly as possible
- Report any incidents to the police
- Be wary about accepting invitations out – these may give out the wrong signal and expose you to the risk of sexual assault
- Always trust your instincts

Health Issues

- See your doctor at least six weeks prior to departure for a full check-up and explain the nature of the trip you are undertaking. If you are likely to travel with specific medications, be sure to observe the law in different countries with respect to possession of medication. It may also be advisable to take a letter from your doctor explaining your condition
- For your own convenience and peace of mind, take a sufficient stock of feminine hygiene products and (if you use them) contraceptives to last for the duration of the trip
- Be very careful not to get dehydrated. This is regarded as a relatively common cause of urinary tract infections which will undoubtedly impact on your ability to ride and travel
- Constantly be aware of the risk of HIV – avoid anything involving needles such as ear-piercing, acupuncture, tattooing or dental work while on the road
- Always practise safe sex

Sometimes you just have to stop and look
📷 KTM

One Woman's
Round the World Story

Unlike most motorcycle adventurers I've met, I'd not been dreaming of riding a motorcycle around the world for weeks, months or years. The thought never entered my mind. I had ridden a motorcycle in the United States about 15 years ago, but those days were long gone. I moved to Australia in 1999, didn't take my old Harley with me, and had no intention of ever riding again. I was happy with the time I'd had on the old bike, and that was that. Ten years on and I had a good job, a beautiful home and a simple, happy life. I really didn't have anything to complain about – life was good! – but I did begin to feel I needed a challenge. Good is better than bad, but it can be boring too. I had been looking for either a business to create or one to buy for a few months, and nothing was working out or exciting me. One day I came home from work and felt I needed to put my foot down. The time had come for a change – I closed the curtains, sat down on the couch and vowed not to get up until I had made a decision about what to do. I either went into meditation mode (or took a nap) and when I came to, the idea of riding a motorcycle around the world was in my head. What? That's crazy! I sat there on the couch arguing with myself…

Then I thought I should at least look into it. Doing some research on the Internet I found the website of a woman who had ridden a motorcycle around the world several years previously. I looked at her photos and became excited. Yes! This is what I'd been looking for! But I was still arguing with myself. I'd say, "I can't go, I have no experience, I don't even have a motorcycle! What about my dog, what about my house?" I was coming up with every excuse and argument in the book.

One thing I learned many years ago is that if I wanted to do something it was best just to take baby steps. Make enquiries. Go to a motorcycle showroom and just 'see' what the bikes look or feel like. The more I started asking questions about this crazy idea I had, the more positive endorsements I got from people who wanted to help. I took that as a sign that I was on the right track; it made me think I might be able do this thing!

Well, from that time to the day I actually pulled out of my Australian driveway on a motorcycle trip around the world was a mere six months. Why did I leave so soon, rather than planning my trip for years and years like many people I've since met? Because I have no patience! Before I set off I trained a new person for my job, remodelled my house to take tenants, researched the available motorcycles and adventure gear, placed my orders, figured out a route plan, organised visas and travel documents, and did a good job of driving myself, my friends and family crazy in the process.

⬇ **Enjoying some European scenery – the Grimsel Pass in Switzerland**

📷 Sherri Jo Wilkins

My departure day arrived in a flash: 1 June 2010. I couldn't sleep, tried to perfect my luggage and bike but couldn't get it quite right and then, in a panic, just threw whatever I couldn't fit on the bike into the shed, locked the door and left town. I was completely scared out of my mind!

Lesson learned? I couldn't tell you today what it was that I threw in the shed, so I obviously didn't need it. I have since learned there were lots of things I didn't need but thought I did. I remember learning from others how to pack my bike and then throwing out 50% of what I'd packed. But I honestly didn't know which 50% until I was living on the road. I had to learn everything along the way because not only was this all brand new to me, but I'd also been too busy to do the recommended test run before the big trip in order to work out what should stay or go.

The bike I eventually chose was a KTM 690 Enduro R. I researched all my motorcycle options and it seemed the best and most common choice for my kind of journey (a long adventure) was the BMW 650, 800 or 1200 GS. However, I learned from listening to other female round-the-world riders, who all seemed unanimous that if they were to ride the world again they would prefer a smaller bike; many of them had started out on a BMW 650 or larger model.

Where I was living in South Australia, there were four makes of bike available for me locally at the time – I wasn't interested in ordering from overseas – BMW, Yamaha, Aprilia and KTM. Finally I whittled it down to either the BMW or the KTM. I'd thought I would choose the BMW 650 GS, given its good reputation, but in the end I didn't, for two reasons. First, it weighs 199kg (438lb) dry, whereas the KTM 690 weighs 138kg (304lb) dry. That is a huge difference for a bike with similar power, plus the KTM is light enough for me to be able to pick it up myself, which is important. The second reason was that the manager at my local BMW dealership wasn't taking my questions seriously, whereas the guys at the KTM dealership were more than enthusiastic in being a part of setting me up.

When I rode that bike home for the first time I was beyond nervous, and shaking. The KTM 690 is a very tall bike. I'm 5'9" and even this wasn't enough to get my feet on the ground. My only other riding experience had been on a very low Harley-Davidson many years ago. I practised and practised but the KTM and I were not getting along because of my height, especially if I had to stop on a hill, either going up or coming down. When I left on my trip I was still having a difficult time riding it confidently, but fortunately with my gear loaded the seat height dropped and that made it easier. I was really scared during the first ten days of my journey. In the

↑ **Modeling my new Rukka riding gear!**
📷 Sherri Jo Wilkins

end, though, as with most things in life, you learn to live with the issues and then they become normal.

Speaking of fear, high on my list of priorities as a solo female rider was, of course, my personal safety. Where would I sleep at night? What would happen if I broke down alone? I had an absolute panic about that before my trip, but I felt if I didn't face my fears I'd just stay home the rest of my life and miss out on the world. Picture yourself aged 90, sitting in a rocking chair on the porch – are you happy with what you've accomplished? I do it fairly often – and that's what made it easy for me to walk out of the front door and get on the bike.

Two years later, and still on the road, I can tell you that 99.9% of my nights are comfortable and safe, whether I'm camping in bear territory or staying in a host's home, a hostel or the shack in somebody's backyard. I've experienced just two nights when I couldn't sleep for fear – and even then, nothing happened. Another big lesson I was taught before I left was to trust my instincts, especially if it's about a place where you plan to spend the night. I had bad vibes at the two places just mentioned, and I'll walk away when somewhere

⬆⬆ Pitching camp on the Nullabor in South Australia

⬆↗ A river crossing in Siberia

⬆ On the Arctic Circle on the Dempster Highway in Canada. After being warned by the truckers to turn back I went ahead and glad I did!

📷 Sherri Jo Wilkins

doesn't look or feel right. On the other hand, I have stayed in some really questionable areas but I felt the people were good. I have been right about that so far, too.

Another important safety factor I needed to address was my riding gear, because I had no idea which riding suit to pick. I did some online searching and determined that the best gear I could get my hands on would be Rukka, made in Finland. Even better, once I contacted them they agreed to sponsor me! To this day they have been one my strongest supporters, and I can easily and happily report that the research must have been right, because for all the times I've fallen down while riding over the last two years, I've never had a bruise. Rukka gear's safety pads are positioned perfectly and I am always amazed, every time I get back up on my bike, that nothing on my body hurts – and the suit also keeps me warm and dry.

I am no mechanic, but while some would say you need to be able to take your motorcycle completely apart and put it back together again successfully before you even consider taking a round-the-world trip, I beg to differ! I agree totally that knowing something about the workings of your bike would be beneficial for most people, including me, but I also

know that even if I learned how to do something mechanical, unless I did it regularly, I would be no good at it. And on top of that, I would probably make the problem worse by attempting to fix it.

There are mechanics all over the world, and lots of generous ones at that. Any time I've needed to get something fixed, it has been fixed by somebody who does that job most days of their lives. I watch, and I learn what I can. It's even fair to say that I have learned a lot on this trip and can discuss tyre choices, chain lube, pistons, valves and even sprocket choice, all of which I knew nothing about at the beginning. I also chose a bike with a good reputation for being well made, buying it new on purpose so that, hopefully, I wouldn't be breaking down any time soon. I guess that strategy worked because I have had very little bike trouble in 62,000 miles (100,000km), hopefully because I made a good choice of bike and mostly had services done by KTM mechanics.

I have been asked time and time again why, as a woman, I am doing this trip alone. I've really had to convince the people who ask me that I am doing it because I can. I don't have any children that I need to stay home and raise, and I don't need to prove anything to anyone other than myself. I'm a pretty conservative and traditional sort of person, but I grew up in a household that didn't dictate you should be one way or another. I am not a feminist; I don't need to feel I am doing this for empowerment because I am empowered enough already. I have built my life myself, and I am proud of where I am. And I like being a woman! I didn't feel like I was a lesser person when I left, and I don't feel like I'm better than anyone else now, I truly just love the adventure of it all and that's what excites me and gets me out of bed early every morning.

Another lesson was that you don't have to have everything worked out before you go on a long journey. Of course it makes sense to check out what you are getting into, which countries you are going to visit and their entry requirements, but it's really important not to plan too far ahead. My good friend Clare reminded me about my own philosophy – 'baby steps' – and suggested I just focus on the first three countries I would be riding through: Japan, South Korea and Russia. In the latter I knew I would be meeting Walter Colebatch to ride 2,500 miles (4,000km) with him on the dirt roads of Siberia, so I felt comfortable that this part of the journey was planned and organised. After that, if I didn't like what I was doing, there was no law that said I couldn't come home. If I felt I wanted to continue the journey, then Clare suggested I work it out as I went along – and two years later her advice holds good. I'm still on the road and I take each part of the world as I meet it. I don't plan, or think about another continent until I'm getting close to it and have accomplished my previous goals.

I have to say that riding a motorcycle around the world has been the greatest decision of my life. To be able to see, feel, smell and taste all the different cultures in person rather than through a book or via a television screen has been an awakening. People are not nearly as bad as they are portrayed in the media, and there is much less to fear on this planet than I imagined.

I've learned that I can do so much more than I thought I was capable of, and not just in terms of riding the motorcycle. Mental and physical challenges have been huge teachers for me. I have enjoyed getting to know, and becoming part of, the large international adventure motorcycling community. I am also grateful to the many people who've helped me, from my very first question to those I still ask 24 months down the road, and am always amazed at how generous folk have been and continue to be. In every country I've visited I have been supported by strangers who have treated me like family, so I look forward to returning the favour to travellers when I am back home.

Emerging from the super hot, tough rubble tracks of Death Valley National Park, California
Sherri Jo Wilkins

For more information log on to: sherrijowilkins.com

The annals of adventure motorcycling are full of famous women who have achieved tremendous feats on two wheels. These three intrepid adventurers all have their own unique stories and typify the spirit of adventure motorcycling:

Elspeth Beard →

Elspeth Beard is one of a select band of bold women to ride a motorcycle around the world, and she was the first Englishwoman to do so. She achieved this feat a quarter of a century ago, in the days before satellite navigation, Internet, e-mail and mobile phones, and she did it mostly alone. The bike she chose for the trip was a used 1974 R 60/6 flat-twin, for which she paid £900 in 1980 – a substantial sum at the time, especially for a machine that already had 30,000 miles (48,000km) on the clock.

Elspeth used the bike for her first long solo rides to Scotland and Ireland, then to mainland Europe and Corsica, racking up over 10,000 miles (16,000km) in her first two years of ownership. Then it was time for 'The Big One'. Aged 24, Elspeth put her architectural studies on hold and put her savings into the trip of a lifetime. By the time she got back to her native London Elspeth had been away for three years and added 48,000 miles (77,000km) to her R60's odometer. She stripped and completely rebuilt the engine herself and still has the bike in running order today.

With thanks to Paul Blezard for his insight on Elspeth's journey.

Photo kindly provided by Elspeth Beard

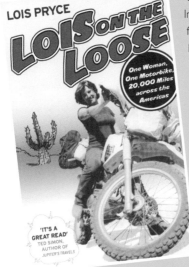

← Lois Pryce

In early 2003 Lois Pryce gave up a job at the BBC to follow her dream of escaping and rode her trail bike from the northernmost point in Alaska to Tierra del Fuego, the southernmost tip of South America. Her online diary of the journey became a cult hit and led to her first book, *Lois on the Loose*. She has recently returned from a trans-African expedition on a Yamaha TTR 250. Following her 20,000 mile (32,000km) journey across the Americas, she commented: "My journey hasn't so much cured an itch, as given me an incurable disease."

Cover image kindly provided by Lois Pryce

Benka Pulko →

In January 1997 while lying in bed staring at the ceiling, Slovenian-born Benka Pulko made a life-changing decision – she was going to ride a motorcycle around the world. She had never travelled on a motorcycle before, let alone knew how to ride one. But this did not deter her from the grand plan. Five months later she rode off on a 1996 BMW F650 which she describes as "the friendliest bike in the world". She planned to travel for two years and returned five-and-a-half years later! During this time, she logged over 111,000 miles (179,000 km), experienced 75 countries on all seven continents and had her name listed in the *Guinness Book of World Records*. Benka does things that most people only dream of and some swear cannot be done. Her story confirms that anybody with a steel determination can reach a chosen goal.

Photo kindly provided by Benka Pulko

Keeping in Touch

One of the things which Ted Simon remarked on having completed his latest journey was the spread of communications technology and the availability of the Internet. He was of course comparing it to his last round-the-world trip in the 1970s, but the growth of the Internet has revolutionised communication and made it easy to keep in touch with friends, family and developments back home from almost anywhere in the world. If this is an important factor for you, then there are several ways of doing so:

Internet Cafés

Internet cafés are widely available and offer the chance to send and receive e-mail and catch up on world events. You can also use online phone accounts (such as those offered by the likes of Skype – www.skype.com) and messaging services. Also consider setting up a website or 'blog' which can act as an online travel journal, easily updated with news and photos in chronological order thereby keeping friends and family up to date with your progress.

Mobile Phones

Taking a mobile phone is really a personal choice but using it comes at a cost and it's just another item to keep track of. If you plan to take one make sure you're on the best possible overseas tariff available from your service provider and use it primarily for text messages. Purchase calling cards for local landline phones if needed.

Satellite Phones

These are great if you are travelling remotely where there is no mobile coverage but even though purchase prices have come down recently, satellite phones are still bulkier than mobiles and call charges remain expensive. Plus this is yet another high value item to be carrying around and looking after.

Receiving Packages

If for example you need to get some urgent spares or copies of vital documentation sent from home, consider using a hotel to receive the parcel. If this is not an option, consider using the *Poste Restante* ('to be called for') option whereby the local post office will hold mail until you call for it. It is a common way to get mail delivered to someone who is visiting a particular location and has no way of having mail delivered directly to their place of residence at the time. Timescales vary from country to country according to local practice and it's worth checking if parcels are accepted.

Navigation

Touratech

Successful navigation requires various elements to be used in conjunction with one another. Relying on just one aspect can leave your navigation open to error and when riding in remote areas in particular, this can create unnecessary and sometimes significant problems. The elements being referred to include good quality maps, a GPS unit, route notes and descriptions, the motorcycle trip meter and a compass.

In the book entitled *Chasing Dakar*, Jonathan Edwards MD and rally veteran Scot Harden comment that used correctly, these various elements will "help to keep you on the correct trail, prevent you from getting lost and may even save your life". They rightly state that "riding with and using navigation equipment is multi-tasking in its highest form; one must learn to shift one's attention from the trail to navigation without compromising your safety".

With this in mind, always remember to position your navigation equipment on the bike in such a way that it is easy to read and you are able to maintain a focus on the terrain which lies ahead. Switching between the two becomes something of a skill that develops over time. ◼

Compass Navigation

A compass is a good back-up if your GPS fails or as a second resource to confirm your position. Make sure you understand how a compass works and how to use it in conjunction with your maps. Maintaining a constant sense of orientation in terms of north, south, east and west is a useful start. Once you are comfortable, a compass can be used to determine your location on a map (orientation) and then to plot and maintain a set course (navigation). In order to do this you will typically need a topographical map, compass, protractor, ruler and a pen. Remember your compass will need to be calibrated as different areas on the globe have a different magnetic declination – the further north you go, the bigger the declination becomes.

Maps

Maps are a vital ingredient for an adventure ride but don't take for granted that what the map says is indeed what you will find. While the road systems in some areas are being upgraded and this can provide a nice surprise, other roads suffer from serious neglect and may be very different to what you are expecting. Some sealed roads may in fact be quite difficult to negotiate, with potholes, sand, broken sections and rock falls. There will be extreme variations in some roads that are indicated as being the same on a map – a 'gravel road' in, say, Botswana or Namibia, is likely to be better quality than one in Tanzania or Ethiopia though they will both have been identified as similar in quality by the map's legend.

Try to cross-check your route with other maps and sources of information. Consider likely weather conditions and the impact this may have on the roads and travelling times and always factor in more time for the route as a result of poor road conditions. Before heading off ensure you are comfortable with basic map reading, understand how co-ordinates are defined, and how map scales, latitude and longitude work.

Maps are best carried in a clear sleeve in the top of your tank bag where they can easily be seen while riding. Waterproof, tear-resistant versions are more expensive but worth the investment if you can afford it.

Map reading and compass skills are useful, particularly if your GPS fails
Chris Smith

Global Positioning Systems (GPS)

GPS is a satellite-based navigation system, developed and controlled by the US Department of Defense. It provides remarkably accurate measurements of position and altitude relative to sea level 24 hours a day anywhere in the world.

The system of satellites gives every square metre on the planet a unique address, making it an extremely accurate tool for navigation. By using signals from a series of the satellites simultaneously, accurate data relating to your position is provided.

Without a good map though, a GPS on its own is of little use and under no circumstances should you rely on a GPS unit as your sole method of navigation. Flat batteries, inputting incorrect information, the inability to access a clear satellite signal or mistakenly deleting vital data can create some real problems and potentially render the device useless. Always carry a good map and constantly cross-reference this with the GPS. Read the instruction manual and familiarise yourself with how the unit works before you leave home, ideally putting it (and yourself) to the test on early shakedown runs. Also, prepare yourself with the knowledge and skills required to find your way with elementary materials such as a map and compass before setting off.

Though some in the field of adventure motorcycling appear to discount the value of using a GPS, there are a number of reasons why one may indeed find it useful:

With very few landmarks, off-road navigation requires focus at all times
📷 Waldo van der Waal

Verifying your position – Assuming you know where you are, you can work out how to get to where you're headed.

Providing information and data – Speed, distance travelled, direction and time on the move are just some of the data streams provided and can be used to cross-correlate with your map reading and to assess progress on any given route.

Plotting points of interest – You can use the GPS to plot specific locations (known as waypoints) for future use. Once plotted, the point is stored in the unit's memory and can be renamed to make it easily identifiable (eg 'water well' or 'cross roads'). Points you are still to visit can be stored and recalled (some guidebooks will provide GPS co-ordinates for use on adventure trips and co-ordinates for numerous routes are routinely available on the Internet).

Navigating to a waypoint – The GPS can guide you directly to a specific location and will provide lots of other useful information in the process, including the direction and distance to the waypoint from your current location and the time it is going to take given your current riding speed. It constantly recalculates the direction and distance to the waypoint as you progress.

Tracking back – A GPS unit will constantly log data relating to your position and this information can then be used to re-trace your route. This is a particularly useful tool if you get lost or need to head back to your last known position.

Routes – By linking waypoints together it is possible to generate a complete route. The GPS can follow a pre-programmed sequence which you can define in advance simply by linking the waypoints together.

Road signs are useful but verify your route with GPS data and maps as some can be confusing
📷 Waldo van der Waal

Upload new routes to your GPS from your laptop and keep a record of your journey
📷 Touratech

Given the nature of an overland motorcycle expedition, not only in terms of the speed and functionality required, but also the stresses and climatic extremes that the unit may be placed under, you are probably going to want a model that offers a fair bit more than an introductory level unit.

There are a number of different brands available on the market to choose from and at least five key criteria to consider before purchasing a GPS unit:

Durability – A rugged GPS unit that can cope with the rigours of a motorcycle expedition is essential. It needs a durable, waterproof casing capable of withstanding harsh conditions without compromising its functionality.

Memory – Choose a GPS which has sufficient memory capacity and check if the unit is expandable – if not, this can impact on future upgrade potential.

Reception and Accuracy – Look for a GPS unit which uses a 12-channel parallel receiver system (this will allow access to more satellites giving quicker and more accurate calculations).

Mapping Capabilities – If you would like to view maps in higher levels of detail then a GPS unit with advanced mapping capabilities is preferable. Get advice on what maps are available for the areas you plan to travel to and the amount of detail they offer.

Power – Running a GPS off battery power will give you anywhere from 8–24 hours of constant use depending on the type of unit and what functionality you make use of (some features have a tendency to decrease battery life). It's best to hard wire the GPS into the electrical harness on the bike or run it off the bike's 12-volt supply with a suitable adaptor.

GPS TIPS

Some travellers advise removing your GPS from view before making a border crossing as it could be confused for a transmitter of some sort and may get the local security services interested.

Some fellow travellers should be in a position to provide GPS co-ordinates to guest houses or other useful points which can be very helpful when headed into a large city or into unknown territory.

I'm sure we should have got to that junction by now...
www.vueltamundoaventura.com

ADAM LEWIS ON THE MERITS OF USING A GPS

We have used a Garmin 276c GPS unit on our round-the-world trip and have found it to be a good navigational aid but of little use on its own for this kind of trip. Whilst Europe, North America and Australia have 'turn-by-turn' maps available, the rest of the world doesn't. We've installed and use the Garmin World Map software but it certainly doesn't provide enough info to navigate by in a number of regions. Indeed, we often find ourselves on roads shown on the World Map and yet the GPS unit says 'No roads at starting point'.

Surprisingly, just because a road appears on the World Map doesn't mean it's a sizeable one. In the far reaches of Northern Cambodia we were heading cross country to join a road shown on the map which turned out to be a 12ft (4m) wide sand track!

A lot of big cities between Eastern Europe and India don't have ring roads – you ride into the centre and back out. We often exit these cities on a compass bearing provided by the GPS. The track logging facility is very useful and allows us to retrace our steps if we get lost.

The trip computer functions are also very helpful. We use the bike's trip meters purely for monitoring fuel usage and the GPS trip meters for everything else. It's surprising just how low our average speeds were in Asia – indicated by the Moving Average Speed and Total Average Speed features on the GPS – and these helped in deciding a day's destination as we progressed. Sunrise and sunset times are also useful, especially when crossing so many time zones.

We've even used the trip meters to navigate by. In the mountains around the source of the Ganges north-east of Rishikesh in India there is a huge network of roads and villages that don't appear on any maps and whilst the road signs display distances in kilometres, the names are written in Hindi.

In a guest house we found a wall-mounted map with accurate distances marked between all the villages. I wrote down all the distances and for two days we navigated by reading distances on road signs, adding and subtracting distances to go and distances covered, to determine which road to take. This was only made possible by having an accurate trip meter that we could set to read in kilometres.

Having said all that, of the 16 other overlanders we have met en route to Malaysia, only seven of them were using a GPS.

Tips from the Expert

Riding in the Dakar Rally, Nick Plumb has a lot to think about. In addition to keeping his heavy BMW rally raid bike upright across some of the toughest terrain in the world, he also has to constantly navigate at high speed using a combination of GPS, compass, trip meter and rally road book – a scrolling sheet that fits in a holder and can be advanced backwards and forwards. This contains vital route information including potential hazards, checkpoints, fuel stops, GPS waypoints and distance markers.

"Riding off-road is great fun, but add in the element of navigation and suddenly you have a whole new dimension to deal with," says Nick.

He believes successful navigation comes down to a combination of four key things:

- Confidence is needed right from the start and comes from good basic preparation and an appreciation for where you are headed
- An awareness of the geography around you, the distances and the scale involved
- Always reading the map to the terrain, not the other way round
- If there is any doubt about your location, stop, assess the situation and if necessary turn back

On his first Dakar Rally, Nick was tracking the arrow on his GPS and mistakenly headed down a narrow canyon. "Fortunately it wasn't long before I knew this was the wrong place to be. The nerves certainly kicked in quickly though – this was my first Dakar and at one stage I thought it might be my last if I couldn't find my way out. The panic and disorientation which follow in a situation like this have a knock-on effect and heightens the pressure you're under. It takes your concentration away from two key things – riding confidently and finding your way back to the right route," says Nick.

"Recognising early that you're lost is essential – if you have any doubt, stop and reassess the situation as the longer you keep riding the more fuel you're using, the more energy you're using up and sooner or later you begin to question your decisions. It's easy to make errors when navigating but if you can correct the mistake quickly, you've got a good chance of getting back on track. In this type of situation, try to stay calm and use your common sense, the tools available and the terrain to work your way back to the last known point."

Author's Note:
Nick Plumb started riding when he was 14 years old and has participated in the gruelling Dakar Rally four times aboard a BMW F 650 GS. He has also competed in the Dubai, Qatar and Tuareg Rally events and is Managing Director of Touratech UK, the aftermarket overland adventure specialists.

Maintenance & Repairs

📷 Mihai Barbu

You will be crossing arduous and unpredictable terrain in varying weather conditions and at the same time carrying a heavy load which will place significant stresses on the machine, so a basic level of motorcycle maintenance and technical know-how is required.

For this reason alone daily checks are essential and must include the obvious: fuel, oil and coolant level checks, appropriate tyre pressures and a good 'once-over' of the bike for anything obvious which needs attention. A trip can succeed or fail on the performance of the smallest component, but in the main a regular maintenance schedule can avoid all but the unavoidable! You will potentially need to carry out a range of repairs or at least provide temporary solutions until a professional mechanic can fix the problem and having a basic knowledge of your bike is thus essential.

Your tour could grind to a halt owing to an inexplicable electrical failure which may be something as simple as a blown fuse so knowing where the fuse box is is the first step to solving the problem and getting back on track. A couple of hours spent with the owners' manual in the comfort of your garage before leaving is the place to learn about your bike, not out on a baking hot piste when you're up to the axles in soft sand!

Engine & Chassis

A good basic service is not a guarantee that engine or chassis trouble won't strike at some point on the journey but there is a lot of basic routine maintenance which can help to reduce the risk of something going wrong. Routine engine and chassis maintenance en route should include the following:

Control cables are often taken for granted, but a few minutes taken to check and lubricate them is time well spent

Check all luggage system fixing bolts are secure as heavy panniers and racks will place high loads on the bike

Check coolant levels regularly

Check brake fluid levels, brake discs and cleanliness of calipers

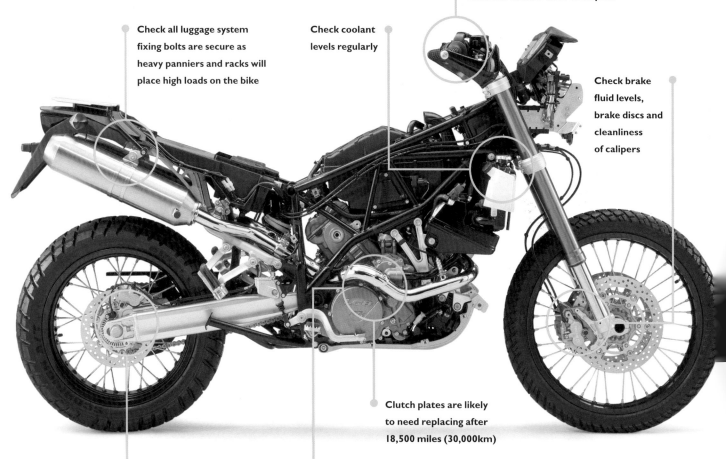

Clutch plates are likely to need replacing after 18,500 miles (30,000km)

Give the bike a clean as regularly as possible. Try to avoid making use of high pressure washers – amongst other things they can damage the grease packed into the bearings which will accelerate wear

Check oil level regularly – excessive oil consumption is indicative of a potentially serious issue that will need attention. Assuming the engine is serviced correctly before departure, an oil change is unlikely on shorter trips. For long distance trips an oil change may be needed every 3,000 miles (5,000km) together with an oil filter change (this may necessitate carrying your own oil or being sure you can source what you need en route)

📷 KTM

Electrical Systems

It is a fact that the electrical systems on motorcycles are more prone to giving problems than any other single sub-system so it is vital that they are checked for integrity on a regular basis. Complete a thorough check for loose and frayed wires that can cause intermittent problems or short circuits. Look for any areas where the wiring loom can chafe against the frame – the greatest risk area is going to be around the headstock. Make it a routine exercise when maintaining your bike on the road to look over the electrical system carefully – wires can get trapped under the tank or seat so it's worth a look there too if you run into trouble.

Electrical systems have become more sophisticated in recent years but if you have modified the basic wiring harness to accommodate, for example, power for a GPS unit or your on-board communications system, you may be at more risk of something going wrong. Electrical connections are prone to moisture and corrosion. A little dielectric grease applied to the terminals when assembling or reconnecting the loom simplifies reassembly and also protects against the ingress of moisture. A water displacing spray can also be used to good effect in less accessible areas when needed.

Get some sound advice from your dealer before leaving about essential spares – fortunately they tend to be relatively small and easily stored. It is vital to know where your fuses are located as you may well be required to replace a defective one at some point on your journey. Quite often a faulty fuse can be the culprit when an electrical component stops working.

The fuse box is generally located in a reasonably accessible position (perhaps under the seat or inside a fairing panel) and most bikes have a set of spare fuses next to the ones in use. Inside the box you should find information about what each fuse does.

Finally, unless your bike is reasonably new, it may be worth investing in a completely new battery for the big trip.

↑ Make sure the electrical system forms part of your maintenance routine

📷 GlobeBusters

← The KTM 990's fuse box is conveniently located and well marked

📷 Robert Wicks

→ **Fill up**
at every
opportunity
📷 Nik Boseley

⬇ **'Are you**
certain that's
Premium
unleaded?'
📷 Johan Engelbrecht

Fuel

Fuel en route may come from various sources and will certainly vary in terms of quality. Low octane fuel is fairly prevalent in many Third World countries and this is not ideally suited to the modern motorcycle engine. It may be an idea, particularly if you are heading off on an extended journey, to consider reprogramming the bike's ECU to better cope with regular amounts of low octane fuel. On bikes with conventional carburation it may be worth considering other methods which will allow the bike to run better on lower octane fuel. These may include the use of fuel additives such as octane boosters or re-engineering the engine by lowering the compression ratio. Bear in mind that doing any of these will result in a reduction in power.

Fitting a larger fuel tank will extend your range considerably and by filling up less often offers you the possibility to at times avoid 'dodgy' looking fuel.

A fuel-related modification undertaken by Adam Lewis and Danny Burroughs on the BMW F 650 GS machines for their round-the-world trip was the replacement of the exhaust. The standard OE system on the bike is fitted with a catalytic converter which they were advised might become blocked and fail when used with leaded fuel. Unsure of what fuel would be available they fitted after-market exhaust systems without catalytic converters.

Similarly, in 2006 when friends Nick Clarke and Nick Graham rode from the Cotswolds in England to Cape Town in South Africa, they undertook the same modification. They had the catalytic converters removed from their BMW R 1150 GS bikes as their local dealer had pointed out that 95 octane fuel might not be that easy to find – the modification was a wise one as they were forced to use 80 octane petrol at times.

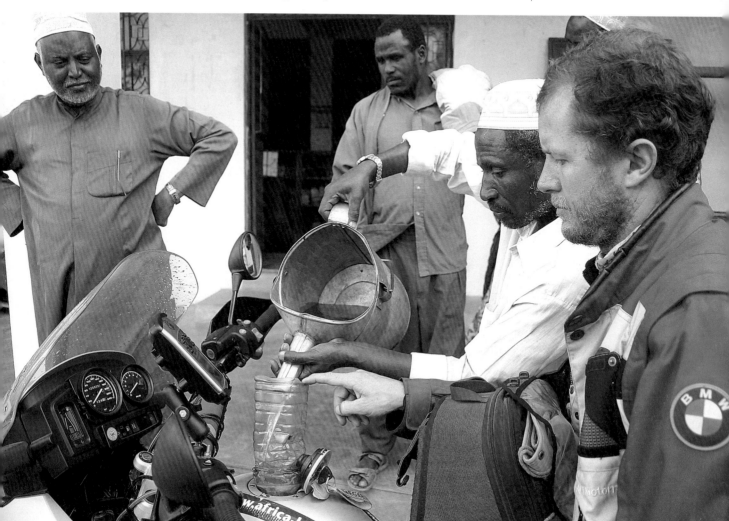

FUEL FILTERS

The bike's fuel filter is designed to screen out dirt and particles from the fuel and en route your fuel may come from a variety of sources – anywhere from normal garages to entrepreneurial roadside sales. It will vary dramatically in quality and octane, particularly in remote areas. Consequently, the fuel filter is likely to need cleaning or replacing. In addition to the main filter on the fuel tap, it is worth investing in an in-line fuel filter. This is a small item that comes at minimal cost but greatly assists in further reducing contamination as the filter medium is considerably finer and thereby more effective. These can be cleaned if needed by reverse flushing with clean fuel.

Air Filters

The air filter in your bike is designed to remove contaminants and provide the best possible air quality for the engine. They are typically made of paper, fabric, foam, felt or a gauze element and will need cleaning on a regular basis, preferably daily when you're riding through dusty terrain. Familiarise yourself with the location of and how to remove the filter. Make use of a high pressure air hose at a local garage to give the filter a good blast from the inside out. In the absence of an air line, the filter can be shaken or tapped to get rid of the worst of the dust as an interim measure.

Sprockets & Chains

Well maintained chains and sprockets are essential to the well-being of your motorcycle and should be in good condition prior to any arduous journey. Assuming they are in serviceable condition, the single most important factor is correct adjustment. Check in your owners' manual for the specific adjustment details, but the chain should never be allowed to run too tight as this places enormous loads on the output shaft bearing. Fully loaded, the chain should typically be able to sag between 0.8" (20mm)–1.6" (40mm) at the mid-point between the two sprockets. This sag is used when the bike suspension moves up and down over uneven surfaces.

You should make allowance for the fact that you will be carrying luggage and traversing terrain that will compress the suspension more than normal, so it's probably better to have the chain slightly slack than a little too tight. Chain condition can be checked by pushing the bottom run of the chain up towards the swing arm to remove any slack, then with the other hand trying to pull the chain off the sprocket. If it lifts appreciably off the sprocket then it will probably need replacing, most likely along with the sprockets.

A visual check of the sprockets will show their condition. The teeth should still be well formed and showing no signs of thinning or hooking. There is a wide choice of replacement chains available, but it is probably wisest to buy the best you can afford, and certainly one of the 'O'-ring types. These have lubricant sealed into the body of the links and as such tend to need much less adjustment and little additional lubrication over their lifetime.

Lubricate the chain often, ideally every five running hours or 200 miles (300km). Spray liberally on the side of the chain that comes into contact with the sprockets. Ensure that you spray both the left- and right-hand sides of the chain. Supplementary lubrication systems should be avoided or turned off whilst off-road, as sand and dirt combined with any kind of oil makes an extremely effective grinding paste – not what you want on your sprockets!

Suspension

Given the likely load you will be carrying and the ease of handling required, the right suspension and related settings are essential on an adventure machine. That said, roadside maintenance is likely to be minimal as neither component is particularly 'repair friendly'. Always ensure that your suspension and associated components (such as fork seals) have been serviced before leaving so that it is in the best possible condition.

Wheels

Wheels take a terrific hammering off-road, and are expected to cope with all types of terrain from tarmac to sand, and mud to boulders. Strong wheels are therefore essential as they bear the brunt of the load carrying, making a regular inspection important. Depending on the route you are travelling, you may have elected to upgrade the wheels to a higher specification.

Spoked wheels rely on even tension to maintain the wheel's strength and integrity. One or two loose or broken spokes can cause rim deformation or even collapse in extreme cases. The tried and tested method of testing spokes is to tap them with a screwdriver. Spokes under

the correct tension will 'ring' whereas a loose spoke won't. The tone of the ring will also show how much tension the spoke is under – the higher the pitch the greater the tension.

The ideal situation is for all spokes to be correctly tensioned, producing roughly the same tone when struck. One or two loose spokes can be tightened without too much worry, but care must be taken when adjusting them not to over-tighten and pierce the inner tube. If you have several loose or tight spokes on one particular side and section of the wheel then it's probably suffered a side impact strong enough to slightly deform the rim. In these circumstances it is imperative that the spokes are re-tensioned to prevent the wheel from buckling or collapsing.

As a final note on spoked wheels, remember that water can seep in through the spokes, causing damage to the rims, spokes and inner tubes.

Cast wheels obviously can't be adjusted, but should be inspected for any cracking around the spoke, hub and rim joins. A damaged cast wheel requires very specialist equipment to repair. It's unlikely that you'll encounter this type of equipment whilst on tour, so it's probably best to avoid any big boulders!

⬇ **Take time out to regularly service your bike**
📷 Liz Peel

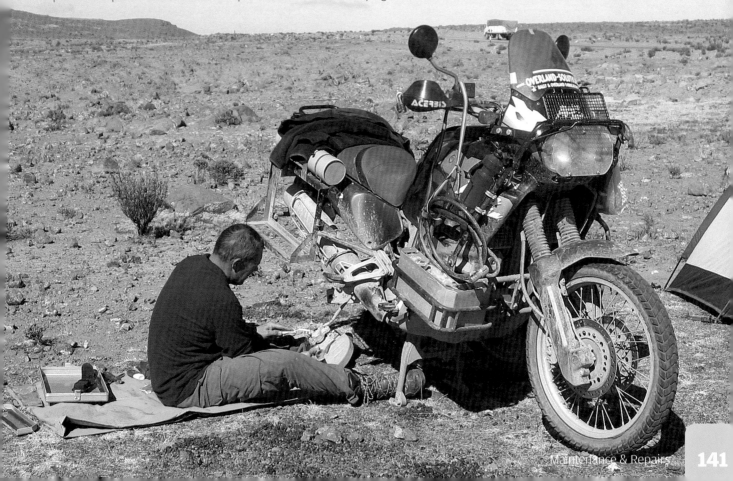

Tyres & Pressures

Tyres and pressures are rarely given the consideration they deserve. As the interface between you and the road, your tyres are expected to perform faultlessly under every road condition encountered and looking after them as well as the relevant pressures should be seen as an essential part of your daily routine.

Opportunities to replace a worn tyre may be few and far between in remote areas unless you are carrying your own replacement rubber so it makes sense to inspect your tyres on a regular basis (at least once daily) for damage and wear.

Arguably the best way to get the most out of your tyres is to vary the pressure to suit the conditions. Tyre pressure is generally a compromise, particularly when it comes to riding off-road. The lower the pressure, the better the tyre is able to 'flow' into and across the uneven surface of the road and the bigger the contact patch is likely to be.

Under-inflated tyres generate more heat and although this helps them grip better, the tyre does not last as long and also tends to wear unevenly leading to poor handling and premature replacement. Over-inflated tyres run cooler and therefore last longer. Tyres, however, need to be warm in order to offer good grip on the road surface.

At high speed they offer better handling and save fuel. They also offer better resistance to damage as a result of impact.

Manufacturers thus recommend pressures which are seen as the best compromise as they have no idea of the type of riding you plan to do, the type of roads you will travel on and the climatic extremes of where you plan to head.

Therefore it is wise to adopt a proactive approach and vary your tyre pressures by a fair margin to suit the relevant conditions. For this to be viable, however, you need a compact 12-volt compressor, accurate tyre gauge and plug point fitted on your motorcycle. With this kit you can quickly and easily match your tyres to the conditions. Consider the guidelines given below. The logic applied is aimed at providing the maximum grip while still protecting your wheel rims, tubes and side walls from damage.

This is perhaps asking a lot particularly if you don't have the necessary kit, but it is essential to maintain the correct pressure at all times as this will greatly assist both your riding and the life of your tyres.

On a final note, always check your pressures when the tyres are cold (pressure increases as the tyre becomes hot). Take the cold reading and check them against the recommended tyre pressures, which you should keep in a handy location.

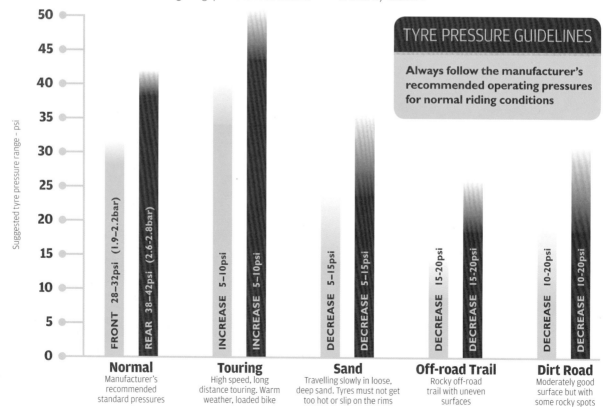

TYRE PRESSURE GUIDELINES

Always follow the manufacturer's recommended operating pressures for normal riding conditions

Suggested tyre pressure range - psi

50 / 45 / 40 / 35 / 30 / 25 / 20 / 15 / 10 / 5 / 0

FRONT 28–32psi (1.9–2.2bar) | REAR 38–42psi (2.6–2.8bar)

Normal
Manufacturer's recommended standard pressures

INCREASE 5–10psi | INCREASE 5–10psi

Touring
High speed, long distance touring. Warm weather, loaded bike

DECREASE 5–15psi | DECREASE 5–15psi

Sand
Travelling slowly in loose, deep sand. Tyres must not get too hot or slip on the rims

DECREASE 15-20psi | DECREASE 15-20psi

Off-road Trail
Rocky off-road trail with uneven surfaces

DECREASE 10-20psi | DECREASE 10-20psi

Dirt Road
Moderately good surface but with some rocky spots

Punctures

Don't leave home without knowing how to fix a puncture. Practise taking the front and rear wheels out and get to grips with what you will need to do to get going again. Punctures come in different guises, from a slow leak or a hole that may be too large to plug, to a sidewall puncture requiring a completely new tyre.

Tubeless Repairs

Most tubeless repair kits enable temporary repairs to be made without having to remove the tyre from the rim. The kit is designed to work for holes that are generally no larger than 0.15'' (4mm) in diameter. Kits will generally contain up to three CO_2 gas cartridges, allowing you to inflate the tyre to a usable pressure. As soon as possible, the gas should be replaced with normal compressed air and the tyre should be replaced at the earliest opportunity. The length of time a repair of this nature will last varies considerably and depends on a number of factors including the effectiveness of the repair, the terrain being covered and your travelling speed.

- Mark the location of the hole using chalk and remove any remaining debris
- Coat the inserting tool with special adhesive
- Insert the tool into the hole and use its abrasive tip to roughen up the edges of the damaged area, making it easier for the cement to bond to the plug
- Slide a rubber plug onto the end of the inserting tool's eyelet
- Apply another healthy amount of adhesive to the plug and insert into the hole
- Remove the tool without twisting it on extraction and cut off any protruding part of the plug with a sharp knife. Be careful not to damage the area around the hole with the knife which could compromise the repair
- Screw the CO_2 cartridges tightly onto the valve and inflate.

A combination of the inflated tyre and the cemented plug should get you back on the road but be sure not to exceed 30–40mph (50–60kph) and certainly no more than 250 miles (400km) before replacing the tyre.

↑ **KTM brand ambassador Joe Pichler from Austria repairs a front wheel puncture on his 990**

📷 Joe Pichler

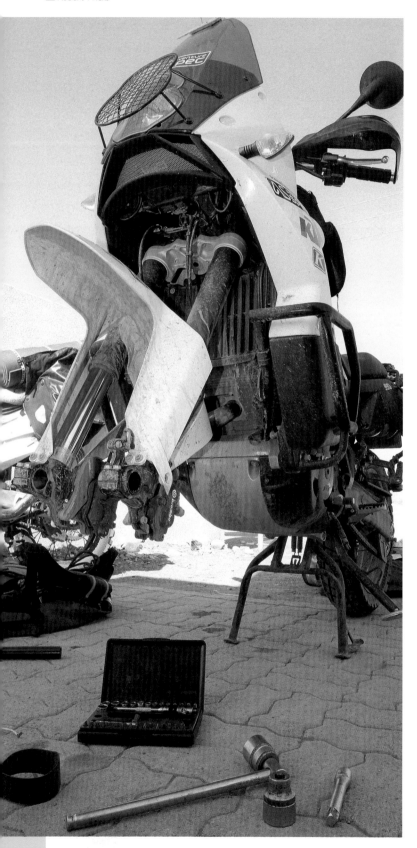

Tubed Repairs

Find a place to commence repairs and ensure you are well off the road. Prop the bike on its centre stand or use a flat rock or even a pannier as a substitute stand. Loosen the wheel nut and remove the rear spindle. Remove the chain from the sprocket and remove the wheel from the bike.

Get rid of any remaining air and loosen any rim screws. Undo the base nut and push the valve back through the rim into the tyre. Apply pressure to the bead of the tyre to loosen it from the rim. Once loose, insert one tyre lever under the bead and repeat with the second lever. Slowly work your way round the circumference of the tyre until one side is entirely clear of the rim. This will give you access to the tube and to the tyre which should be carefully inspected for the cause of the puncture. Make sure to check both the inside and outside of the tyre.

Once this is done, inflate the tube and try to locate the puncture. You will either hear the air escaping or feel it against your skin. Placing the tube into water should reveal a steady stream of bubbles if you are having difficulty finding the hole. Dry the area thoroughly and roughen it up to help bonding with the patch. Coat the area with a thin layer of adhesive and allow it to get tacky before applying the patch with a good amount of pressure. Use talc around the edges to absorb any remaining glue. Reinsert the tube into the tyre and use the levers to leverage it back onto the rim, using a soapy mixture to help the final part of the process along. Be careful not to pinch the tube as you do this. Fit the wheel to the bike taking care to tension the chain as required. Re-fit the base nut, inflate the tyre to the desired pressure and replace the valve cap. If you are stuck without a tube for the rear wheel, you can use a front wheel tube as an emergency to keep you going for a short distance.

Consider replacing inner tubes every 12,500 miles (20,000km) even if they haven't sustained a puncture. This is because the area around the valve deteriorates and small tears can cause a puncture that can be impossible to repair.

In addition to the tools required to remove the wheel from the bike, a good puncture repair kit for tubed tyres should consist of:

■ Two tyre levers (of the 12" or 15" variety for maximum leverage)

⬇ **Clever use of the bike's side stand helps to push the tyre off the rim**
📷 Touratech

⬇⬇ **A tubeless puncture repair kit**
📷 Robert Wicks

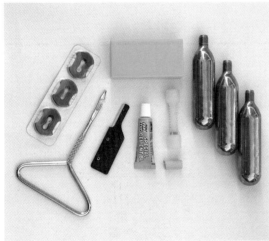

- Fresh glue
- Valve spares (cores and caps)
- Liquid soap – to help mount the tyre on the rim
- Sandpaper – to create a good surface for the patch to bond to on the inner tube
- Talc – to absorb any remaining adhesive
- A high pressure, push-pull bicycle pump or alternatively a 12-volt compressor which can connect to a cigarette lighter socket on the bike (some latest models have this as standard and it is worth considering fitting one for other applications anyway such as powering your GPS). It's worth shopping around for a compressor as some can be very bulky – or strip the plastic case off to reveal just the motor and pump which will save on space
- A small good quality tyre pressure gauge (petrol station gauges can often be inaccurate)
- Spare front and rear tubes.

PREVENTATIVE MEASURES

Tyre Sealant – One option to help with minimising punctures is to consider use of a tyre sealant which can seal punctures up to a certain size (typically around 0.25"(6mm) in tubeless tyres and 0.12"(3mm) in tubed tyres). It is reasonably easy to install and works instantly. It can be installed as a pre-treatment before a puncture occurs and can also be used to repair a flat tyre or a slow leak by removing the valve core from the tyre, injecting the substance and re-inflating the tyre. The substance is squeezed into the tyre through the valve stem. Once installed it remains liquid, evenly distributed by the centrifugal forces at work on the tyre. When a puncture occurs, the escaping air forces the liquid in the puncture wound to seal the puncture with different chemical agents intertwining and clotting to quickly seal the hole.

Tire Balls – One of the latest inventions to come to the market is 'Tire Balls' – a high-performance inflation system composed of multiple cells that inflate the tyre. They differ from conventional inner tubes or tubeless tyres which effectively have one vulnerable single cell. The individual cells are made from state-of-the-art materials that are up to ten times more puncture resistant than conventional inner tubes. The system makes use of progressively increasing pressure created as the tyre impacts with obstacles – the harder the tyre impacts, the higher the pressure builds within the cells, thereby maintaining the overall ride quality. Lower initial inflation pressure means a plusher, smoother ride over rough terrain. This is a relatively new product but certainly worth considering as an added precaution against punctures in tubeless tyres.

📷 Tire Balls

Emergencies

Chris Smith

Despite the best planning and being alert to all manner of potential situations, you could face an emergency and will need to know how to deal with it. Typical emergencies could include getting lost, having a serious accident or succumbing to the elements. If your bike is out of commission then it is time to think about yourself and ensuring your survival. The situation is obviously more serious if you are travelling solo. If this is likely to be the case, be fully competent in your survival skills.

Some basic survival skills are discussed in the next section but there are a few things you can do as part of a more general routine that will put you in a better position should an emergency unexpectedly arise:

- Be competent in your navigation skills and if you think you are lost, retrace your steps to the last known point

- Make regular inspections of your bike to spot potential problems early

- Be familiar with your planned route each day, the distances involved and vital points where help may be at hand

- Carry reserves of fuel, food and water

- Ride well within your own limits, don't take chances and don't ride at night

- Know your bike from a basic technical perspective – know how to repair a puncture, find simple faults and carry the tools needed to carry out the repairs

- Always try to maintain visual contact with your riding companions

Basic Survival

For anyone faced with an emergency survival situation, fear is very much a normal reaction. Fear tends to then trigger panic which in turn can lead to pain, cold, thirst, hunger and fatigue. It is extremely important to calmly assess the situation and not allow any of these issues to interfere with your survival. To increase your chances of survival, you should always adhere to these basic rules:

- In the event of an injury, deal with it immediately before it becomes more serious. Ignoring an injury could severely compromise your ability to survive
- Stay calm and use your common sense together with the tools available to try and determine your position and the nearest place you can find help
- Never stop moving or allow yourself to fall asleep without adequate shelter
- Do not ignore the early signs of dehydration. Carrying an adequate water supply is vital and remember that your intake of fluids will increase quite significantly as you get on the move. Hunger on the other hand is dangerous but seldom deadly
- Be conscious of the onset of fatigue which can be exacerbated by extreme weather conditions
- Try to get to higher ground so you can look out and searchers can see you
- Conserve energy wherever possible and do not consider a steep climb unless absolutely necessary as this will sap your strength
- Depending on your options, it may be best to stay in one location, allowing you to build a fire, establish a shelter and send out distress signals

Take care of yourself and always remain positive.

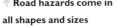
⬆ **Road hazards come in all shapes and sizes**
📷 Global Enduro

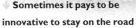
⬇ **Sometimes it pays to be innovative to stay on the road**
📷 Touratech

Essential Equipment

In the event of an emergency, it is a good idea to either have a survival kit at the ready or be in a position to quickly gather the relevant items to take with you. Having a few key items can make the difference between life and death. Also never forget that your mindset and your ability to remain calm and not panic are arguably your most important survival tools.

The importance of carrying an ample supply of water cannot be over-emphasised. Humans will only last a few days without water – so it's worth taking as much with you as possible. The balance of the kit should be waterproof, compact and lightweight to include:

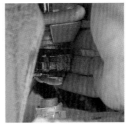

- Water
- Water Filter and Purification Tablets
- Food
- Emergency Blanket
- Torch
- Sharp Knife
- Compass
- Map
- Pen or Pencil
- Lighter or Matches
- Heavy Duty Plastic Bag
- Wire
- Basic First Aid Kit
- Personal Medication

Section 3
Typical Adventures

Touratech

As the earlier chapters have shown, overland adventure rides can take many different forms – from travelling solo or in a small group to participating in larger commercial expeditions over a few weeks or months, or perhaps even putting your normal life on hold and embarking on the ultimate round-the-world adventure.

This final section of the book is designed to give a sense of the scope of what can be contemplated. It highlights a number of very different adventures and indicates what is possible given time and budget constraints as well your own personal ambitions.

The first two tales from the saddle come courtesy of the author and fellow adventure rider and writer Greg Baker and detail their exploits in Morocco and more recently in Oman. In both instances, careful planning ensured reasonably hassle-free trips though it goes on to prove that with adventure motorcycling, it's best to expect the unexpected.

There is the ambitious ride by a group of eleven South African and English adventurers who tackle the challenges of a trans-Africa run from Cairo to Cape Town.

A new addition to the collection is the wonderful story of Mick Wheeler and Sue Wilson who ride overland to Mongolia following the legendary Silk Road.

The chapter goes on to provide an update on the long-running adventure of Adam Lewis who left the United Kingdom in March 2006 to ride around the world and after more than six years and 15,300 miles (250,000km) is still on the road!

The final story comes from Walter Colebatch who set out on an adventure ride with a twist – to set a new motorcycle altitude record.

These are all very diverse trips – different geography, different experiences and different people – but one thing in common: all were the experience of a lifetime!

Two Weeks in Morocco

These distance markers on the piste to Zagora were remarkably accurate

All images: Robert Wicks and Greg Baker

Riders	**Robert Wicks and Greg Baker**
Route	**From Bournemouth (UK) by road through France and Spain to Ouarzazate (Morocco) followed by: Talouine, Tazenacht, Foum Zguid, Zagora, Mhamid, the Draa Valley, Nekob, Alnif, Merzouga, Erfoud, Tinerhir, Lake Isli and Lake Tislit, Msemir, Boumalne Dades and return to Ouarzazate**
Date	**October 2006**
Distance	**1,900 miles (3,000km) plus 1,500 miles (2,500km) from England to the start point in Morocco and home again**
Duration	**15 days (10 days of riding)**
Bikes	**BMW R 1200 GS Adventure** **KTM 950 Adventure**
Budget Estimate	**£1,200 each (excluding bikes, but including costs to get to and from Morocco such as fuel and ferries)**

TIPS

- **Travel as light as possible**
- **Don't ride at night – you're simply asking for trouble**
- **Keep your panniers organised to minimise unnecessary packing and unpacking**
- **A good pair of comfortable boots makes all the difference, especially if you are doing a lot of walking and sightseeing en route**
- **Keep a close eye on tyre pressures and increase/decrease them to suit the terrain**
- **Build in a couple of rest days to regain strength**
- **Chocolate will melt if left unattended in a pannier!**
- **Always interact with locals and fellow travellers, especially those headed in the opposite direction for the most recent information on where you are headed**

Morocco offers a great combination of sealed roads and off-road riding

In late 2005 close friend Greg Baker and I decided it was time for another adventure and, with Morocco on Europe's doorstep, we began hatching a plan to ride in this North African adventure paradise on the fringes of the Sahara. I would ride a BMW R1200 GS Adventure and Greg would be on his KTM 950 Adventure – both very capable machines. Greg left a week in advance with the bikes in a trailer. He would head through France and Spain, over the Straits of Gibraltar and on to Morocco. Given my work commitments, I would fly to Morocco and the expedition would commence from the town of Ouarzazate (translated it means 'the door of the desert') in southern Morocco.

Having ridden in Morocco before, I was thrilled to be going back to a place where there was at least a degree of familiarity with the culture and geography. This time the route would take us much further south, to some remote areas close to the border with Algeria. We both carried GPS units and Greg had sourced waypoints for many of the routes from detailed research online. We supplemented

this with the latest maps from Stanfords in London and Greg also purchased a CD containing some old military maps on eBay which we printed out and laminated, together with some general route directions.

Departure day was soon upon us and we worked late into the last night on final modifications. Bikes, kit, food, tools and camping gear were loaded and Greg set off. Fortunately getting all our paperwork together had been reasonably simple and no carnet was required.

Once we'd met up in Morocco and unloaded all our kit, the first priority was a short shakedown run to check the bikes. This was a very useful exercise as Greg's KTM had developed an electrical fault which took until the early hours of the morning to repair. Bleary eyed but keen to get going we headed out of Ouarzazate on the first morning, full of excitement and trepidation.

Not long into the ride on the second day and Greg hurt his knee on one particularly tough descent through a narrow gorge. With it heavily strapped and uncertain

154 Adventure Motorcycling Manual

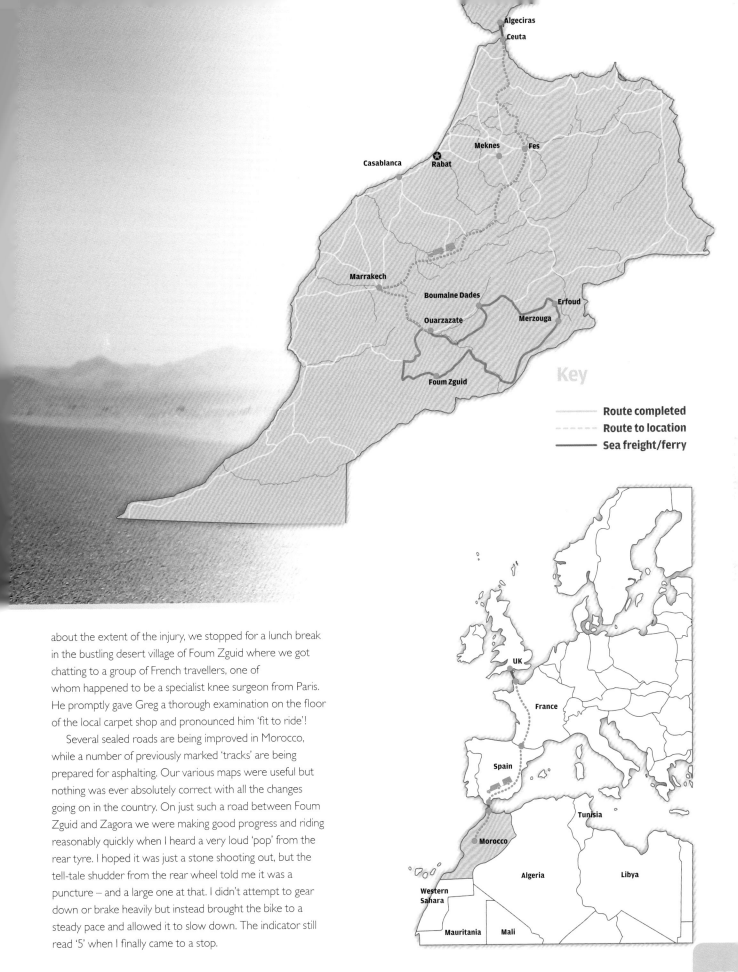

Key

— Route completed
- - - Route to location
— Sea freight/ferry

about the extent of the injury, we stopped for a lunch break in the bustling desert village of Foum Zguid where we got chatting to a group of French travellers, one of whom happened to be a specialist knee surgeon from Paris. He promptly gave Greg a thorough examination on the floor of the local carpet shop and pronounced him 'fit to ride'!

Several sealed roads are being improved in Morocco, while a number of previously marked 'tracks' are being prepared for asphalting. Our various maps were useful but nothing was ever absolutely correct with all the changes going on in the country. On just such a road between Foum Zguid and Zagora we were making good progress and riding reasonably quickly when I heard a very loud 'pop' from the rear tyre. I hoped it was just a stone shooting out, but the tell-tale shudder from the rear wheel told me it was a puncture – and a large one at that. I didn't attempt to gear down or brake heavily but instead brought the bike to a steady pace and allowed it to slow down. The indicator still read '5' when I finally came to a stop.

↑ Overnight in the desert – a secluded camp was a welcome surprise after a long day in the saddle

→ The KTM proved to be a worthy machine for the trip

Greg, who was ahead of me when it happened, didn't realise that I'd stopped. By the time he returned I had the panniers off the bike and was searching for my puncture repair kit. Neither of us was carrying a spare tyre and at this point we must have been some 45 miles (70km) from Foum Zguid and more than 75 miles (120km) from Zagora.

On closer inspection, what concerned me most was the size of the hole – it was almost 0.5in (1.2cm) in diameter – and looked to have been caused by a sharp stone. In retrospect, my tyre pressure was possibly also a little on the high side, which would almost certainly have been a contributing factor. One rubber plug certainly wasn't going to be enough, but with some careful manoeuvring we were able to get a second plug into the hole, with a large helping of cement to try and make it stick. Greg had wisely carried with him a small 12-volt compressor which had the tyre inflated in no time (easier than using the gas cartridges) and we were soon on our way again.

The terrain was very rough in places but we made slow, steady progress, always conscious of the repair and how long it might last. With nightfall fast approaching, we set up camp in an old animal pen with only the stars and a warm fire for company.

The next morning it was a huge relief to see the tyre still perfectly inflated and we set off on the remaining run to Zagora, the final few miles of which were very difficult, with thick sand halting our progress at regular intervals. We could see the town in the distance but it seemed to take hours to cover the last stretch.

When we finally rode into town, like weary cowboys coming in off the hot plains, we were flagged down by a local called Ali who was keen to direct us to a hotel. I explained that fixing the tyre was our first priority and in seconds he was pointing us towards what he called 'the best garage in town'. The workshop was managed by the very hospitable and efficient Mohammed Gordito whose workshop was adorned with stickers and memorabilia from every desert rally in the last ten years. He happened to be a specialist off-road mechanic who regularly provided his services to the Dakar Rally when it passed through town. Mohammed was only too happy to help and his repair would see me through the rest of the trip.

⬆ Desert dust gets everywhere

➡ Breathtaking scenery and not a soul in sight – just what adventure motorcycling is all about

⬇ Cooling down through the Todra Gorge

Very fine dust from the desert seems to get into everything, so we used the opportunity to clean the filters and give the bikes a good going over before heading off. Before departing, we were whisked away to Ali's shop for some obligatory mint tea and a look at the range of crafts and carpets he had on sale – we returned his kindness by purchasing some small trinkets for family back home.

Parts of the country we visited seemed almost forgotten in time, with primitive habits and cultures, vast amounts of subsistence farming and some spectacular scenery. The final leg of our route took us along the famous Todra Gorge and up to Lakes Isli and Tislit, high in the Atlas Mountains. This was undoubtedly one of the highlights of the trip, with spectacular scenery and not a soul in sight for days. From the lakes we headed south down a challenging mountain pass and through the neighbouring Dades Gorge. The pass was very narrow in places, and not wanting to plummet off the sheer drop on the left-hand side during the descent we found ourselves keeping strictly to the right-hand side of the track. At one point I misjudged the line and my pannier struck a rock outcrop. Fortunately the case was not punctured, but the lid was forced open and the pannier was bent out of shape. Some duct tape was used as a short-term fix until we could make a proper repair that evening.

The remainder of our route took us along the fringes of the Sahara, through the Draa Valley with its oases to the spectacular dunes at Merzouga and 'the end of the road' at Mhamid before a return to Ouarzazate. For now the adventure had come to an end, but what it had done for us as individuals and as friends would go on forever.

Weary as we were, we loaded the trailer and bid farewell to our hosts, Peter and Zineb, at the Bikershome in Ouarzazate, a wonderful retreat for any exhausted rider. Morocco is a special place – when you leave you take a little bit with you and it is this which draws you back. It had been a wonderful adventure and would live long in the memory for both of us.

↑ **A running repair got us to a specialist tyre shop in Zagora**

Oman

Robert Wicks

Riders	**Robert Wicks and Greg Baker**
Route	**Dubai (UAE), Musandam (Oman), Fujairah (UAE), Muscat (Oman), Sur, Ras al Had, Wahiba Sands, Nizwa, Al Hamra, Ibri, Al Ain (UAE), Dubai**
Date	**December 2012**
Distance	**1,600 miles (2,600km)**
Duration	**10 days**
Bikes	**KTM 990 Adventure and KTM 450 Rally (kindly provided by KTM UAE)**
Budget Estimate	**£600 per person (including return flights)**
Riding Gear	**Klim, provided by Adventure Spec (adventure-spec.com)**

TIPS

- At the first sign of wet weather it is highly advisable to find shelter on high dry ground and stay put – flash floods move quickly and it is very easy to get trapped by washed-out roads
- Consider fitting mousses (puncture-proof 'inner tubes') to your tyres, or maintain normal to slightly higher tyre pressures when riding in the wadis to prevent sidewall damage and punctures from sharp rocks
- Oman is famous for its historic forts, which are the country's most striking cultural landmarks. Don't miss Bahla Fort at the base of the Jebel Akhdar highlands – it is a **UNESCO** World Heritage Site

- Always test the depth and strength of any water crossing. If it's safe to cross then use a low gear, slightly higher revs than normal and a steady speed
- Don't plan to travel here between the months of April and September, given the heat
- Add 1,250 miles (2,000km) for a run to and from Salalah – the 'perfume capital of Arabia' and Oman's second largest city – in the far south
- Look out for a copy of Explorer Publishing's *Oman Off-road* book – it has lots of good information on mountain, wadi and desert drives, camping locations and maps with detailed GPS co-ordinates

t had been a while since our last decent trip together, so in June 2012 Greg and I started planning an adventure in Oman. I had been spending a lot of time in the Middle East on business and it didn't take long for me to realise Oman's potential as an adventure riding destination. The country has one of the most diverse environments in the region and consequently offers some outstanding off-road riding.

With the support of KTM in Austria and their distributor in the United Arab Emirates (KTM Middle East) confirmed, we began planning a route that would offer us a real flavour of Oman. I secured the support of Dave Lomax at Adventure Spec who liked the idea of seeing one of his brands – Klim riding gear – being used on the ride. Edox Swiss Watches also came on board as a sponsor, and before we knew it we were packing our gear.

However, the closer we came to the starting point, the less likely it seemed we would actually be able to get going. A week before our departure I tore my calf muscle in a freak accident. Lots of physio, crutches and keeping it elevated got me on the road to recovery. Then, just 24

hours before departure, we were advised by British Airways that the flight had been cancelled. This could have had serious consequences, with a public holiday looming in Dubai and the inevitable delays this would cause to our tight schedule. Fortunately we were able to get out to Dubai about ten hours later, on an evening flight. Then, when we were checking in at the hotel, it seemed Greg and his passport had parted company. A mad dash back to the airport police station as well as the lost property office thankfully saw the two reunited. These three unexpected little curve balls had us thinking the 'adventure' had started a little earlier than expected!

A day was spent in KTM's workshop to prepare our bikes – a KTM 990 Adventure and the 'beast' – a KTM 450 Rally bike that had competed in the 2012 Dakar Rally.

We had just over a week to cover a circular route, starting in Dubai and heading north towards the impressive Omani enclave of Musandam with its jagged peaks and azure water located on the Straits of Hormuz just 40 miles (65km) from the coast of Iran. From here we headed east along the coastal

plain to Muscat and beyond to Ras al Had, before heading inland to the desert of Wahiba Sands and the spectacular scenery of the Al Hajar Mountains in central Oman where we enjoyed some of the best riding of our lives.

Known as the 'fjords of Arabia', the route offered breathtaking scenery throughout. From the jagged cliffs that plunge into the Gulf of Oman to the resulting hidden inlets, each new corner on the road made us gasp. Khasab was a good place to stop for fuel and food. The road to the top of the hills surrounding the Musandam Peninsula and down the other side to the fishing village of Khor Najd was the highlight of the first two days of riding. A close second was the picturesque campsite in an acacia forest – we awoke the next morning surrounded by goats!

Campsites are neither prominent nor plentiful in this area, but if you're happy to forego the typical amenities of a shower block and a convenience store, then camping rough is the best option. Guest houses in the smaller towns and desert camps offered some respite from tented accommodation.

We left the isolation of Musandam and re-entered the UAE before heading south to the Omani border, crossing at Khatmat Milahah, just a short run from Fujairah on the east coast. Visas can be acquired at the point of entry into both the UAE and Oman. In addition to your UK licence, an International Driving Permit (IDP) is advised and available from selected post offices while you wait. You will need to purchase insurance at the border when entering Oman, but it's not particularly expensive or time consuming to buy. Officially, a carnet is not needed for Oman; KTM had kindly prepared a carnet for each bike but it was never asked for. If you are heading further afield and a carnet is needed, it can be purchased in Muscat.

The run down to Muscat gave the clearest indication of just how much money is being pumped into the country's infrastructure. The road is significantly congested by extensive roadworks that look to be there for a while, but unfortunately it's the quickest way to Muscat and the mountains. Muscat is certainly worth a visit, although we spent more time in the adjacent area of Muttrah. Before

↑ ↗ Oman is filled with amazing roads and interesting characters

📷 Robert Wicks

the discovery of oil, Muttrah was the centre of commerce in Oman. The scenic port, the corniche road and its extensive souq are all worth a visit.

With the countless villages and towns along the coast one got a real sense of the importance of the sea for Oman, and how much the country depends upon it, both now and in earlier times. Some 93 miles (150km) beyond Muscat lies the picturesque village of Sur, renowned as a major dhow-building town; the very same vessels were used for trade two centuries ago. By the sixth century, Sur was an established centre for trade with East Africa, with local dhows setting sail for destinations as far away as China, India, Zanzibar and Iraq. Be sure to take some time to visit the shipyards, where visitors are welcomed with great pride. Beyond Sur, stop in either Ras al-Jinz or Ras al Hadd – the last point in the east of Oman – where the beaches are a well-known breeding ground for green sea turtles.

Our next stop, and one that gave us an opportunity to do some great desert riding, was the Wahiba Sands. The region is named after the Wahiba tribe and it stretches for 110 miles (180km) from north to south and 50 miles (80km) from east to west – an area of some 4,800 square miles (12,500km²) of rolling and shifting dunes. We entered the desert at Al Mintarib and spent a night at the Al Raha camp, which comes highly recommended for its great food and friendly service. There are other camps too, and these can be used as a great base for exploring the desert, sandboarding, stargazing, meeting local desert folk and even testing your ability as a camel jockey!

If you're feeling really adventurous, it is possible to cross the desert, but this will need considerable preparation. Unless you are a confident desert rider with good navigational skills you will invariably need a local guide. A north/south crossing is advised as an east/west crossing is particularly challenging, given the geographical layout of the dunes.

The desert lies at the south-easterly tip of Oman's famous Hajar Mountains (Arabic for 'stone mountains'). This is the highest range in the eastern Arabian Peninsula, with the mountains separating the low coastal plain of Oman from the high desert plateau, and lying 30–60 miles (50–100km) inland

from the Gulf of Oman coast. The mountains start where we began our journey, in Musandam, and run south-east, parallel to the coast, but moving gradually further away as it goes. The central section of the range is the Jebel Akhdar, the highest and wildest terrain in the country. As we passed through the foothills the dramatic scale of the surrounding mountains became clearly apparent, and we knew we were in for a treat.

There are countless routes to consider, so it's worth taking some time to research what you'd like to see and how best to make the most of your time in the mountains. These were some of our favourites:

Jebel Shams – This 32-mile (52km) route takes you to the highest point in the country at 9,872ft (3,009m) and the views of Oman's own 'Grand Canyon' are some of the most stupendous in the Sultanate. It's an incredibly rewarding ride up a fast, flowing piece of asphalt that seems to get steeper and steeper with every turn. Early on in the ride, where the tarmac ends and the gravel begins, be sure to look across to your right for the abandoned village of Ghul which sits partly

camouflaged against the rock. Beyond this point it's a well-graded gravel road with wonderful views all the way to the summit.

Wadi Damm – This 23-mile (38km) route starts in the foothills of the Hajar Mountains. Riding conditions are easy, with only a short wadi section. There are many local historical attractions worth visiting, including ancient beehive tombs and the spectacular backdrop of Jabal Misht – the peak most coveted by rock climbers on the Arabian Peninsula.

Wadi as Sahtan – This 21-mile (34km) route offers myriad possibilities for exploration. Wadi as Sahtan acts as a gateway to a host of roads that all lead off to interesting sights and villages. The region is sometimes knows as 'mandoos', meaning the 'chest of Oman' and referring to the area's hidden and secluded nature. Be sure not to miss out on the road to Yasab – by far the most spectacular section of road in Oman. The route takes on epic proportions as it climbs to over 5,580ft (1,700m) in less than 2.5 miles (4km). The track is narrow in places and the scenery is mind-blowing so be sure to keep your eye on the road!

Welcome respite after a long day in the desert
Robert Wicks

Wadi Bani Awf – There is not a lot that can prepare you for the start of this ride. Think Stelvio Pass on steroids! This was by far our favourite ride and undoubtedly one of the most spectacular in Oman, with the picturesque village of Balad Sayat a must-see sight. If you start the wadi from the north, do stop at the Al Hoota Cave with its massive subterranean chamber. Riding conditions are challenging in places, with sheer cliff faces, and it's difficult to keep your eye on the road because of the amazing vistas. At 36 miles (59km) in length and given the undulating terrain, don't underestimate the time it takes to complete the route and how quickly the light fades during the winter months.

Wadi Bani Kharus & Wadi al Hijayr – One of the longer routes at 28 miles (45km) and close to Muscat if you're looking for a great day trip. The two wadis share a common entrance from the start near Al Awabi. The views are good, as is the geology if this takes your fancy. There are plenty of terraced gardens, refreshing pools for a swim and even a few abandoned villages to explore.

Wadi Mistall – This is a relatively easy 19-mile (30km) route with several stunning towns accessible towards the end. It's easy to become distracted on one of the many side roads that lead off from the main wadi. Look out for some great examples of 'falaj', an intricate system of channels used to irrigate palm plantations and farm fields.

Sayq Plateau – Unfortunately when we arrived at the start of this amazing 29-mile (47km) route it was not open to bikes following what the officer at the military control post described as 'bad conditions for motorcycles'. Despite our best efforts to convince the authorities otherwise, it seems there had been a couple of two-wheel cowboys who ran into trouble on the steep climb and the route was now restricted to 4x4 vehicles. It's worth keeping an eye out to see if the restrictions are lifted as this vast expanse at altitudes between 6,560 and 7,875ft (2,000–2,400m) has more than 30 villages, a maze of roads and trails, tremendous camping and commanding views. If the restriction on bikes remains, it's still worth considering a trip to the top and there are plenty of locals who will sort out a 'taxi' to the summit.

After some of the best riding of our lives we reluctantly pointed the KTMs away from the mountains and towards the border crossing at Khatam Al Shikhla, near Al Ain. In stark contrast to the sights and sounds of the past week we headed north and finished the journey with the sun setting on the spectacular Dubai skyline. We cannot recommend Oman highly enough – people are welcoming, the food is great, fuel is astonishingly cheap and, most importantly, the riding is out of this world.

KTM 990 ADVENTURE

Engine	Liquid cooled, four stroke, twin cylinder
Drive	Chain
Front suspension	48mm WP-USD forks, 210mm wheel travel
Rear suspension	WP-PDS rear shock, hydraulic spring pre-load, 210mm wheel travel
Front tyre	Pirelli Scorpion – tubed 90/80 – 21
Rear tyre	Pirelli Scorpion – tubed 150/70 – R18
Seat height	860mm
Dry weight	209kg
Fuel capacity	19.5 litres
Navigation	Garmin 60CSX

KTM 450 RALLY

Engine	Liquid cooled, four stroke, single cylinder
Drive	Chain
Front suspension	WP-USD Ø 48mm, 300mm wheel travel
Rear suspension	WP-Monoshock with Pro-Lever linkage, 310mm wheel travel
Front tyre	Michelin Desert – mousse 90/90 – 21
Rear tyre	Michelin Desert – mousse 130/80 – 18
Seat height	980mm
Dry weight	150kg
Fuel capacity	35 litres
Navigation	Garmin Zumo 550

Six Weeks from Cairo to

Cape Town

📷 All images: Johan Engelbrecht

Riders	Clinton Pienaar, Harry van Zyl, Clinton van Loggenburg, Andrew Barrum, Herman Botha, Jeffrey Collins, Piet Potgieter, Hugh Brassher, Patrick Banfield, Rob Kenedy and Johan Engelbrecht (official photographer, riding pillion)
Route	Cairo to Cape Town (Egypt, Sudan, Ethiopia, Kenya, Tanzania, Zambia, Botswana and South Africa)
Date	March–May 2006
Distance	7,760 miles (12,500km)
Duration	35 days
Bikes	2 x BMW R 1150 GS Adventure 2 x BMW F 650 GS Dakar 2 x BMW R 1150 GS 2 x BMW R 1200 GS 1 x KTM 950 Adventure 1 x Honda Africa Twin
Budget Estimate	Approximately £5,000 each (excluding bikes)

With thanks to Two Wheels Magazine (South Africa) and Harry van Zyl for allowing this article to be republished, as well as to Doc Herman for access to his travel diaries from the trip.

TIPS

- Make sure you choose the right kind of bike for the trip you are planning
- Packing is a fine art – try it a couple of times, make it all fit, then throw half of it away!
- The earlier you get started on your paperwork the better
- A GPS is invaluable – even if simply for the security of knowing exactly where you are all the time
- Make sure you are in at least reasonable shape if you want to survive the tough sections and be able to help your mates up out of the sand
- It's an adventure, not a race. So as odd as this might sound, ride slowly instead of trying to imitate the flat-out 'stand up and charge' approach. Two of the group tried this and flew home early because of accidents
- Be wary of suicidal pedestrians

A lone KTM braved the journey south but ran into trouble in Sudan. Repairs in Nairobi were successful and saw it home

Back in December 2002 a couple of friends were watching the solar eclipse near the town of Messina, close to the South Africa/Zimbabwe border, and they got to discussing the fact that the next eclipse would be in Egypt in 2006. "How about going to that one too, and riding home on our bikes?" they thought. There were several minutes of long silence while their minds toyed with the crazy idea, but the seed had been planted and the idea eventually grew into reality. The more they spoke about the trip, the more like-minded individuals they came across. The final group consisted of seven South Africans and three friends from England who would ride from London across Europe to North Africa for a rendezvous in Cairo before heading south.

Planning sessions commenced in December 2005, as did the practice runs, which if anything served to indicate just

how much was involved in the expedition. One of the first decisions the group made was that this was not going to be an 'organised tour' with a team leader, support vehicle and someone to blame when things went wrong – instead this would be a bunch of guys riding together, being responsible for themselves and taking each day as it came.

The team set aside six weeks to complete the trip, but this timetable was soon in turmoil when the bikes were held for an extended period, reinforcing the old adventure adage of not planning too far ahead, particularly in what is a very different Egypt now from the one they rode through in 2006.

What follows is a series of extracts published in *Two Wheels Magazine* in South Africa.

Why do grown men leave everything and go on a journey like this? For me this is some kind of pilgrimage. Ever since I

Key

—————— **Route completed**

- - - - - **Air freight**

can remember, I have been fascinated by the idea of travelling the length of the African continent. If you don't do it at some point, you will always be able to come up with excuses not to go – never enough time, never enough money, and always too many responsibilities and reasons why not to.

Egypt: 'Sea and Sand'

Looking down from the Egypt Air flight at sunrise all that was visible below was sand, so we went across to the other side of the aircraft to look down and saw more sand and at that moment the reality of our trip kicked in. Up to now it had been all planning and theory, but now we were about to set off for real.

Cairo is a large bustling city with a huge pollution problem, and like most other cities has good and bad areas. The main tourist spots and hotels are very neat and tidy, but this all turns very dirty as soon as you go around the next corner. The city noticeably comes to life later in the evening with the millions of inhabitants all trying to earn a buck, from pavement shoe shiners to the many sidewalk restaurant owners, not to mention the thousands of black Fiat taxis vying for road space with donkey carts delivering coal. The car hooters never stopped and the general rule was whoever hooted the loudest and took the gap first, won.

We chose not to eat at hotels, and instead dined with the locals. This was a winner and we experienced everything from goat stew and beans from sidewalk vendors, to excellent roast pigeon and tender lamb.

In Cairo it was great to be reunited with our bikes, and

after assembling them we headed directly to the pyramids at Giza. Egypt is not very user-friendly for self-drive holidays or for the independent traveller – it is geared more for large tour groups in coaches. We had to get a 'Permit to Travel' from the authorities and were often stopped and checked by the tourist police at the entrance to towns, and then escorted in convoy to be handed over to the tourist police in the next town.

This was a frustrating process as some convoys only did an agonising 40mph (65km/h) on open desert highways, while others travelled at a very dangerous 80mph (130km/h), with lights and sirens blazing, through towns of busy streets teeming with pedestrians, traffic and animals. The roads were generally good and the countryside was all sand except for the lush green belt on the banks of the Nile.

After two nights in Luxor we headed south to Aswan and the port on the Aswan High Dam. From there we had to catch the passenger ferry for the 18-hour crossing to Wadi Halfa in Sudan. The ferry is the sole means of crossing directly from Egypt to Sudan, and the customs formalities took forever. The bikes were eventually loaded on to a much slower cargo barge alongside bags of cement, fridges and Egyptian linen, which was to arrive in Wadi Halfa a day later than the passenger ferry. The ferry's dining room, ablution facilities and meals were very poor so we all slept on the deck and opened our emergency can of sardines!

Sudan: 'Desert and Dust'

It's funny what effect one's expectations and perceptions can have. We expected the worst from Sudan but were all pleasantly surprised by the friendly and efficient manner in which all the border formalities were concluded. We booked into the 'best hotel' in Wadi Halfa – to say the facilities were basic was an understatement – with three hand-made beds to a room, a low steel door and a small padlock. The toilet block consisted of two shower cubicles over 'long-drop' toilets without running water. Some of us got used to the smell, but others preferred the long walk into the hills.

A day later we got our bikes off the cargo vessel and cleared customs in no time at all, thanks to our 'fixer' who was recommended by his counterpart in Egypt. He charged a handsome service fee but it was worth it. We then found a general dealer who had some drums of petrol so we hand-filled all our tanks as we prepared the bikes for the long ride across the Nubian Desert.

We left Wadi Halfa early the next morning on a confusing system of tracks – all leading more or less to the south. We had planned to cover about 250 miles (400km) to Dongola this day, but before we were 5 miles (8km) into the route all of us had dropped our over-laden bikes several times in the thick sand. We soon realised the target distance was a bit optimistic – we would only get to Dongola two days later.

Trouble struck the very next day when the Honda Africa Twin was forced to retire with electrical problems and a broken shock absorber, and one of the BMWs developed a nasty oil leak and had to be taken on to the next town by a passing Bedford truck. The hospitality of the Sudanese along the Nile was really wonderful and very unexpected.

Little did we know what lay ahead of us. On the map was just a thin line, and according to the notoriously unreliable local knowledge, a sealed road all the way to Khartoum. The reality was quite different – sand, serious corrugations, road

⬇ Crossing into Sudan from Egypt – the weekly ferry is the only means to do so

⬊ All aboard at Aswan

construction and very slow going from sunrise to sunset. We fell over more times than any of us care to remember – accepting yet again that the bikes were way too heavy and that picking them up often did as much damage as the falling. With temperatures of at least 45°C (113°F), and with fatigue and dehydration setting in across the group, the psychological impact of falling and getting up and then riding assertively again soon became severe. Back home during our planning phase we knew it would be more of a mental than a physical exercise, but our limits were now being sorely tested.

Somehow we made it through a very tough day and, exhausted, we rolled into a dusty Khartoum in a scene reminiscent of the movie *Black Hawk Down* – lots of crazy traffic, searing heat and wind. When we left the energy-sapping heat of Khartoum we headed for Gedaref, the last town before Ethiopia, some 95 miles (150km) away.

Ethiopia: 'Beauty and the Beast'

Metema must rank as one of the weirdest border posts ever. Little mud huts in different locations across the village made up passport control and security. This also turned out to be one of the most painless crossing exercises we had been through, with the security officer even ordering tea for us! Customs was another 15 miles (25km) away.

The road from the border to Gonder had some really beautiful mountain passes, which climbed continually towards the highlands and the Simien Mountains. The roads were badly rutted with very deep pebble and shale to contend with. It was at this point that Doc Herman lost control and 'high-sided' just outside the little town where the customs office was situated.

In trying to avoid the locals who were rushing up to help, a couple of us took the wrong line in the dust and careered

↑ **You soon get tired of picking your bike up out of the sand** right over the downed bike, with another one of us heading into the gravel in the process. The Doc's GS was quite badly damaged, but we managed to 'bend' everything back into place for the run to Gonder.

The northern part of Ethiopia, up in the highlands, appears still to be living in biblical times, with a subsistence economy being the way of life. People were tall and slender with big round eyes and gaunt expressions. Herders tended their donkeys and goats while peasants walked the roads on the way to market with bushels of wheat, hay or sticks on their overloaded, hunched backs. Scattered around were wrecks of many Russian tanks and armoured vehicles, remnants of the war in the 1980s.

The southern part of the country along the Rift Valley was more sub-tropical and fertile. The population here was very different, darker and more tribal, and as in the north everyone converges on the main road to do their business – but with a difference; most people here seemed to be chewing miraa leaves, a narcotic plant which left them high for the rest of the day.

When riding through the towns and villages there were quite a few cases of stones being thrown at us as we passed by and a couple of instances where people seemed to deliberately push domestic animals, and even other people, directly in front of us to try and cause an incident from which they might claim some 'compensation'.

From Gonder there was a new, smooth as glass, tarred

road that continued for about 185 miles (300km) past Lake Tana to Addis Ababa, and we passed through many little villages where the people seemed quite excited to see the bikes. Stone-throwing persisted at times, however, and the perpetrators were mainly young boys spurred on by their mates to throw sticks and stones and even jump into the path of the oncoming bikes. The inevitable finally happened and unfortunately one of us hit a pedestrian crossing the street. He wasn't badly injured but he did have a fractured leg and that soon meant some of us almost became victims of mob justice before the police finally arrived. They detained us for the night, insisting that we camp at the police station to 'protect' us from the village mob.

It was Easter and many folk were bringing sheep and produce to the markets in preparation for seasonal feasts. Three of us were unexpectedly invited to the home of the police inspector for lunch, which turned out to be a very tasty traditional pancake served with spinach, tomatoes and beans followed by strong coffee, roasted and ground while we had our meal.

It took another two days to sort out the 'compensation agreement', and after paying lots of people we were finally on our way, feeling somewhat aggrieved. Most of us were getting a bit tired of Ethiopia with all the jeering, stone-throwing kids and rip-off artists – like the hotelier who told us the room rate was double because we were foreigners.

After our unpleasant experience we tried to cover as

⬇ Roads in Africa are unpredictable and constantly changing as networks are upgraded

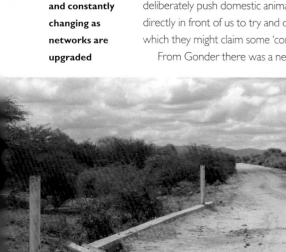

much distance as possible, continuing on to Addis Ababa through wonderful countryside with massive communal farmland giving way to lush tropical forests and open savanna. Ethiopia is beautiful, with a rich and colourful history and religion that goes way back – some churches we visited were built in the mid-seventeenth century. Everything also appeared to be bigger here – the mountains were higher, the valleys wider and the gorges deeper. And one good thing left behind by the Italians who colonised Ethiopia is the art of making good pasta and coffee! The smallest shop in a backwater town will have a proper espresso machine that turns out the best caffeine fix this side of the equator.

Kenya: 'The 300-mile (500km) Hellrun from Moyale to Marsabit and Isiolo'

The first two days in Kenya turned out to be extremely rough on both man and machine. We had heard all the stories about this being bandit country and a definite no-go area during the April/May rainy season – and it was now the third week of April! Fortunately the rains

held back, but the roads were extremely rough, with stones and protruding rocks.

Halfway through the first day the sub-frame on Doc's bike cracked. We transferred most of his luggage to the other bikes, but 30 miles (48km) from Marsabit it finally broke right through on both sides and he could go no further. Some good Samaritans from a drought relief agency picked him up and we loaded his bike on the back of their truck so we could get it to a local garage and begin the job of repairing it.

The next leg to Isiolo was somewhat better but still took most of the day, passing through villages so remote that you really felt like a celebrity with all the attention. Just before the town we were caught in a heavy rainstorm, soaking us to the bone, but at least bringing some respite from the dust and heat.

The following day took us past Mount Kenya and across the equator to Nairobi. This felt like a milestone and our spirits were high – this was the halfway point of our journey and it would be all downhill from here – so I gave away my last two cans of sardines!

Running into difficulty in Ethiopia – fortunately nobody was badly hurt

**Covering
tough terrain
like this took the
group far longer
than they
anticipated**

Generally the roads in Kenya were in a poor state, the gravel roads in desperate need of grading and the tarred roads full of potholes. At the first village my riding gloves went missing and at the next someone went running off with one of our helmets, so we really had to be on our toes at times.

Tanzania: 'Kilimanjaro Smiles'

The border crossing into Tanzania was uneventful and we headed on to Arusha with Mount Meru looming over us in the distance. After lunch we carried on to Kilimanjaro with rain clouds gathering above us. Unfortunately the volcano was shy and kept itself hidden under a thick blanket of storm clouds, which disappeared as darkness fell.

The roads and the scenery kept improving and we enjoyed hassle-free biking until the turn-off to Bagamoyo. Our group split into two here, with most guys braving the sand road to the coastal resort town of Bagamoyo for a dhow crossing to Zanzibar. As we turned on to the gravel the heavens opened and we were soon drenched; we hadn't put our rain gear on, thinking it would blow over soon.

Most of the roads in Tanzania are in very good condition, with only the occasional pothole, and the population also had better road sense than we'd experienced in Kenya. The people were all very friendly and we loved Bagamoyo, an historic little town where David Livingstone's remains were carried by his two trusty men, which still oozes history and mystique.

The next day we headed off to Mbeya and on to the border with Zambia. The rain persisted and the ride was uneventful, but the border crossing was rough, with touts literally fighting each other to get our attention. On the Tanzanian side they were soon dispersed by a whip-wielding official, but they simply reconvened on the other side of the border and we were forced to change money with them in order to pay insurance and the carbon-tax charge before entering Zambia.

Zambia: 'Livingstone or Bust'

At the Zambian customs station we convinced the 'carbon-tax lady' that all our bikes had catalytic converters and didn't produce any

carbon, so the US$50 tax was waived; she wasn't going to issue a receipt anyway. We did have to pay the third-party insurance, although nobody was sure what we were insured against. Overall it was a rather unpleasant three-hour ordeal, but it was the only way to cross into Zambia.

We set off down the Great North Road via Mpika and rode alongside the border with the Democratic Republic of Congo, and then on through Lusaka to Livingstone. It was slow going as rain accompanied us most of the way and everything was now damp and smelly. Also, Clinton had a blown rear shock which forced us to keep the speed down even more. Our progress was further limited by a number

↑ **A shared goal meant the group worked well together**

of horrendous truck accidents and massive diesel spills, and there were roadblocks at every town and junction. The officials were openly bent, constantly checking for non-existent roadworthy issues or requesting documentation that wasn't required in order to solicit a 'penalty' payment. When I firmly told the officer that I wasn't paying anybody any penalties, he replied that it 'was very cold today, give me your jacket'. I shook my head and we pulled off. At another roadblock they wanted the spare tyre I had been hauling all the way from Cairo. They didn't get that either!

Just footsteps from the raging Zambezi River we met up with friends who had ridden north to join the final leg home. This was a journey of discovery and self-discovery, with a lot of time to reflect and to become more at peace with the continent and its population – to adapt, to accept and to appreciate Africa for its diversity and also the dignity and pride of the people whom we had the privilege of encountering.

There was so much generosity and friendliness that overshadowed the bureaucratic hassles we'd experienced. I can only speak with appreciation and high regard for the people of Africa generally. Arriving in Cape Town felt like a hollow victory. Our adventure was over and we didn't want it to end. We wanted to service our bikes, put them on a ship for South America and keep riding.

<< Africa is unlike any other continent and offers some of the best adventure riding in the world

← Road accidents such as this are reasonably commonplace in Africa. A good reason not to ride at night

↑ 'I know it's getting late, but let's ride on a few more miles before we make camp for the night!'

↓ The raging Zambezi River – with this in sight the riders knew they were close to home

Silk Road

On the way to Karakol, Kyrgyzstan

All images: Mick Wheeler and Sue Wilson

Riders	**Mick Wheeler and Sue Wilson**
Route	**UK, Belgium, Germany, Poland, Belarus, Russia, Mongolia, China (arrested and returned to Mongolia), Mongolia, Russia, Kazakhstan, Kyrgyzstan, Uzbekistan, Turkmenistan, Azerbaijan, Georgia, Turkey, Greece, Macedonia, Kosovo, Montenegro, Croatia, Bosnia, Croatia, Slovenia, Austria, Germany, France, Germany, Belgium, UK**
Date	**March–September 2005**
Distance	**19,212 miles (30,918km)**
Duration	**6 months**
Bikes	**BMW F650 GS Dakar and BMW F650 GS**
Budget Estimate	**£5,000 each; this included all petrol, insurance, visas, hotels and other incidentals, the only exception being the purchase of the bikes**

TIPS

- Most Russian cities and major towns have at least one active motorcycle club. Research beforehand or just flag a motorcyclist down – they will look after you like long-lost friends and take you to places you would never find yourself
- It's probably not worth camping – the hotels and home stays are very good value for money
- Visit Dulaanhaan in northern Mongolia to see Mongolian bows and arrows in the old traditional way
- The Caravanserai at Tash Rabat (south of Naryn) in Kyrgyzstan is well worth a visit. You can stay in a traditional yurt (tent) at an altitude of 10,500ft (3,200m) in the mountains close to the Chinese border
- The Bibi Khanym Mosque in Samarkand and the old town of Bukhara in Uzbekistan are memorable places and well worth a visit
- The cave complex at Postojna in Slovenia is amazing
- Save your photographs to at least two separate places. We had written photographs to CDs, duplicated these but kept them together, and we lost a lot of images when they were stolen!

Every true motorcyclist nurtures a dream, a wish, a desire, to ride off into the setting sun. For most people a long overland trip is out of the question – or maybe just a possibility, a dream, something to talk about. Careers, relationships, mortgages and children always intrude and only the lucky (or selfish) can sell up and leave everything behind them in the fulfilment of their own personal dream. We ran out of excuses in the end, because there was nothing preventing us from leaving the UK behind for several months.

Sue's brain was stirring, wheels and cogs had started to turn … maybe we could ride overland to Mongolia, perhaps follow the old Silk Route she had read so much about. There were no issues for me – anywhere would be just fine, I was a motorcyclist, the destination was a mere excuse for the ride. Yep, Mongolia would be just fine.

The idea and plans snowballed, with the dream quickly turning into reality. It didn't help the cause (or perhaps it did) when friends asked us when we were setting off and how long we would be away. We were committed and in up to our necks. Sue was a great organiser, having been a PA for an international firm for many years; I could strip an engine down blindfold, so the various tasks ahead were easily allocated. Sue sorted out the various visas that would be required and it was my job to prepare the bikes. A Collins 1cm to 120km map of Asia was purchased and using the knuckle-to-knuckle joints of the index finger as a day's travel distance guide, a route and rough time schedule were planned.

I organise group tours to Germany and, over the years, had got to know the team at Wunderlich quite well, taking many BMW riders through their doors and to the goodies counter. Wunderlich readily agreed to help us with the provision of parts and extras for our trip. Tyres, suspension and panniers were just a fraction of their involvement. They really couldn't do enough for us.

With a send-off from Johnnie Walker and Sally Traffic on BBC Radio 2's *Drive Time* the previous evening,

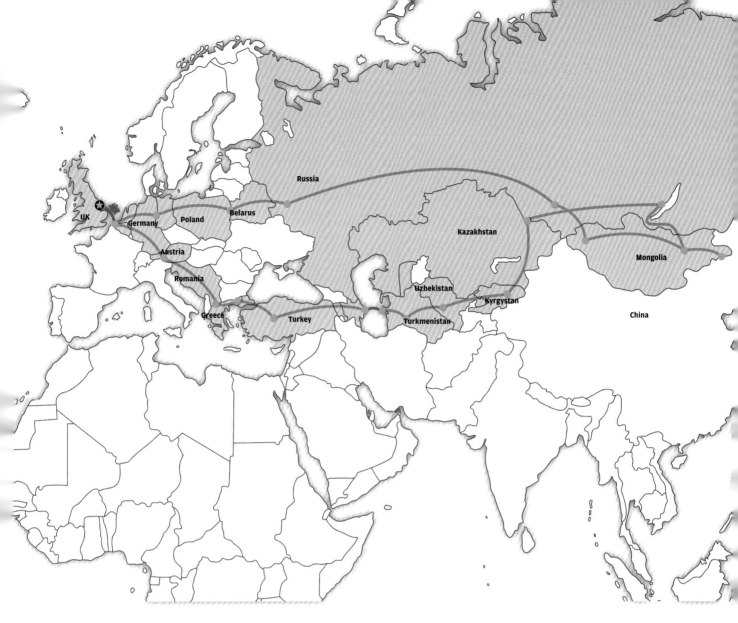

Thursday 24 March saw us meeting up and setting off from Rainbow Motorcycles, Rotherham, for the overnight ferry from Hull to Zeebrugge. We were off on our trip of a lifetime, our very own 'Long Way Home' as we were to call it. It was going to be approximately 6,000 miles to our most easterly destination and 12,000 miles for the return!

We were heading through Belgium and Germany when a leak from the oil pressure switch of my Dakar worsened. Chewing gum, superglue and two-pack adhesive failed to solve the problem, so we headed for the BMW dealership Autohaus Jacobi in Pritzwalk where they kindly removed a new item from a showroom bike and fitted it to mine, and also gave us fresh coffee. Soon on our way again, with no charge because the bike was still under warranty, we headed towards the Masurian Lakes and the Bialowieski National Park in northern Poland. Crossing into Belarus at Brest we only had a transit visa to cross the country and exit at Gomel on the Russian border, some 340 miles (547km) away.

We play a game at border crossings, taking it in turns to guess the time it'll take to pass through, with the other then going over or under that figure. I very quickly learned to smile and look happy at borders, taking my lead from Sue. "These guys are here all day; they've got all day, and if they don't like us they'll keep us waiting for as long as they want!" Sue said, kicking me on the shin as I started to get grumpy. I smiled and the border guard stamped us through. We were in Russia.

I loved Russia. I loved the country, the people, the welcome – but if our only experience of Russia had been our first town of Bryansk then things might have been very different. None of the hotels wanted us for some reason, so we headed out of town and found an old railway station to camp on. Sue had a gut feeling that we would be visited, that all was not well, and so when a police car came zooming in, tyres screeching, and pulled to a stop right next to us she was proved right. Armed police jumped out, two containing the scene by pointing their Kalashnikov

A not-so-soft 'soft sand tumble', near Khovd in Mongolia

machine guns up and down the road, while the driver kept saying "No, no" and "Dangeroos" over and over again, beckoning us to pack our gear and go with them. We felt like miscreant school kids playing truant. Why the old station was dangerous we'll never know – bears or robbers perhaps! Anyway, they took us to a hotel in the woods that we had actually been trying to find when we saw the railway station.

Each day we headed east, riding towards the early morning sun, and we would ride all day, only stopping to make coffee or eat at some roadside café. It was now April but very cold, with snow still high at the roadside, any water frozen solid, the roads becoming more potholed and in a terrible state of repair the further east we headed. We'd both had this romantic notion of heading east and following spring, but spring was still behind us. The ground was too hard for tent pegs, but we needed no encouragement to seek out hotels and motels which could be had for anything from £10–15, with the added bonus of usually good security for the bikes. No contest, then!

For almost three weeks we rode east each day, at each time zone putting our clocks on an hour – Orel, Tambov, Penza, Samara, Ufa, Kurgan, Isim, Omsk Novosibirsk and so to Barnaul. Riding into Penza we flagged down another motorcyclist who promptly took us to the Penza motorcycle club headquarters where we received a very warm welcome and a hotel was found for us. This more or less set the scene for the next few days because as we left one town they would phone our next stop and a couple of bikers would be waiting for us at the town limits, ready to take us to a hotel and offer terrific hospitality.

Into Omsk and we were again welcomed by the local bike club. We were interviewed and filmed by the TV station there, which made a great thing of our trip – but also filmed by them was our being stopped for speeding the next morning as the local police inspector, himself a member of the Penza bike club, escorted us out of town! We would be stopped several times a day, every day, while riding through Russia for either routine matters or alleged transgressions of the law, but there was always a smile and a handshake when they saw that we were a geriatric couple from another land. I had taken a supply of police tie-pin badges, cap badges, etc. and these were very gratefully accepted – and gratefully offered, I might add, when we were allowed off our alleged speeding or white-line offences.

We were now well into Siberia, with its bitter east wind blowing across the steppes, and then came the Altai Mountains, one place where Sue and I will hopefully return, for it is unbelievably wild and beautiful. The last town before the Mongolian border was like a Wild West shanty town, but we found another very warm welcome.

Riding into Kow-Array we were looking for somewhere to eat and so walked into a busy café, thinking if that was where the locals ate it must be okay. We ate well and the owner, Nina, wouldn't take a penny; in fact we were told in no uncertain terms that we must go back later. Well, I wouldn't argue with this lady! We set up camp nearby, for Nina had told us that the only hotel was awful, and went back to the café early in the evening; it was closed for customers, but not for us. The tables were set with large amounts of food, beer, and vodka, and Nina, her sister and two staff looked after us like long-lost friends. Again Nina wouldn't take a penny. Bearing in mind we spoke no Russian, and they no English, we busily chatted all evening … the marvels of communication! The next morning we went to bid our farewells and how we all hugged and cried.

We exited Russia without a problem and then came 10km of no man's land to find the Mongolian border control. The roads in Russia had been terrible, the rear plastic mudguard chain guard extensions of both our 650 GS bikes had long since fractured and broken off – but now there were no roads, only dozens of tracks disappearing in different directions. Ahead of us a four-wheel drive was stuck at a river crossing so we found an alternative route and eventually came upon the border control, more perhaps by good luck than judgement. Very

smart and efficient border officers, who simply couldn't believe that we had ridden through Russia unscathed, stamped us in.

Mongolia is a land of no fences, and no roads, and we'd ridden overland to get there. We were smiling and hugging, the thoughts of "what happens if…" having long disappeared. Within hours Sue had taken the first of many SSTs, or 'soft sand tumbles' as I call them. Her bike was well laden and heavy, and a real handful in the soft sand. At the first town we came to, Olgi, I changed the Continental Escape tyres for the knobblier more off road orientated TKC's we were carrying, only to find that one of Sue's front wheel bearings was totally shot. We obtained a replacement from a nearby bike bits place – it was sealed at one side with metal, open the other; maybe it was a gearbox application, but it would do for now and got us out of trouble.

"What happens if …." was to be put to the test time and time again. Another SST put Sue into the hospital in Khovd for an X-ray on a suspected broken ankle. It turned out to be severely bruised but kept us 'holed up' in the town for a week while the swelling went down. Then, 15 miles after leaving Darvi, Sue's bike ground to a halt. The gearbox sprocket would not move at all; the gearbox had apparently seized. I retraced our tracks into Darvi and

Magical Cappadocia, located in the centre of the Anatolian region of Turkey

↓ **Taking in the**
view of the
Tien Shan
Mountains,
Tash Rabat

eventually found a lorry leaving for Altai, our next town. A deal struck, I headed back out to let Sue know all was sorted and that a lorry would be coming shortly, but my GPS had packed in some time ago, after the bikes had been power washed by our biker pals in Omsk, and I couldn't find my way back with so many tracks to choose from.

Eventually I found Sue, just minutes before the lorry arrived. Even then, as we struggled to raise her bike on to the top of the lorry, the penny didn't drop that the only working GPS, and the only map we had, was being raised ten feet into the air to continue the journey on the lorry. I had made a serious blunder. The lorry was slow, we would be travelling at night, so I cut out and went on ahead, little knowing that the lorry kept breaking down behind me. I was now navigating alone across the Altai Desert and Mountains with nothing but the memory that Altai was due east, plus the use of an old Silva walking compass I always carried. The lorry eventually made it to Altai late the next day and, with

the bikes ensconced in the hotel foyer, we were relieved to find the cause for Sue's gearbox malady to be nothing more serious than a stone between the gearbox casing and sprocket, locking everything up.

We spent a week in Ulaan Bataar before heading south through the Gobi Desert to the Chinese border at Zamyn-Udd, some 550 miles away. It took us five days, staying in hotels at Choir and Sainshand and also camping. The night sky seen from the Gobi Desert was incredibly beautiful. We had the necessary visas for crossing into China and spent a day trying to get through, but the motorcycles didn't have the vital – and difficult to obtain – paperwork. The next day we found a friendly truck and, with some help from the Mongolian border officials, loaded the bikes and were cleared by them to cross the border. Well, there wouldn't have been a problem but for a young border official, vying for promotion maybe, who spotted the bikes. We were promptly arrested. They

should have thrown the book at us, for we were clearly guilty of a severe transgression of the law, but the Chinese border officials helped us all they could before finally returning us to Mongolia.

We had a single entry visa for Mongolia and yet we entered, and exited, three times! It was late when we were returned from China – the Mongolian side would be closing their gates in ten minutes and we didn't want to be stuck in the two kilometres of 'no man's land'. While the young border guard was closing the Chinese gates for the night, his radio blaring out to let us pass, Sue got all excited and promptly fell off her bike. The lad didn't know whether to go to her help or reopen the gates, the panic written on his young face.

We eventually made it back to the Mongolian border where familiar faces greeted us as the barrier went up, and then dropped down behind us, for the last time that day.

Our planned route was now out of the window. We'd

planned to ride through China following the southern Silk Route via the Taklimakan Desert to Turpan, and then cross the Tien Shan Mountains to the tenth-century Caravanserai at Tash Rabat in Kyrgyzstan. Now we would have to go north.

We returned through Mongolia to Ulaan Bataar via the night train. Negotiating our passage on the train and the loading of the two motorcycles would have been impossible had it not been for the young guy and his girlfriend who tapped me on the shoulder at the railway station and asked if they could help. He was Mongolian, could speak excellent English, and was to spend the best part of the day with us. The friendship of strangers never ceased to amaze us. We had to give 'baksheesh' to the stationmaster, for the bikes were well over the allowed weight for 'hand luggage'.

In Ulaan Bataar Russian visas were obtained and we continued our 'Long Way Home' north to Lake Baikal, Irkutsk and then headed south for Kazakhstan's Semipalatinsk (where the Russians tested their atom bombs in the 1950s) and Almaty. Into Kyrgyzstan we headed for Lake Issyk-Kul, with Naryn and Tash Rabat in our sights. We would be back on the old Silk Route again, picking up our original planned route.

We had a couple of days at Karakol, where we took time out for a swim in Lake Issyk-Kul, teaching the local kids how to dive down and pick up a stone from the bottom of the lake. They found this fascinating and clearly had never done it before.

Keeping on the old Silk Route we headed towards Naryn and then to Tash Rabat where we stayed for a couple of days in a Ger while we walked in the Tien Shan. Tash Rabat is an ancient fortress, a Caravanserai, where the camel trains would rest up and be protected from marauding robbers.

En route Sue's bike began to slow down, with a very noticeable loss of power. The cause was soon found to be the rear brake master cylinder sticking, causing the pads to bind on the disc. The piston couldn't be freed off sufficiently, so the caliper piston was shoved away from the pads and, for the time being, Sue wasn't to use the rear brake. My offer to swap our rear brake master cylinders was refused so, to be fair and to keep things equal, I volunteered not to use my rear brake either. Descending a steep gravel track road I honestly intended not to use it but, whispering an apology, I applied it just at the point when Sue, riding behind me, crashed to the ground amid a shower of gravel and curses. Later we were able to collect and fit a replacement master cylinder in Osh, our friends at Rainbow Motorcycles in Rotherham having sent it out to us by DHL. This was the second time Rainbow and DHL had come up trumps. While in Ulaan Bataar DHL ferried us out to the airport to collect a replacement GPS unit and help us with the paperwork and customs clearance.

Still in Kyrgyzstan, we had four days resting up in Osh, fitting the rear brake master cylinder and climbing Mount Suleiman, which rises up steeply from the Fergana Valley. The sacred Mount Suleiman is a UNESCO World Heritage Site and has been a place of pilgrimage for centuries. We had befriended Mira and Erkin from the hotel and learned much about Kyrgyzstan and its people from them.

Leaving Osh we were almost immediately into Uzbekistan. We played our game at the border and Sue said 90 minutes. I went under and we were through in 45 minutes, something of a record. In Tashkent, Uzbekistan's

'Arrested' by friendly Russian bike cops

Altai Desert, Mongolia

capital city, we sought out the five-star Intercontinental Hotel to change some money, but then Sue came out and announced we would be staying there. Why they should welcome two grubby 'overlanding' motorcyclists with dirty, dusty kit I don't know, but welcome us they did: we were treated like royalty and the manager even got the bellboy to change us some money via the back door of the bank, and at a better rate than if we'd gone through the front door. The bikes were looked after by the hotel's very conspicuous police presence.

Now we were heading west and the time zones were retreating. We had been eight hours ahead of the UK while in eastern Mongolia, where we had been on the same longitude as the North West Cape of Australia. In Samarkand, a UNESCO World Heritage City described as 'the crossroads of cultures', we were five hours ahead of

GMT. We visited the Bibi-Khanym Mosque and just had to touch the beautiful mosaic tiles. It was difficult to believe that we had ridden here, to this ancient city in Uzbekistan, by motorcycle. We were living a dream.

In Bukhara I learned another lesson from Sue. We pulled up to look for a hotel and immediately a taxi stopped and offered to take us to one. At the same time a young lad had left his small stall of chewing gum and cigarettes to come over to help us. I was all for the taxi driver but Sue persuaded me to go with the boy, so we followed him down back streets, one-way streets (the wrong way) and thus to the Hotel Nodirbek where we were made very welcome and the bikes were parked inside. It happened to be Sue's birthday, and later all the staff turned out to sing 'Happy Birthday' to her.

We each saw a carpet we liked, in separate shops, and

↑ **Servicing the bikes in Ulan Bataar**

↑ Safe parking in the Khovd Hotel

cross in order to get to Turkmenbashi, where we were hoping to blag a lift across the Caspian Sea to Baku in Azerbaijan. The police stopped us regularly and each time all our details were hand-written down in giant ledgers – it took time and it was hot! – but we were offered balls of salt the size of gobstoppers to suck on at each checkpoint, to replenish that lost in sweating.

We rode into Turkmenbashi to see a large train-carrying ship moored up where the railway lines finished. We looked at each other and, smiling, gave the thumbs up and I shouted across to Sue, ''That'll do nicely!'' Huge amounts of paperwork were generated, all stamped several times by different people in different offices, and we were ready to exit Turkmenistan – but not before customs wanted all the panniers, roll bags and so on unloaded for searching. I was thinking 'carpets' as I began to unfasten the first strap, but fortunately the officials on the boat wanted us to board 'pronto', so we were ushered forward. The customs people wouldn't have noticed my deep sigh of relief as we rode up the ramp between the railway lines, but euphoria soon turned to fear as the guy indicated for us to move across to the other side of the boat. This necessitated crossing two sets of railway lines on a greasy ramp and at an incline, but neither of us fell off and we'd soon secured the bikes between large railway oil tankers. It was grubby and smelly, but we were out of Turkmenistan.

The boat was secured for sea but still we didn't sail for another eight hours. It wasn't a passenger ship, just an oil freight train tanker ship, but we did manage to secure one of the crew's cabins for a very modest US$20, and that meant a reasonably comfortable crossing. Eventually, at 1am, we reached the port of Baku in Azerbaijan, some 30 hours after boarding.

We rode into the night, unwilling to pay US$250 for a hotel in Baku, and eventually found a truck stop where, at 4am, we were offered cushions to crash out on for an hour or two, on the seats alongside a picnic table. I had a beer and there was a pot of tea for Sue before we catnapped. When I went to pay the owner before we left he wouldn't accept any payment and even gave us breakfast 'on the house'.

We were on a roller coaster now, heading west, heading home, and pulling the time zones back. From Azerbaijan we rode through Georgia, Turkey, Greece, Macedonia, Kosovo, Montenegro, Croatia, Bosnia and Slovenia. We stayed with old friends in Turkey and in Slovenia found the Hotel Lucija in Most-na-Soci, which I now use for my tours.

A reception committee was waiting for us at the Hotel Forsthaus in the German Eifel, and again at Hull when we

bargained for them with no thought of how to get them home. We weren't sure about the lead identity seals tagged on to the carpets, or if there were any restrictions on taking them out of the country, so we removed the seals, kept them 'just in case', and then folded and hid the carpets in our camping gear, where they remained until we reached home.

The border with Turkmenistan was just 60 miles away but it took us five hours to get through it. We only had a transit visa for Turkmenistan and so had to stop on a designated route, which took us into Mary, the provincial capital city, in the dark. At a checkpoint the police immediately stopped the next car and instructed its driver to take us to a hotel, which he did quite willingly, but by then it was too late for food, the barman was miserable, we were tired and there was no hot water. The barman poured me a drink from a bottle of beer I'd identified as being suitable, but it took Sue to tell me that there were still a couple of inches left in the bottle when he put it down, out of sight, behind the bar. That didn't happen the next time!

After Ashgabat we had the Peski Karakum Desert to

alighted from the overnight ferry. We were escorted back to Rainbow Motorcycles where it had all begun six months earlier. We'd been on the road for six months and had covered 19,250 miles (30,918km) through 25 countries. While the 'what ifs' were dismissed from our minds within a couple of weeks of starting the trip, incidents did happen, but we soon learned that there was nothing that couldn't be sorted. The words of advice from Kevin and Julia Sanders were ever present in our minds: "Plan, plan by all means, but don't plan too much because it will restrict your itinerary. The problems you envisage will not be the problems you encounter, the problems you'll encounter will be a total surprise to you." How true that was!

Sue and I were both nudging 60 when we set off and we had absolutely no idea what we were getting into. An Indian girl studying in Semipalatinsk couldn't believe that we could manage to get by in so many countries without speaking the lingo. I didn't tell her my trump card was cartoon drawings – someone snoring in bed, a tent with a motorcycle alongside, a petrol pump, a knife, fork and spoon – all laminated and produced when necessary, and always eliciting the required result!

One everlasting memory of this trip, confirmed again with a later trip through Iran and Pakistan, is the overwhelming hospitality of total strangers. The less people have the more they share with you.

For more information, log on to: adventure.gs

MICK WHEELER

Mick Wheeler – Aged 59 and a bike cop for most of his 30 years' service in the police; retired at the age of 49 as a Police Class 1 Instructor. With motorcycling in his blood from birth, Mick started his own 'Advanced Riding Techniques' advanced rider training school, even flying out to Turkey to train motorcycle groups there. His wife died in 2003.

SUE WILSON

Sue Wilson – Aged 56 and married, Sue had pedal-cycled everywhere in a former life, including all round Australia, and backpacked around Iceland. Realising that with an engine one could travel further and with much less effort, Sue took up motorcycling rather late in life, at the age of 48. She passed her Institute of Advanced Motorcycling test in July 1999 and went on to be an official IAM observer. As a child she had read of Genghis Khan and the Mongol Empire and, for some reason, Mongolia remained in her subconscious mind for many years. With her new-found wings her motorcycling would have to take her somewhere far and distant.

Somewhere over the rainbow, Mongolia

Six Years Around the

World

All images: Adam Lewis

Rider	**Adam Lewis**
Route	**Round the world**
Date	**Departed March 2006 and still on the road...**
Distance	**155,300 miles (250,000km) as of January 2013**
Duration	**Uncertain, but 53 countries visited so far**
Bikes	**BMW F650 GS, then switched to Suzuki DR650. Suzuki DRZ400 as of March 2013**
Budget Estimate	**£11,000, per annum (excluding original bike purchase)**

TIPS

- Don't over-plan – things will change constantly once you're out on the road
- A bike cover is a wonderful security device – you will be amazed by how invisible it makes your bike
- Hide a small amount of money and perhaps a credit card somewhere on the bike so that if you get mugged while out on foot, all is not lost
- A Tupperware-style box is useful for tools to stop them corroding
- Take an adaptor that not only plugs into everything but that everything can be plugged into
- Ensure you can bank online
- Make sure your carnet starts from when you first need it, not from when you first leave home as it is only valid for 12 months
- Travel light – it means less to carry up the six flights of stairs to where the 'cheap' rooms in the hotel are usually located

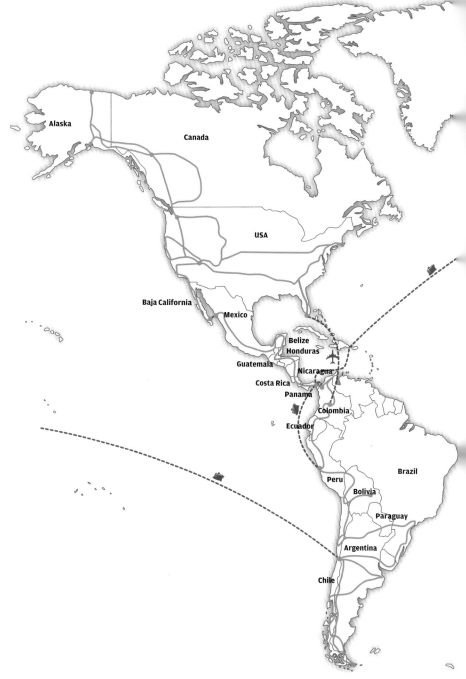

Key

—— **Route completed**
—— **Route continued**
----- **Air / Sea freight**

Alaska

Canada

USA

Baja California

Mexico

Belize
Honduras

Guatemala

Nicaragua

Costa Rica

Panama

Colombia

Ecuador

Peru

Brazil

Bolivia

Paraguay

Argentina

Chile

When I left home with my friend Danny Burroughs back in 2006 I had no idea that by mid-2013 I'd still be travelling. Our original plan had been to send all our snowboarding gear to New Zealand, spend a year riding there (on two modified BMW F650 GS machines), a winter season snowboarding, then a year riding through the Americas, eventually shipping the bikes back to the UK from eastern Canada or the USA.

We left on St Patrick's Day 2006 and rode through some serious snow across Germany, swapping our bikes for snowboards for a day in Slovenia before cruising down the beautiful Adriatic coast through Croatia, Montenegro and Albania. In Istanbul we bought tyres, procured Syrian and Iranian visas (the Iranian one had been arranged online via an agency in Shiraz) and spent a couple of days at the MotoGP.

Joining the dots of various archaeological sites we worked our way around the country in an anti-clockwise direction, punctuated by a southerly detour into Syria and finishing up under the shadow of Mount Ararat at Dogubeyazit, where we crossed into Iran.

In Pakistan we skirted the Afghan border for 400 miles (645km) through the tribal region of Baluchistan to Quetta. From there we were sent on a 1,000-mile (1,610km) detour to Peshawar as the direct route was deemed too dangerous. Finally, among the stunning Karakoram and Hindu Kush mountain ranges, we could relax. We camped on the Shandur Pass and watched polo matches, broke our bikes on the Babusa Pass, and got sick after living on goat's cheese while trekking in the Hindu Kush.

Three months later we rode within 31 miles (50km) of where we'd been on the Deosai Plateau, only on that occasion we were on the Indian side of the border having ridden the famous (for good reason) Manali to Leh 'Highway' in Ladakh. Our passion for the mountains meant that during our three months in India we didn't venture south of Risikesh, itself some 125 miles (200km) north of Delhi.

With Burma (Myanmar) closed to through traffic we headed for Kathmandu and, after trekking in the Annapurna region, we air freighted the bikes from Kathmandu to Bangkok and spent Christmas on the beach, en route to the emotional roller-coaster ride that is Cambodia. We entered Laos through its most southerly border and exited through its most northerly, riding the length of Thailand en route to Malaysia, from where we

shipped the bikes to New Zealand. At this point we'd been on the road for 13 months.

Once in New Zealand we bought a van for travelling to and from the mountains on a daily basis, rented a house in Queenstown with two young English party animals that we'd met along the way, and collected our season passes. Unfortunately New Zealand's 2007 winter season proved to be the worst in years. In fact it only snowed four times all season and so, in August, I loaded my bike and spent two weeks riding and camping along the west coast.

By the time the season came to an end Danny had found a job and decided to stay on in New Zealand. For me it was decision time – 'go home or go it alone'. It was an easy decision, though, and in early October 2007 I said goodbye to the lads and set off solo. A month later I air

↓ Treacherous road conditions block the route to Kranska Gora in Slovenia

freighted my bike from Auckland to Sydney and within three hours of landing I rode out into the Sydney traffic, where I promptly ran out of gas!

I went on to spend nine months 'Down Under' and rode 22,400 miles (36,000km), including many of the famous outback roads such as the Great Central Track and the Gibb River Road. I took in a 'lap' of Tasmania, the World Superbike race at Phillip Island and the Horizons Unlimited Travellers' meeting at Tintaldra.

Along the way I hooked up with Englishman Tim Hobin, whom I'd first met in Pakistan in 2006. He'd recently bought a well-prepared DR650 in Sydney and we rode together for a few months, bumping into English legend Linda Bootherstone (aka Bick) along the way. Linda (who was also DR650 mounted) had ridden from Germany, celebrating her 60th birthday in India along the way.

The price of accommodation not only forced me into camping but also, more specifically, into 'bush' camping as the Aussies call it (free/rough camping to everybody else) and I soon became hooked. I didn't spend a single night in a hostel, hotel or roadhouse and less than a handful on commercial sites. I was taken in by several friendly local families on my travels and was fed and watered by many more as I made the most of the Australian '24hr max stay' in roadside parking areas. On many occasions I would finish pitching my tent among the camper vans only to be met with: "You don't wanna be cooking/making your own fire/drinking warm beer, etc. … come over and share ours." Australians certainly know how to enjoy the outback and they make foreign travellers extremely welcome.

My anti-clockwise loop took me to Darwin at a time when oil had reached US$130 per barrel. The quote I'd

received for air freight from Sydney to Santiago in Chile was from a time when it was 'only' US$100. The financial crash of 2008 was starting to have an effect on the sterling exchange rate and the interest on my savings had become negligible. I needed a new plan. As I researched the cost of sea freight as an alternative I learned that there was no direct shipping route from Australia to South America. Everything went via Singapore or Hong Kong. My immediate thought was "I can ride to Singapore!"

Aware of a ship that sailed from Darwin to Dili (and on to Singapore) I aborted my plan to return to Sydney and shipped my bike to East Timor. Without a return/onward plane ticket, obtaining a visa for Indonesia took a bit of negotiating. After much arguing with the guy in the embassy I finally persuaded him to converse with a colleague over my claim that my Carnet de Passage (CDP) was sufficient proof that I would be travelling overland and enter/exit via land/sea borders respectively. A 60-day visa was duly issued.

The original CDP had expired while the bikes were at sea, en route from Malaysia to New Zealand, and Danny had collected new ones when visiting his parents in the UK prior to flying to New Zealand. With the help of Paul Gowan at the RAC I was able to extend my second CDP in Australia, but only until the expiration date of my visa. Fortunately I had a year's visa and so the extension meant I had three months in which to get my bike aboard a ship in Singapore.

The smell of rotting rubbish and open sewers slapped me in the face as I walked into Dili town for the first time. It was good to be back in Asia. Dili itself was still overrun by UN officials and, as many will know, that generally means overly inflated prices, so as soon as I collected my bike I rode out into the countryside.

⬆ **Albania brought the first taste of gravel roads**

⬇ **'Danny of Arabia'**

↑ Submerged boulders are no fun when you're 5'4"

↓ There was a convoy of these around the next bend

→ Another water pump failure on the F 650 – Adam replaces his in India

East Timor shares the island of Timor with West Timor (Indonesia), the two separated by a friendly (to foreigners anyway) land border. Over the next few months I took my life in my hands as I skipped from island to island aboard hand-me-down ferries long since decommissioned from the Greek islands. Timor – Flores – Sumbawa – Lombok – Bali – Java and finally Sumatra; each place had its own flavour, food and religion. From hiking a live volcano to snorkelling a wreck and trekking through the jungle in search of orangutans, Indonesia has a lot to offer. I do, however, recommend avoiding Ramadan on Sumatra or you'll be rather hungry, as I was.

With no vehicle ferry operating between Sumatra and Malaysia, leaving the world's sixth-largest island took some researching. Eventually I ended up handing over my bike and a huge wad of cash to a guy in a warehouse following a meeting in a taxi drivers' café. Any concerns were soon quashed when I arrived at the port in Butterworth and saw 'Lady P' sitting in the warehouse, with no ill-effects from her time aboard the timber ship she'd arrived aboard.

With my bike finally in a crate in a warehouse in Singapore it was time to make my way to Chile. Plane tickets via Australia were so expensive that I ended up flying via the Middle East, Europe and Brazil, visiting my sister in Jersey along the way – all for less money than the Australia/New Zealand option.

Axel Heilenkotter, importer of Sherco motorcycles into Chile (and a 2013 Dakar competitor) helped me retrieve my bike from the port in Valparaiso before we headed to Argentina for New Year in Buenos Aires and the start of

Khardung La, Ladakh, India: The world's highest motorable pass

the inaugural South American Dakar Rally. We followed the rally for four days until it reached its most southerly point at which time I said 'Hasta luego' to Axel and turned south for the ferry to Chaitén, the Carretera Austral, Ruta 40 and the notorious winds of Patagonia.

After a few days in Ushuaia I followed Ruta 40 north to Mendoza before turning east to Uruguay and following the Atlantic coast to Rio de Janeiro. The Iguazu Falls were followed by Paraguay and a blast across the plains back

to the Andes and an east–west crossing of Paso Sico to Chile and a west–east return crossing of Paso San Francisco to Argentina.

Little did I know it at the time, but Bolivia was to prove a huge turning point in my journey. After spending some time in Sucré, in an attempt to learn some Spanish, I set off around the country, celebrating my birthday camped alone in the middle of the Salar de Uyuni, the world's largest salt flat – a truly spectacular experience.

It was on a track to the north of the Salar that my Ohlins rear suspension unit broke – again. Danny and I had incurred multiple failures in India, Cambodia and Malaysia and after much 'negotiating' Ohlins had agreed to repair them both under warranty as a 'token of goodwill', and the supplier begrudgingly undertook the work. Now mine had failed again, snapping the side off the aluminium U-bracket at the base of the unit, among other issues. Despite contacting every Ohlins dealer in South America and both the USA and UK importers, nobody had that part in stock. Ohlins Sweden (the manufacturer) refused to deal with me directly, insisting that I had to go through one of their importers. Both my visa and Temporary Import Document (for the bike) were running out and eventually I managed to find a guy who stick-welded the aluminium U-bracket back together as a temporary repair.

Back at the hostel I was in the throes of refitting the shock when the needles belonging to the roller bearing in the rear

STATISTICS

- **Hottest day:** Multan–Peshawar, Pakistan 48°C (118°F)
- **Hardest day:** Babusa Pass, Pakistan – it took 13 hours to ride just 45 miles (73km) and many parts were broken or damaged
- **Worst day:** Sukkur–Multan (Pakistan) with a police escort
- **Worst food:** Pakistan
- **Most sick:** Pakistan
- **Cheapest petrol:** Venezuela – so cheap I didn't even calculate it! 0.1Bolivar/litre. On the black market I got 8 Bolivars for U$1. It was basically free!
- **Most expensive petrol:** Turkey £1.25 per litre
- **Longest Day:** 1109km from Valparaiso north to a bush camp
- **Highest altitude:** Khardung La, Ladakh (India) – 17,552ft (5,350m)
- **Longest continuous rainfall:** Shrinigar, Kashmir (India) – 72 hours
- **Longest time without seeing rain:** MacLeodganj (India)–Nong Khiaw (Laos) – five months

↑ 'Glad I wasn't coming the other way!' Mahendra Highway, Nepal

↗ The road disappeared into the water – then we spotted the ferry. Loading up in Nepal

→ Don't carry all your eggs in one pannier!

linkage fell out and rolled all over the floor. That was the final straw. I'd already replaced all the linkage bearings four times since leaving England. Along with a stretched pair of link-arms I'd also replaced the steering head bearings four times (despite fabricating a tool to allow their fitting, as per the BMW service manual), four water pumps and numerous batteries.

If I wanted to continue along the routes I'd planned to follow I needed a more suitable, lighter, off-road-friendly set-up. To cut a long story short, that's exactly what I did. I stayed on the tarmac from La Paz to Lima on Peru's Pacific coast and shipped my BMW to Hamburg. I'd already decided that (based on the experiences of Tim Hobin and many others I'd met along the way) a Suzuki DR650 was the bike for me. An online search pulled up a few potentials and I eventually settled on a three-year-old model with 2,400 miles (3,860km) on the clock and a fair list of modifications. The owner was an aircraft engineer and the bike looked immaculate in the photos. A deal was done and I flew into Salt Lake City, registered it and rode it to a friend's house near Boston. I then flew to Hamburg, collected my BMW and rode it to my sister's in Jersey where I spent Christmas before returning to Boston to prepare my DR650.

In the spring of 2010 I boarded 'Rosie' and set off around the USA, Canada and Alaska, before turning south to 'fill in the gap' between there and Peru. My new set-up, complete with soft bags, was somewhere in the region of 198lb (90kg) lighter than my previous machine. It was a revelation and completely transformed my journey.

No longer did I need to consider the potential for getting stuck before heading off the beaten track. On Rosie I could go anywhere, and camp anywhere, in the knowledge that I could get myself out of any situation in which I found myself. None of the 'dual-sport route-arounds' were necessary on the Trans America Trail, while the sandy trails of Baja were fun rather than traumatic. Accessing parking spots in guest houses was a breeze, as was loading Rosie on and off several tiny boats.

I went on to spend a further two years in the Americas, taking a boat from Panama to Colombia and exploring areas of the High Andes I'd previously only dreamt of. I crossed the Amazon on the Trans Amazonican 'road' from Porto Vehlo to Santarem, took a boat to Macapá and rode north through the Guianas, taking in New Year's Eve 2011/12 in Suriname along the way.

With no land border between Guyana and Venezuela I returned to Brazil and finally entered Venezuela through the magnificent Gran Sabana. Back in Colombia I air freighted Rosie from Bogota to Miami, Florida and rode up the east coast of the USA to my friends near Boston, arriving almost two years to the day after leaving in 2010.

It had been six years, 53 countries and 155,300 miles (250,000km) since leaving home, and I had finally completed the journey I'd set out on.

So What Have I Learned?

Lots. It has been and continues to be the greatest education of my life. On a daily basis I am shocked, bewildered, frustrated and humbled. I have learnt how even the simplest of pleasures taste sweetest when hard earned, but most of all I have learned how fortunate I am to have been born in a free country and to hold a passport that is accepted the world over.

Mine was a journey within a journey. Obviously there was

⬆ **Solitude – surrounded by 10,000km² of salt flats on Bolivia's Salar de Uyuni**

⬇ **Frustration – stuck...again on the 'road' to Lake Eyre, Australia**

the physical journey, but the evolution of how I travelled, the bike I rode, the equipment I carried and how I carried it can be construed as a second journey. I'm pleased to say that neither is concluded.

The best decision I've made since leaving home was to continue solo when faced with the alternative of returning home. The second was the decision to change my bike and thereby the way in which I executed my journey.

After the first four years I started thinking about the countries I'd passed through during the early years. Many (including Iran) I'd like to return to; I was a very 'green' traveller in those days and I feel I would 'get among it' more if I were to return.

How the World Has Changed

The world's political climate, though, is constantly changing and as one door (country, border) opens so another closes. I have very fond memories of both Syria and Pakistan. The latter was a real adventure and it's sad to see that many of the areas we travelled through are now deemed off-limits and dangerous. Syria is a tragedy. The people are wonderful and the country full of history, from the castles of Krak des Chevaliers and Saladin to the water wheels of Hama and the Great Mosques of Aleppo and Damascus – buildings dating back 900 years. I'm glad I had the opportunity to visit these fascinating countries when I did.

During my initial research, back in 2004, I received a reply to an email I'd sent to the workshop manager of BMW Iran asking about the opinion of the people regarding the West. The reply I received read: "People are people and politics are politics. Be sure to visit us when you come."

When we entered the country in 2006 it was World Cup year and Iran had made it into the competition. "We'll be knocked out in the group stages, but when we are we'll be supporting England" was a statement we heard on several occasions, regularly followed by chants of "Beckham!!!" and "Rooney!!!" I wonder if we'd receive the same reception now that the UK has allied itself with the US with regards to sanctions.

Bikes and Equipment

As I've said, changing my bike changed my journey and so choosing the right bike is an important decision. What's right for you undertaking a given journey may not be right for someone else. If you want to cruise along the Pan American Highway from one Wi-Fi-enabled hotel to the next then ride what you want and pack what you want. If you want to get off the beaten track and explore then there's no substitute for a light(er) bike and kit.

As for camping gear, I wouldn't be without it. Apart from my initial ride from Salt Lake City to Boston, a journey of 2,400 miles (3,800km) for which I was

Western Bolivia – the riverbed was soft sand so I chanced the bridge

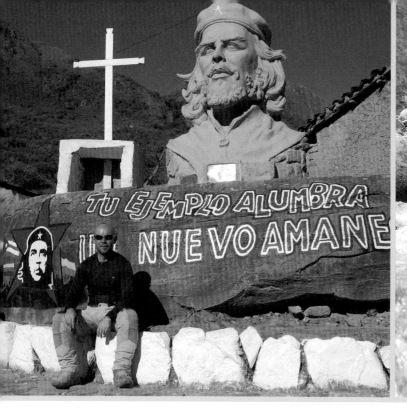

A day to remember – together with American John Martin (aka Throttlemeister) we became the first foreigners ever to visit the next village along this trail in the Colombian heartland. Hard to believe it ended with a few beers in a thermal spring!

Chillin' with Che. La Higuera where Che Guevara was finally captured in 1967 (Ruta del Che) in Bolivia

There's a new bridge between Brazil and French Guiana. Why it remains closed depends on whose story you believe. I took a boat

My view for 1,600km – riding Brazil's Transamazonica

FIND OUT MORE

For further reading, or to follow my journey into 2013 and beyond, visit:
www.ShortWayRound.co.uk and www.facebook.com/ShortWayRound

unprepared, I didn't spend a single night in a hotel/motel/ guest house throughout Australia, the USA (including Alaska) and Canada. The budget connotations alone are obvious, never mind the sense of freedom and satisfaction I get from being able to sleep pretty much wherever I want.

Over the years what I carry and how I carry it has evolved, and continues to do so. Some gear has broken or worn out, other gear has been replaced with my adoption of the 'less is more' approach. Just the realisation that I didn't need to be able to completely strip and rebuild my bike roadside (anything major would require a pick-up truck ride to town) combined with a more tool-friendly Japanese bike reduced my toolkit weight from 12.6lb (5.75kg) for the BMW to just 3.85lb (1.75kg) for the Suzuki. All up, my kit weighs 66lb (30kg), including tools and spares but not food and water. Almost 13lb (6kg) of that is made up of electronics, including a laptop, DSLR camera, second lens and associated paraphernalia.

The Future

It was always going to be a transitional year in 2012 – I needed to carry out some maintenance on my house that I rent out, top up my funds, and plan and prepare for the next 'leg' of my journey. With my maintenance work completed I headed to the Indian Himalayas where I spent the summer working as a tour guide for Blazing Trails Tours, a position to which I shall return in November 2013, combining it with my ongoing travels.

As I look ahead to 2013 I realise how 'spoiled' I was as a European riding through the Americas. With the exception of Suriname (ironically, the former British Guyana) I obtained every visa at the border. Now, as I contemplate the next stage of my journey in Central Asia, Siberia and Mongolia, I am faced with not only securing visas in advance but also 'letters of introduction', transit visas, visas valid for specific dates and a host of regional permits. All of this means I need a plan, something to which I have become rather unaccustomed.

Adam and Danny undertook a significant number of modifications to their BMWs as illustrated by the following table:

MODIFICATION	REASON	SUPPLIER	COMMENTS
21" Front Wheel	Better handling off road & more ground clearance	Talon rim & spokes built on original hub	Use in conjunction with modified rear shock
Stiffer fork springs	Better handling particularly when loaded	Touratech	
Fork sliders	Protect fork stanchions from stone chips	Touratech	Can use gaiters
2003 Dakar screen	Improved wind protection	BMW	Needs home-made adaptor bracket if using on 2004 model as previous models use a 3-hole fixing
Radiator guards	Stone protection	Touratech	
Handlebar risers (65mm)	Gain clearance between handguards & clocks; More upright riding position when standing	Touratech	Requires longer front brake hose
Magura oversize handlebars	Strength. Magura are only company that make heated grip compatible bars	Touratech	Can use any brand if not using heated grips
Handguards/Brushguards	Protect levers in crashes	Acerbis	
GPS Mounting bracket mounting	Braceless handle bars	Homemade	
GPS Mounting bracket	Vibration proof lockable mounting	Touratech	Mounts to handlebar brace – see above
Large fuel tanks (39-litre)	Balance loaded bike. Patagonia/Australian outback	Touratech	Supplied unpainted. Replace breather hoses with approved fuel pipe. Carry spare O-ring for Q/R fittings
Auxiliary wiring	Charging laptop, camera batteries, phone etc	Homemade	Use ignition-fed circuit to avoid blown fuses
Hawker battery	Long life. Deep discharge.		Adam's failed in Iran – faulty.
Sump guard/bash plate	Protect engine cases	Overland Solutions	
Engine crash bars	Protect engine in a crash	BMW	Had to modify to use with Touratech 39-litre fuel tanks as both items use same mounting point in front of engine
Footrests	Larger size for better foothold	Racespec	Motocross size footrests. Require custom mountings
Sidestand/Footrest mountings	Improved design. Weight pushes through length of stand. Larger foot for soft ground. Mountings to suit non-standard footrests	Overland Solutions	

MODIFICATION	REASON	SUPPLIER	COMMENTS
Centre stand	Needs lengthening to suit suspension mods	Overland Solutions	Dakar models come without a centre stand
Rear suspension unit	Improved ride quality especially when loaded	Ohlins	Dakar shock shortened to mid point between GS and Dakar length. Plain bearing fitted in cylinder head. Sprung and re-valved to suit load
Pannier frames and rack	For effective load carrying	Overland Solutions	Custom made. Inc 'hidden' tool/spares boxes. Adjustable to allow for a pillion
Pannier boxes	For effective load carrying	Touratech	Modified by Overland Solutions. Anodised, lockable clasps to suit frames. Stronger lockable lid clasps
Registration plate brace	Strengthen mudguard assembly	Touratech	
Chainguard/Speed sensor protector	Replace bulky enclosed OE item	Touratech	
Exhaust system	Remove catalytic converter for using leaded fuel	Remus	
Scottoiler	Extended chain life	Scottoiler	Use large 'touring' kit. Carry a few spare 'injectors' and the screw-on nozzle for re-filling
Grease nipples	Longevity. Ease of servicing		Fitted to swing arm and bottom suspension linkage
Braided steel brake hoses	Extra length required for handlebar risers. Improved braking performance	Venhill	
Headlight bulb	Improved performance bulbs		
Flexible indicators	Bend in a crash	Touratech	
Folding gear lever	Fold up in a crash	Touratech	Modified to operate correctly when wearing boots
Clutch lever – adjustable span	To suit small hands	Wunderlich	
Bike-to-bike jump start kit	Easy jump-starting of bikes	Wunderlich	Access to battery requires removal of rack, seat and cover. Add a fuse
Auxiliary power socket mounting	Requires moving when fitting 39-litre fuel tanks	Homemade	
Communications system	Bike-to-bike communications. Music via MP3	Autocom	

World Altitude Record

↓ Ojos Del Salado, 6,361 metres, the
highest a motorcycle has ever been
📷 Lukas Matzinger

Riders	**Walter Colebatch (UK/Australia), Barton Churchill (USA), Lukas Matzinger (Austria)**
Route	**La Serena, Copiapo, Ojos del Salado**
Date	**March 2012**
Distance	**932 miles (1,500 km) return**
Duration	**3 weeks**
Bikes	**Husaberg 570FE**
Budget Estimate	**1,000 pounds per person (excluding shipping and equipment)**

HUSABERG 570FE

- **565.5cc single-cylinder competition-level enduro bike**
- **Haan wheels, cush drive, Golden Tyre GT 216 tyres and mousses**
- **Rekluse auto-clutch**
- **ProMotoBillet/Fastway Adventure foot pegs**
- **Highway Dirtbikes handguards, bar risers, integrated mirrors and switches**
- **Akrapovic titanium exhaust**
- **BurnsMoto weatherproof USB power sockets**
- **Giant Loop Coyote tail bags that need no rack**
- **Bullet Proof Designs radiator, swingarm and disc guards**

PERU

BOLIVIA

PARAGUAY

CHILE

Atacama
Desert

Copiapó   Ojos del Salado

Vallenar

ARGENTINA

La Serena ⭐

⭐
Santiago

Adventure rides don't come much bigger than this. In March 2012 three hardened explorers – Walter Colebatch, Barton Churchill and Lukas Matzinger – embarked on an epic challenge to set a new motorcycle altitude record. The current record belonged to the North Calcutta Disha Motorcycle Club, a group of Indian bikers who reached 20,489ft (6,245m) riding Hero Hondas. After years of planning, Colebatch and his team headed for Chile with the aim of beating the long-standing record. This is how they did it…

After shipping three Husaberg 570FEs to South America, we completed our final preparations at the KTM dealer in La Serena. From there we rode north along the highway to Copiapo, the last town before the real adventure in the mountain wilderness began.

On arrival at Copiapo, altitude 1,230ft (375m), we stocked up on 300 litres of drinking water and 200 litres of petrol. Copiapo is where civilisation ends, and just a few miles out it became crystal clear that we'd arrived in the stunning Atacama Desert. From here on in there was no water, no trees, no animals, no mobile phone coverage, no Internet, nothing – just an old road that begins to climb as soon as it leaves the city limits.

⬇ **Starting point was sea level, the beach at La Serena**
📷 Andes Moto Extreme

Reaching the landmarks of 1,640ft (500m), 3,280ft (1,000m), 4,920ft (1,500m), 6,560ft (2,000m) and 8,200ft (2,500m) was easy and just part of a very gradual climb along a series of poorly surfaced asphalt roads. But by 9,840ft (3,000m) the adventure began to feel very real – civilisation was now a long way behind us and we were already making our way into the high mountains.

Just over two hours later the three of us, along with our support crew of Sherri Jo Wilkins driving the 4x4, pulled into our first acclimatisation camp – Laguna Santa Rosa, located at 12,369ft (3,770m). Despite being some 8,200ft (2,500m) off our target, the altitude and lack of oxygen were already taking their toll; there was only approximately 65% of the oxygen that we'd enjoyed at sea level.

In an effort to give ourselves the best possible chance of breaking the record, we knew we had to take time to acclimatise to the altitude. After 48 hours we moved on to Ojos del Salado, the world's highest volcano at 22,615ft (6,893m), a few miles from the Argentine border. We were now at Camp Murray, 14,852ft (4,527m), with oxygen at 55% of what you'd experience at sea level, making everything we did literally twice as difficult.

We changed to our mountain wheels, sprockets, tyres

⬆ **Camp Atacama, at 5,265 metres is the base camp for mountaineering expeditions on Ojos del Salado. Even in the peak of summer morning temperatures were around –10°C**
📷 Walter Colebatch

⬇ **Three separate GPSs confirm the record, 6,361 metres (20,869 feet)**
📷 Walter Colebatch

and mousses and were able to make an initial reconnaissance ride up the mountain. Despite the thin air, the fuel-injected Husabergs behaved perfectly, firing up and idling without issue. Our initial ride took us up to 19,505ft (5,945m). Getting to this height wasn't a problem, but anything above that was going to be difficult because, wherever we looked, we were met by a wall of sand, rock and ice. On returning to our Camp Murray base we decided to move further up the mountain to Ojos base camp – Camp Atacama – at 17,244ft (5,256m) in preparation for our final push.

We now had the mountain all to ourselves. A group of Chilean climbers had left two days earlier and a German group was just leaving. We were now down to 50% of sea-level air density, so regular pulse and blood-oxygen checks were compulsory to ensure we were all coping with the altitude and fit enough for what lay ahead. By 17,225ft (5,250m) we had reached the limits of human ability to adapt to the conditions – no-one lives higher, and mountaineering base camps worldwide all lie at or below that limit. Any nights spent higher weaken the body.

We were under no illusion about the magnitude of the challenge ahead of us, to reach and beat the magic 20,489ft (6,245m) record, so to prepare we took further exploratory rides daily. We were able to get to 19,642ft (5,987m), but we were unable to find an easy way across the steep belt of sand and rocks on Ojos del Salado.

Our final reconnaissance mission was on foot, walking up a route that had been used by Matthias Jeschke when he set a car world altitude record in 2004. It was a long way round, and covered in snow, but it took us directly to a small peak of about 20,869ft (6,361m). It was there that Jeschke had built a tiny cairn of rocks with a foot-long piece

The peaks of Tres Cruces loom over Laguna Santa Rosa from our viewpoint at 4,000 metres
Walter Colebatch

of bamboo sticking out of it. We nicknamed it 'Jeschke's Noodle' and it became a possible target for us. That evening we sat down to discuss our tactics to beat the record. It was going to be tough and we estimated that it would take between two and three days to reach Jeschke's Noodle. And it was at this point we decided to take only one bike, because manhandling all three would be impossible.

We were now at the point on the mountain that would define our adventure. It was the moment to find out whether our months of preparation and training would be good enough and, ultimately, set a new world record. Lukas was well up for the challenge.

He jumped on the big Husaberg, hit the throttle and, in an effort to gain as many vertical metres as possible before traction and momentum gave way to gravity, bucked his way up to 19,521ft (5,950m). From then on it was down to hard work and willpower, and it took five hours of haulage and labour to get over a steep sand and rock section to reach 19,751ft (6,020m). From there Walter rose to the challenge and blasted to 19,882ft (6,060m). We were now completely exhausted and, with the sun going down, decided to call it quits for day one of the final push.

WALTER COLEBATCH (UK/AUSTRALIA)

- **Age 43**
- **Team captain**
- **Experienced motorcycle adventurer who has ridden on every continent and guided tours across Siberia**
- **Accomplished author who sits on the Ted Simon Foundation Committee of Advisers – committed to furthering adventure motorcycling and promoting the spirit of adventure**
- **Featured prominently in Robert Wicks's books *Building the Ultimate Adventure Motorcycle* and *Great Adventure Motorcycle Routes***
- **Has published books and DVDs on adventure motorcycling in Siberia and Mongolia**

BARTON CHURCHILL (USA)

- **Age 38**
- **The team's high altitude and mountain specialist**
- **American adventure motorcyclist who in 2010 rode around the world solo on a KTM 640 Adventure. The ride started and finished in Montana, covering 21,000 miles (33,500km) in total, of which 11,500 miles (19,000km) were off-road**
- **Highly experienced mountaineer, high mountain back country skier, rock and ice climber**
- **Has worked as a back country ski guide, mountain search and rescue ranger, and wilderness emergency medical technician with the National Parks Service**

LUKAS MATZINGER (AUSTRIA)

- **Age 30**
- **The team's motorcycle and mechanical specialist**
- **Former commando in the Austrian Army**
- **Motorcycle and adventure travel background in over 40 countries on five continents**
- **Proficient rock climber with high altitude experience in South America (various 6,000m peaks)**
- **Motorcycle technician with a very high level of mechanical skills, including several frame-up adventure bike builds**

After a day's rest we were full of energy and enthusiasm to finish the job. Barton, the team's mountaineering guru, put a schedule in place: we would wake at 2am and be prepared to ride, pull and push our way up the mountain. He told us to be prepared for an 18-hour day. It was Barton's turn to ride and we quickly got to 20,013ft (6,100m), but from here a massive glacier blocked our progress.

The ice was breaking up and the surface was very rough and riddled with crevasses. It would be extremely challenging and physical work to get the bike across, but Lukas took up the challenge. With Barton and Walter testing the glacier and path-finding, Lukas amazed us all with a brilliant ride that took the team across the entire glacier.

We were all completely exhausted after the crossing. At 20,013ft (6,100m) the air was down to 45% of that at sea level, with recovery from even moderate exercise taking a good 10–15 minutes. There were more glaciers ahead of us and we stopped at 20,374ft (6,210m) to survey our options. The slope in front was covered in snow, yet there were a few lines that could be taken. We were now just 115ft (35m) from the existing world record – 20,489ft (6,245m). Walter saddled up and, spotting a potential line, roared up the hill. When he stopped, a look at his GPS showed that the job was done … 20,568ft (6,269m). The world record was now ours!

The Husaberg Adventure Team had come through. It was now a question of how much we could improve it; certainly 79ft (24m) was not enough. We wanted to be more decisive than that. We looked at several potential lines and found a ridge exposed to the sun with a thin line of exposed gravel. Barton launched himself up the hill. It was a little gem of a ride that, in about 90 seconds, seemed to score the team another 165ft (50m) of vertical.

It took 20 minutes for Walter and Lukas to catch up, but when they did they saw the GPS was now reading 20,725ft (6,317m). We were 236ft (72m) above the old record.

Lukas took over the reins and was determined to extend that to 328ft (100m), though how he was going to do it was a mystery. Barton had stopped on a small gravel knoll, but all around was deep snow. Lukas had an idea, dropping the Husaberg into a small gully, but he soon became bogged down in the snow. Then a few hands on the Kriega haul loop we had fitted on the bike and he was through, finding a path up to another rocky peak with a spectacular view.

Lukas had taken the bike to 20,820ft (6,346m), so we had topped the old record by over 328ft (100m). Yet one small hill, about 328ft (100m) away, seemed 32ft (10m) or so higher, but it was covered in snow. It was Walter's turn to saddle up. He had done deep snow riding before, in Russia, as a guest of the Off-Road People Club. The Russians had passed on plenty of good advice and Walter blasted through the snow, bouncing his bike along as a huge white tail shot out from under the it. When he finally stopped the GPS was reading 20,850ft (6,355m) and the hill we had been aiming for was now clearly identified as Jeschke's Noodle.

This had been our optimistic goal – and we were now just a few yards away from it! Next it was Barton's turn on the bike, but while he could comfortably have ridden up to the summit of Jeschke's Noodle he turned to Lukas and Walter and suggested we all take the bike and push it the last few yards to the summit, together. It was a fitting way to arrive at the new world record.

We checked the GPS units. They were all showing an accuracy of +/–3m. Readings fluctuated on all units between 20,862ft (6,359m) to 20,875ft (6,363m), but the most common reading was the middle one, at 20,869ft (6,361m). We had broken the old world record by 380ft (116m).

The crew reached a minor peak that they christened Jeschke's Noodle, in honour of a small straw left in that summit by Matthias Jeschke on reaching an earlier 4WD world record at exactly the same spot in 2005
📷 Andes Moto Extreme

Overcoming a short steep section of ash and boulders at 5,975 metres, manually
📷 Walter Colebatch

Taking a break at 6,000 metres
📷 Walter Colebatch

Listings

The following websites and books are useful places to start research on routes, bike choice, tours and equipment.

Useful Websites

General Advice

www.adventurebikerider.com
www.adventuremotorcycle.org
www.adventure-motorcycling.com
www.advrider.com
www.berndtesch.de
www.dualsportnews.com
www.flamesonmytank.co.za
www.haynes.co.uk
www.horizonsunlimited.com
www.rac.co.uk
www.visordown.com
www.whitehorsepress.com

Tours and Expeditions

www.bikershome.net
www.globalenduro.com
www.globebusters.com
www.globeriders.com
www.ktmadventuretours.com
www.kuduexpeditions.com
www.motoaventures.com
www.nicksanders.com
www.transamtrail.com

Gear and Equipment

www.acerbis.it
www.adventure-spec.com
www.camelbak.com
www.cotswoldoutdoor.com
www.dainese.com
www.garmin.com
www.happy-trail.com
www.hein-gericke.com
www.hyperpro.com
www.klim.com
www.kriega.com
www.ortlieb.com
www.overland-solutions.com
www.metalmule.com
www.pac-safe.com
www.pelican.com
www.rayz.nl
www.rukka.com
www.touratech.com
www.traveldri-plus.co.uk
www.wunderlich.de

Useful Reading

Adventure Motorcycling Handbook
Chris Scott

Chasing Dakar
Jonathan Edwards & Scot Harden

Desert Travels
Chris Scott

Dreaming of Jupiter
Ted Simon

Heading East
Andreas Hülsmann

Into Africa, Under Asian Skies, Distant Suns, Tortillas to Totems
Sam Manicom

Jupiter's Travels
Ted Simon

Lois on the Loose, Red Tape and White Knuckles
Lois Pryce

Long Way Down, Long Way Round
Ewan McGregor & Charley Boorman

The Longest Ride
Emilio Scotto

Mondo Enduro
Austin Vince

Motorcycling Abroad
Peter Henshaw

Obsessions Die Hard
Ed Culberson

One Man Caravan
Robert Fulton

Riding the World
Gregory Frazier

Rough Guide: First Time Around The World
Doug Lansky

Sahara Overland
Chris Scott

10 Years on 2 Wheels
Helge Pedersen

Tea with Bin Laden's Brother
Simon Roberts

The Motorcycle Book
Alan Seeley

Two Wheels to Adventure
Danny Liska

Zen and Art of Motorcycle Maintenance
Robert Pirsig

Charities & Campaigning Organisations

The Ted Simon Foundation
Encouraging those who adventure into the world to go the extra mile and transform their experiences into something of value for the world to share.

Motorcycle Action Group
MAG is a volunteer-led riders' rights organisation, representing the voice of riders in local and national government. It defends all that is good about biking.

Motorcycle Outreach
Working to introduce effective healthcare delivery in remote areas of developing countries.

To contact the author, please e-mail:
adventuremotorcycling@gmail.com

Index

📷 BMW Motorrad

Index